Vocal Technique

A Physiologic Approach for Voice Class and Studio

Vocal Technique

A Physiologic Approach for Voice Class and Studio

Jan E. Bickel, D.M.A.

PLURAL
PUBLISHING
INC.

SAN DIEGO
OXFORD
BRISBANE

5521 Ruffin Road
San Diego, CA 92123

e-mail: info@pluralpublishing.com
Web site: http://www.pluralpublishing.com

49 Bath Street
Abingdon, Oxfordshire OX14 1EA
United Kingdom

Typeset in 10½/13 Garamond by Flanagan's Publishing Services, Inc.
Printed in the United States of America by McNaughton and Gunn

Library of Congress Cataloging-in-Publication Data:

Bickel, Jan E.
  Vocal technique : a physiological approach for voice class and studio / Jan E. Bickel.
    p. cm.
  Includes bibliographical references (p.   ).
  ISBN-13: 978-1-59756-190-7 (alk. paper)
  ISBN-10: 1-59756-190-8 (alk. paper)
 1. Singing–Physiological aspects. 2. Singing—Instruction and study. 3. Voice—Care and hygiene. I. Title.
  MT821.B53 2007
  783'.043–dc22

                                                                    2007049340

Contents

HOW TO USE THIS BOOK EFFECTIVELY

As a voice teacher for 30 years, I have worked with many students with varying interests regarding the technical aspects of singing. Most of my students have had graduate school and professional singing goals in mind when beginning studies at the undergraduate level, but some have wanted to become professional teachers of singing, and others only to improve their vocal technique so they could find more personal fulfillment from their endeavors as singers. This book is an appropriate beginning for all of them.

I am of the opinion that a singer must know and understand the anatomic and physiologic functions connected with the speaking and singing process in order to feel "in control" of that process. In addition, this knowledge enables the singer to maintain optimum technical skill and vocal health throughout a long singing or teaching career. A singer who knows and understands his or her own body will necessarily be a better singer and a better teacher of singing. This book is based on that premise. Knowledge is power.

This book is intended for use in a first-year voice class at the college or university level. Portions of it may also be suitable for a voice class at the high school level, where students are interested and dedicated to learning a strong vocal technical foundation. As you read this book, do not hesitate to utilize the exercises given here as well as those given by your teacher in class. Practicing outside of class what you are learning in class is the only way to improve dramatically. You must come to know your voice intimately in order to utilize it to its fullest potential. You can only do this with many hours of practice in the privacy of your own home or practice space.

I have found, over the years, that vocal progress is somewhat different from the progress made by instrumentalists studying technique. Singers seem to make great strides as they initially learn about and begin to understand the technical aspects of the process, and then the process slows somewhat while the brain and muscle connection "catches up." Do not be frustrated by seeming plateaus in your learning. As the muscles learn to obey the commands of the educated brain, the complex interworkings of the anatomic system will begin to come alive and work for you. It takes time, patience, and perseverance.

Use this book to gain as much knowledge as you possibly can in regard to the technical aspects of singing; that is, anatomy, posture, breath management, physiology, articulation, and resonance. Use it also to help you learn to apply the important International Phonetic Alphabet (IPA) to the Italian and English languages, and to help you learn about good health and nutrition for all people. Take all of these concepts and make them your own. Apply as much information as you can to your own situation, and think carefully about how the information can help you to become the best singer you can be. Then, be a discoverer. Go out and read more books and articles on the subjects contained in this book. Gather more facts and opinions, which will help you in establishing your own personal vocal technique.

Those who aspire to be professional singers or teachers of singing should pay particular attention to the health and nutritional aspects of this book. You are your instrument, and being a professional singer, or a teacher of singing requires a tremendous amount of energy and excellent health in order to be successful. Begin now to study the appropriate eating and exercise suggestions, and begin to make them a habit for the rest of your life. A healthy body is a necessity for a life in the professional world of singing and the teaching of singing.

Following a voice class, you should expect to go on to study privately with a voice teacher for many years. A class in vocal technique is merely a beginning to a lifelong process, which requires daily practice and study to achieve success. After you finish this class; however, you should have a strong foundation on which to base your choice of voice teachers and vocal techniques. There are probably as many vocal techniques as there are voice teachers, and choosing the right teacher and technique for you is very important. Use the body of information you gain from this book to make decisions in this regard, but also continue to read books on technique and interpretation, as well as poetry and foreign languages. You will want to read other books in the area of music as well if you wish to become a professional musician. Begin now to be a lifelong learner.

I wish you well in your vocal studies and hope you gain much knowledge and insight from using this book.

Jan Bickel

Acknowledgments

I have so many people to thank, that it would be impossible to acknowledge all of them on this page. I am greatly indebted to my own voice teachers; particularly Madame Sonia Sharnova of the Chicago Conservatory of Music, and the Chicago Opera Company, Kathleen Kaun, who worked with me at Northwestern University, and Wilma Osheim of the American Conservatory of Music. Their careful guidance and encouragement of my own vocal technical and interpretive skills can surely be witnessed in these pages. I am also indebted to my first voice teacher, Susan Stevens at Saint Mary's College at Notre Dame, who discovered that I had a voice worthy of the singing profession, and taught me to be a lifetime learner and discoverer.

I am indebted to the many colleagues whose presentations, seminars, writings, and quiet conversations led me to put these words on paper. I have benefited frequently from individual members, as well as collectively, from the work of the National Association of Teachers of Singing, and the Voice Foundation's annual conferences in Philadelphia. Although Dr. Robert Sataloff, M.D., D.M.A., does not know me personally, he has had a tremendous influence on my singing and my teaching of singers, and I thank him for his tireless efforts in reaching the pedagogic community with his medical and vocal expertise through seminars and print media. In addition, I have been strongly influenced by the work of Richard Miller and William Vennard. I have read their works in depth, and even though I know it is impossible to learn to sing well from a book, it is not impossible to gain insight into the complex process through their writings, and I thank each of them for their pioneering work.

I am also indebted to the students in my voice studio, and my vocal technique classes at Saint Xavier University, where I have taught for 25 years. Their patience and enthusiasm regarding this book have been most rewarding for me as a teacher and a writer.

My deepest thanks goes to my colleague and friend, Martha M. Morris, Director of Instrumental Studies and Music Education, at Saint Xavier University, with whom I am engaged in very rewarding research regarding the application of vocal resonance techniques in wind and brass players. Thank you for your unending support and encouragement in my work as an educator, a singer, and a writer. This book could not have come about without you.

I am also indebted to my outstanding illustrator, Douglas Klauba. Thank you for your generous assistance, your keen eye, and wonderful artistic skills in making the technical concepts perfectly visually clear for the teachers and students who will use this book.

The Linguist's Software, Inc. font IPAKiel used to print the IPA portions of this work is available from Linguist's Software, Inc., P. O. Box 580, Edmonds, WA 98020-0580; tel: (425) 775-1130; www.linguist-software.com . This software is easy to work with, and has saved me countless hours of work. I highly recommend it to my colleagues as a workable software program for you and your students as you are teaching and learning to work with the International Phonetic Alphabet.

My thanks to everyone who encouraged me to write this book and to pursue publication.

Singer Information Sheet for Voice Class

Name _____   Age _____

Voice Category _____ SOPRANO _____ MEZZO-SOPRANO _____ ALTO

_____ TENOR   _____ BARITONE   _____ BASS

1. Have you had any vocal training?   ___ Yes ___ No

   a. class voice lessons   ___ Yes ___ No

   b. private lessons   ___ Yes ___ No

   c. within choral organizations   ___ Yes ___ No

   d. through a church choir   ___ Yes ___ No

   e. through a school choir   ___ Yes ___ No

2. How would you rate your vocal technique?

   ___ Excellent   ___ Good   ___ Moderate   ___ Poor   ___ None

3. If you have had private voice lessons, please list your last two teachers, and the number of months or years you studied with each teacher.

   Teacher 1 _____ _____ Months or Years

   Teacher 2 _____ _____ Months or Years

4. Do you sing regularly in a choral or other vocal ensemble?   ___ Yes ___ No

   If yes, what type(s) of ensemble: _____

   _____

5. How long have you been singing? _____ (months, years)

6. Have you ever had any vocal problems such as the following?

Hoarseness (scratchy sound and feel) ___ Yes ___ No

Fatigue (voice tires or changes quality after singing) ___ Yes ___ No

Trouble singing ___ softly ___ loudly ___ making sound at all vocally

Loss of range of voice (low or high notes) ___ Yes ___ No

Breathiness in sound (cannot produce a clear tone) ___ Yes ___ No

Pain in throat while singing ___ Yes ___ No

Difficulty in warming your voice up to sing ___ Yes ___ No

Other—please explain briefly _____

_____

_____

7. What are your career goals as a singer?

___ Premier operatic career   ___ Premier pop or Broadway career

___ Classical singer   ___ Pop singer

___ Amateur performer   ___ Amateur singing for personal pleasure

___ Music educator   (___ College   ___ High School   ___ Elementary)

___ No real interest in singing as a career

8. Have you ever had training for your speaking voice?   ___ Yes ___ No

Acting voice lessons   ___ Yes ___ No   If yes, how long? _____

Speech Therapy   ___ Yes ___ No   If yes, how long? _____

If yes, what was the purpose of your Speech Therapy? _____

_____

9. What are your personal career goals outside of the art of singing? _____

_____

_____

10. Do you play a musical instrument(s)?   ___Yes   ___No

    ___ Keyboard   ___ String Instrument (Violin, Bass, Cello, Bass)

    ___ Guitar   ___ Brass Instrument (Trumpet, Horn, Trombone, Tuba)

    ___ Single-Reed Instrument   ___ Double-Reed Instrument

    ___ Flute, Piccolo   ___ Percussion

    ___ Other: Please specify _____

11. How often do you do vocal exercises? _____

12. If you practice singing regularly, how long are your practice sessions?

    _____ minutes   _____hours   _____ daily   _____weekly   _____ other

13. Do you regularly practice sitting down?   ___ Yes   ___ No

14. Do you warm up your voice before singing music?   ___ Yes   ___ No

15. Do you have any allergies or medical problems?   ___ Yes   ___ No

    If yes, please explain _____

    _____

    _____

    _____

16. What medications or over-the-counter products do you take regularly?

    _____

    _____

17. Do you have any problems with your voice?   ___ Yes   ___ No

    If yes, please explain _____

    _____

    _____

18. Do you smoke?   ___Yes   ___No

    Do you live with smokers?   ___Yes   ___No

    Do you work in a place where you regularly
    inhale second-hand smoke?   ___Yes   ___No

19. Do you drink alcohol?   ___ Yes ___ No

20. Do you drink caffeinated beverages?   ___ Yes ___ No

21. What is your personal goal for yourself in this course? _____

_____

_____

_____

_____

This book is dedicated to my family, students, and colleagues.
Without your constant support, encouragement, and patience
this book would not have been possible.
I thank you from the bottom of my heart for standing by me
until this work was completed, and hope that it meets your expectations.

Chapter 1

SOME ANSWERS TO QUESTIONS BEFORE WE BEGIN TO LEARN HOW TO SING

I'VE HEARD THAT PEOPLE ARE "BORN SINGERS"—CAN ANYONE REALLY LEARN TO BE A SINGER?

Anyone who has a normally functioning speaking voice can learn to sing! The physiologic requirements are nearly the same for both processes. Many would-be singers are unnecessarily anxious or nervous about singing because they lack experience in singing. This feeling of anxiousness or nervousness can be overcome easily by learning the "how to's" of vocal production, a "vocal technique."

Just as an Olympic runner takes the basic skills of walking and develops them to a high degree, a professional singer takes the skills and coordination process of speaking and develops them into those needed for singing. If you can speak—you can sing. As a matter of fact, learning to sing will improve the quality and projection of your speaking voice. Many lawyers and other professional voice users study singing in an effort to improve their ability to speak persuasively and dynamically in public.

SO WHAT IS VOCAL TECHNIQUE?

Vocal technique is the specific learned process through which a singer controls the coordination of the four physiologic systems (respiration, phonation, articulation, and resonation) to create a beautiful tone quality. When we speak of vocal technique, we are primarily concerned with these four physiologic systems necessary to the production of a cultivated vocal tone quality. Thus, a singer acquires a vocal technique through the study, development, and coordination of the respiration, phonation, articulation, and resonation systems involved in producing vocal tone.

At first these terms may seem formidable, but in actuality, they are processes that are used every day by human beings. By *Respiration* we mean simply the act of breathing. More specifically, respiration includes "the physical and chemical processes by which an organism supplies its cells and tissues with the oxygen needed for metabolism and relieves them of the carbon dioxide formed in energy producing reactions" (Webster, 2005, p. 1061). Much time is devoted to this important physiologic process in Chapter 4. *Phonation* can also be explained simply as the process of producing vocal sounds, especially speech. The term takes its root from the Greek *phone* meaning voice or sound. Thus, to phonate is to make vocal sounds through the application of breath energy to the vocal folds (in humans), causing them to vibrate. *Articulation* as it applies to singing and speaking, is the process whereby vocal sounds produced are affected or changed by the position and motion of the lips, jaw, soft palate, and tongue as well as the position of the larynx (or voice box) itself. Movement of each of these body organs changes the shape of the vocal tract, which allows us to produce the vowel and consonant combinations we recognize as language. Finally, *Resonation* is the process that amplifies the sound produced through phonation, using specific shapes within the vocal tract to create additional sympathetic vibrations. In the case of speech or singing, as the vocal tone passes through the various portions of the vocal tract, it is intensified and enriched by supplementary vibrations achieved there. William Vennard, in his *Singing the Mechanism and the Technic*, states: "To the physicist, resonance is a relationship that exists between two vibrating bodies of the same pitch" (Vennard, 1967, p. 13). Thus, resonating the singing voice means learning to control the shape of these cavities above the larynx as well as controlling the larynx itself. More specific information on the extremely important process of resonating the voice is discussed in Chapter 7.

The physical production of singing tone requires the use of all of these physiologic systems—in precise coordination with, and consciously and consistently guided by, the ear and brain of the singer. This is only the physical or physiologic aspect of the technique of voice production, however. In order for a singer to make vocal sounds worthy of the concert audience, the singer must also engage the body's *psychological system* as well as allowing his or her individual personality to shine through; allowing the creation of vocal sounds which achieve the highest form of artistry while singing.

How Long Will It Take to Become a Singer?

The answer here depends on how disciplined you are and what you wish to achieve. If you wish to be a singer in a choir or to be able to produce pleasant vocal sounds for your own enrichment, you can learn to do this rather quickly. Everyone should be able to learn to produce pleasing vocal sounds using a good vocal technique, within the time period allotted for a voice class. When we speak of achieving vocal artistry, we include the use of the interpretive

and imaginative side of the brain (the psychologic system) as well as the perfect coordination of the four physiologic systems into a highly skilled level of vocal technique. A student of singing must first master the physical aspects of vocal production and will then be able to move on to study the artistic elements involved in achieving this high level of vocal artistry. If a singer wishes to achieve a level of competency that can be used professionally in public performance, his or her studies will continue until a high level of vocal artistry is developed. This generally means going on to study privately with a good voice teacher and continuing to develop many additional skills as well as refining the vocal technique to an artistic level. A world class singer possesses not only an excellent physical vocal technique, but has also achieved a high level of musicianship, as well as interpretive, theatrical, and language skills to make the singing process complete and more meaningful for the audience as well as the singer. Mastery of the most advanced stages of vocal technique is a prerequisite for achieving vocal artistry.

Renowned vocal pedagogue Richard Miller, in *The Structure of Singing, System and Art in Vocal Technique* (1996) states:

> Technique represents the stabilization of desirable coordination during singing. Technique can be 'computerized' in the brain and the body of the singer. No singer ever should be in doubt as to what is going to happen, technically, in public performance, unless illness interferes. Knowing how the singing instrument works, and knowing how to get it to work consistently, is the sum of technical knowledge. That is why a systematic approach to vocal technique is the most successful route to artistic singing. System and art conjoin to produce the professional sounds of the singing voice (p. xvi).

Lotte Lehmann, considered one of the greatest interpretive singers of her time, writes in her book *More Than Singing—The Interpretation of Songs* (1945):

> Not only your voice sings—no, you must sing with your whole being—from head to toe . . . your eyes sing, your body, animated by the

rhythm of the music, sings, your hands sing. How great is the power of expression conveyed by the eyes and the hands! . . . you should learn to feel what you are singing with every nerve (p. 13).

Later in the introduction to her insightful book she states: "Do not sing just a melody, sing a poem. Music lifting the poem from the coldness of the spoken word has transfigured it with new beauty" (Lehmann, 1945, p. 15). These are the words of a *vocal artist* rather than a vocal technician. These are the words of a woman who went far beyond the achievement of masterful vocal technique, achieving what we have learned to appreciate as world-class artistry.

In this course, the emphasis is on the introduction and development of the foundation needed for a strong and reliable vocal technique—to help you achieve a basic understanding of what the requirements are for mastering the physical coordination necessary to produce beautiful vocal sounds. Following this course you may choose to go on with your studies—to work with a private vocal teacher as you continue to develop your own personal vocal technique. If you do not go on to study further, you will have gained a basic understanding of what is necessary to achieve the most beautiful vocal quality you are capable of producing as well as having learned about the anatomic function of the singing mechanism and some exercises for training and coordinating the physiologic and psychologic systems to produce that desired tone quality.

WHY STUDY SINGING IF I DON'T INTEND TO BECOME A PROFESSIONAL SINGER?

The National Association of Teachers of Singing (NATS) offers the following reasons for studying singing. You should consider them before you begin to learn to sing.

1. Singing is a very healthy form of aerobic exercise, which will help you tone muscles, purify your blood, and develop your lungs.

2. Learning to sing properly will promote good posture and give you a graceful carriage.
3. Learning to sing properly will improve your speaking voice, making it fuller and richer.
4. Learning to sing properly will help you to develop self-confidence and poise as you overcome the difficulties associated with singing for others.
5. Learning to sing properly, although it requires patience, energy, and enthusiasm, is fun and aids in your emotional development.

The most important consideration should be: "Do you want to be able to sing to the best of your ability?" This does not mean you necessarily have the desire to be a professional singer, but only that you have a desire to be the best you can be. If you have this desire, you are already on your way to becoming a singer.

HOW DO FEAR AND ANXIETY AFFECT THE VOICE?

Because you are your instrument, your physical well-being as well as the emotions you feel will affect the vocal sounds you produce. Later on in your vocal studies you will learn to use this fact to your own advantage, but for now, learning to deal with unwanted emotions such as anxiety or fear will be important to your study and improvement. No one wants to fail or make a fool of him or herself in front of peers or colleagues. This is not only a concern for those at the student level but for the entire human race. In the case of singing, we will remove this fear of failure by improving our concentration on the elements of correct vocal production and developing a vocal technique that can be relied upon even when we are nervous or under stress.

When you are afraid, your mind has a tendency to wander from one subject to the next; "what if my voice cracks?"—"what if I sing flat?"—"what if I sing the wrong notes?"—and so on. Let us call this the "What if" syndrome. These are all legitimate questions that can be answered and put out of your mind as you learn a correct and reliable vocal technique. Once you have put away the "what if" syndrome, you will be ready to concentrate on developing your own vocal technique. Let us answer some of the questions posed to allow a bit more understanding as you begin your efforts to develop a strong vocal technique.

WHAT IF MY VOICE CRACKS?

Perhaps understanding why the voice "cracks" will make this event less frightening. As the untrained singer attempts to sing an ascending pattern of notes, a sort of "tug of war" is going on between two sets of vocal muscles, the cricothyroid and the thyroarytenoid muscles. With each ascending pitch, tension mounts, and more muscular effort and breath power are required to sustain the higher and higher tones. When the limit of this individual's vocal muscular strength is reached, the muscles give way, or "let go" and the voice becomes quite "light" sounding as it changes to an involuntary *falsetto*. This is what we feel and hear as a "crack." The feeling is uncomfortable as it would be if you over-stretched any muscle in the body, and the embarrassment comes from the loss of control of the tone. However, there is nothing to be embarrassed about, this simply means you were using too much of what is commonly described as *chest voice*. This term is discussed at some length later on in the book. For now, we describe it as a "heavy voice" which uses too much muscle in the vocal folds during the phonation process. In this course you will learn to carefully bridge the *head voice* (a more relaxed use of the vocal folds) with the chest voice so that this "cracking" sensation will not occur. The correct process will allow the vocal folds as well as the cricothyroid and thyroarytenoid muscles to gradually adjust as you move up and down a scale so that they can be used properly and without strain. When you have learned to *support* your voice properly and consistently with breath, there will be no cracking. Until you have developed this skill, however, don't worry about your voice cracking. This automatic adjustment on the part of the musculature actually prevents you from injuring the muscles in your efforts to sing.

WHAT IF I SING FLAT?

Excellent singing requires good *intonation*, the process whereby we sing "in tune," or precisely on pitch. Many things can cause a singer to be *flat* or under pitch. If the tone is not properly focused with the breath, the tone may be flat. If the vowel formation is incorrect, the tone may also be flat. "Holding" the muscles of the voice box or larynx tightly will make the tone "straight," or lacking in *vibrato* and can also give the impression that the tone is flat. A straight or "vibratoless" tone allows no *ring* or *overtones* in the voice, and thus produces a sound that is under pitch or flat. Correcting flat singing is a matter of learning a good reliable vocal technique and is not usually a difficult problem to correct. It is a problem that is cured by learning proper breath support and good vocal technique, appropriate coordination of the respiratory, phonatory, and resonatory systems. Perhaps the diagram in Figure 1–1 will help you to understand the appropriate vibratory relationship between a straight tone, a *wobble* or *tremolo*, and an acceptable vocal tone with vibrato.

We can identify a pitch by letter name (for example, the international concert pitch: A on the treble staff). This pitch produced by any instrument will vibrate 440 times per second. This sound, as

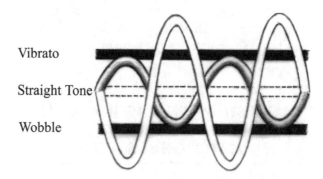

Figure 1–1. This diagram demonstrates the visual difference between a *straight tone* (represented by the center dotted line between the pitch lines), *acceptable vocal tone with vibrato* (demonstrated by the shaded wavy line within the pitch lines), and a *wobble or tremolo in the voice* (demonstrated by the unshaded wavy line which travels outside the pitch lines).

heard by the human ear, may be graphed in a wave as shown. Acoustic scientists have proven that sound does not move in a straight line, but rather in peaks and valleys, or what are called *compressions and rarefaction* (as shown). Thus, it is more natural for the vocal sound to have *vibrato* (a slight pulsation of pitch—approximately six or seven pulsations per second) rather than no pulsations whatsoever. In singing, vibrato is caused by the intermittent supply of nerve energy to the sound producing mechanism—the larynx. When the respiratory and phonatory muscles of the vocal instrument are in perfect coordination (a regular pattern of nerve energy is applied to the larynx), the sound moves in regularly patterned waves as illustrated. When the same respiratory and phonatory muscles are not coordinating perfectly, the sound produced will be either straight, having no patterned waves at all, or may produce what is called a tremolo. A wobbly or tremulous tone allows the wave pattern to go too far outside the normal wave pattern of the particular pitch and thus would force the tone to be *sharp* (above the pitch) at times and *flat* (below the pitch) at other times.

Lack of singing experience may cause a singer to be out of tune, that is flat or sharp. Because this is the case, training the ear is as important as training the vocal production itself. Courses in sight-singing and aural skills are taught in some high schools, and most colleges, and universities. This is a good place to begin to learn pitch-matching skills if you have not already acquired skill in this area. Of course, listening to other highly trained professional and semi-professional singers is extremely important for all aspiring singers and will help here as well.

According to William Vennard, internationally recognized vocal pedagogue and singer, "vibrato is a perfectly normal phenomenon," and "acoustically, the vocal vibrato is a fluctuation in pitch, intensity, and timbre . . . the ear ordinarily hears only a mean pitch, which is in tune with the rest of the music. The other pitches one mistakes for timbre, and one is likely to call the presence of vibrato 'richness,' or 'resonance,' or even 'overtones'" (Vennard, 1967, p. 193).

During your study of vocal technique, your voice will gradually acquire a natural vibrato as the various vocal muscles and physiologic systems learn to coordinate appropriately. Don't worry about too much or too little vibrato in your voice now. Focus your attention on proper posture, breath control, and coordination of the various muscles and you will soon notice a natural vibrato entering in an effortless manner. Remember that vibrato is a normal function of the voice and will be correct when the voice is freely produced and coordinating well.

WHAT IF I SING THE WRONG NOTES?

Singing wrong notes is usually an indication that the singer's concentration is not as strong as it needs to be or that the song was not practiced and learned when the singer was concentrating carefully. Developing good pitch memory takes time, patience, and practice just as developing a good golf swing or learning to throw a curve ball require repeated attempts to achieve success. A singer must be sure that he or she is concentrating carefully when learning a new song or exercise to ensure a perfect delivery of the song in performance. Mistakes learned during practice time, whether rhythmic, melodic, or otherwise, are difficult to correct once they are "programmed" into your mind, ear, and voice. Careful and concentrated practice time as well as patience in learning the skills of vocal technique will help to rid you of potential errors in performance. Using the process for learning a song will also aid you in this quest for good musicianship.

HOW CAN I GET OVER THE FEAR OF MAKING MISTAKES IN PUBLIC?

Here are four easy steps to help you get over the fear of making mistakes. Begin to study and practice using them right now.

1. Concentrate

This means in your practice as well as your performance. "Program" yourself to sing the material to the best of your ability by learning it slowly, carefully, and correctly, whether it is an exercise, an art song, an aria or a section of a choral work. Think carefully about what you are doing and be organized in your approach.

2. Prepare Yourself Well

Your vocal instrument is made up of bone, cartilage, muscles, and other living materials rather than wood, silver, or brass. These living cells respond to the commands of the brain and need practice and exercise every day in order to become fluid in the coordination process. In addition to your vocal exercises, learn the words and music of your song literature slowly and carefully. Remember, good singing is a balancing act of many muscles with the brain guiding every action. The brain must send the proper signals and the body must learn the correct patterns of response to each of those signals. This learning process takes time, patience, and repetition! When you learn a song or an exercise, you are really "programming" the correct muscular action into your body both physically and mentally.

3. Take the Stage

You want to learn to sing or you would not be reading this book, so let your audience know that you want to perform for them and that you have something important to say. This attitude will give you the necessary confidence in your own abilities as a singer. "Taking the stage" means walking to your performance position with confidence quickly, and with an assured smile that says: "I am well prepared and ready to perform for you. Thank you for coming to hear me sing."

4. Expect to Do Well

What you think and feel definitely affects your voice and your performance because you are your instrument. Think positively. Practice *visualizing* your success. You will be surprised at how much this helps your sense of control and your ability to per-

form. Athletes have been using the technique of visualization for years. Watch an Olympic skier standing at the top of the hill: eyes closed, going through all the motions of the course ahead with precision and the exact finesse he or she intends to use when actually moving over the course physically. This *visualization technique* is just as important for singer/performers. Visualizing yourself on the stage singing your vocal material to the very best of your ability and then receiving graciously the applause of the audience can have great benefits both psychologically and physically.

HOW DO I GAIN MORE CONFIDENCE IN MY SINGING?

Lack of confidence comes from lack of knowledge or the feeling that you lack knowledge in a particular subject area. You naturally feel more confident when you feel you know a good deal about the subject. Singing is no different. You will be least confident when you don't know what your voice is going to do, and most confident when you are in complete control of your voice due to a good understanding of how it functions. When you have a good understanding of how your voice functions, and have carefully practiced exercises to help you gain control over these vocal functions, you will find yourself growing more and more confident.

HOW DO I GAIN THIS KNOWLEDGE AND CONTROL?

You learn as much about your vocal instrument and how it functions as you can and attempt to acquire a strong vocal technique, based on all the knowledge you have gained. In learning this technique you need someone in whom you have confidence as a singing teacher, a well-tuned piano, a mirror, a recording device, a metronome, and a great deal of patience and perseverance. There are as many techniques of singing as there are teachers teaching them. It is important for you to find a teacher who inspires you, and in whom you have faith. Singing is a very personal endeavor that requires a great deal of trust on the part of the student. Thus, you must look carefully for a teacher in whom you can have confidence and in whom you can place your trust. Later on in this book you will find a listing of attributes you should look for as you seek out an excellent voice teacher. You need a teacher to guide you as you learn to use your voice properly. This is difficult to do on your own. As you probably are already aware if you have heard your speaking or singing voice on a tape recorder, you do not hear your voice in the same way that others hear you. Learning to sing means learning to trust someone else's ears and your "feelings." That is, the feelings and sensations of vibration, certain muscular feelings, such as those associated with expanding and maintaining a lift in your rib cage, relaxation in the shoulders and jaw, sensations of vibration in the nasal cavities, and so on. Your voice teacher will carefully guide you toward these correct sensations, and will help you discover and acquire an excellent vocal technique.

You need a mirror in your practice area to observe signs of muscular tension, facial expression, posture and hand gestures, and your overall presentation among other things. This is often one of the most difficult aspects of learning a strong vocal technique. Very few people are comfortable watching themselves in a mirror. You will find it easier if you do not make eye contact with yourself in the mirror. Instead, be your own best critic; feeling as though you are standing outside of yourself and objectively analyzing the technique, and not the person you are watching. In subsequent chapters, you will learn exactly what to watch for in the mirror.

A recording device is a valuable tool that will enable you to hear yourself more accurately. Recording lessons and classes as well as practice sessions will help you to remember the correct notes and rhythms of the exercises as well as the purpose of each exercise. Listen for corrections made by the teacher as you attempt to sing the exercises and song literature. Frequently, when a student is concentrating intensely on one concept, some very important information or corrections may slip by unnoticed. If your voice lessons and class sessions are recorded, such moments will not be lost, as you will hear the information or correction when you replay the recording at a later time. A good habit to form

would be to record each class or lesson and soon after, listen to the recording, writing down in a notebook or diary important points from the session, difficulties, exercises learned, as well as the purpose for each, and corrections made. As you listen to your recording, you may discover questions that you did not ask in the lesson. These questions should be brought forward in the next session with your teacher. The body of information you gather by keeping this vocal diary will prove to be a valuable resource for you as you continue your studies. When you are learning a technique, part of the learning time is spent sitting quietly and studying the music and the poetry or listening to professional vocal artists performing the literature. This time is as important to learning to sing well as the time you spend actually singing. It often gives the mind time to gain a deeper understanding of the various aspects of the technique. Do not neglect this important aspect of your vocal studies.

HOW DO I KNOW WHAT AND HOW TO PRACTICE?

Remembering that your instrument is made up primarily of muscles is important. Just as an athlete would not attempt a difficult maneuver without doing stretching and warm-up exercises, so the singer must warm up as well. The voice is a delicate instrument, and should be used with care and intelligence. Warm-ups for singing work as they do in athletics, stretching the muscles to prepare them for work without injury. Many otolaryngologists, and speech-language pathologists recommend *Vocal Function Exercises*. These are "a series of direct systematic voice manipulations (exercises), similar in theory to physical therapy for the vocal folds, designed to strengthen and balance the laryngeal musculature, and to improve the efficiency of the relationship among airflow, vocal fold vibration, and supraglottic treatment of phonation" (*Clinical Updates in Voice: Voice Therapy for the Twenty-First Century*, Symposium, October 24, 1999). You will find these specific vocal function exercises on many Web sites, including the one sponsored by The Milton J. Dance, Jr. Head and Neck Rehabilitation

Center at Greater Baltimore Medical Center in Baltimore, Maryland. The Web site where you will find vocal warm-ups is: http://www.gbmc.org/voice/vocalwarmups.cfm. I recommend that every singer use these warm-ups and cool-downs prior to attempting exercises for vocal development. In addition, be sure to follow the vocal warm-up procedure given by your teacher. Throughout this book you will find a series of vocal exercises that can be used to warm-up the voice. Eventually, you will develop a specific warm up procedure that works well for you personally.

As the athlete trains for years to gain control and flexibility of his or her muscles, so the singer must practice vocal exercises to build control, flexibility, beauty, and power into his or her voice. Developmental exercises are given to you throughout this book, and may be supplemented by your teacher. Practice each one carefully and regularly to develop your vocal instrument. Developing and nurturing your voice now will enable it to last for years. Initially, it is wise to practice for shorter more frequent periods of time; approximately 30 minutes to an hour per day should be sufficient for the duration of a voice class. Check with your teacher about any specific practice requirements he or she may have for your sessions. Of course, careful and concentrated practice will enable you to improve more quickly. Practice should always be done when you are well rested, healthy, and in a place where you can concentrate completely on what you are doing. Never attempt to practice when you are exhausted, ill, or in some physical or psychological way indisposed. Your practice room should have a well-tuned piano, a full-length mirror, a recording device, a metronome, and plenty of fresh air and quiet.

NEVER SIT AT THE PIANO TO PRACTICE: ALWAYS STAND!

Your voice needs the full support of your body, and standing to practice will help you to develop this consistent support more adequately. You do not need to play the notes of your exercises as you sing them. It is much better to memorize the pitch patterns, and give yourself only the first pitch for each exercise. This will also help you to acquire the aural skills necessary for excellent singing. Stand in front of the mirror and check frequently for muscular tension, correct posture, breathing, and mouth position as well as incorrect habits you may have acquired without realizing; for example, standing with the body weight more on one foot than the other, or opening the mouth to one side rather than dropping the jaw evenly from both joints. Your physical appearance is important for correct vocal technique as well as for audience appeal on the performance stage. Removing undesirable physical patterns or techniques early in your vocal technical development is much easier than waiting until these patterns have become habit. If you have particular problems or difficulties in your practice sessions, get into the habit of writing down the problem and asking your teacher about it as soon as possible.

WHAT IS INVOLVED IN DEVELOPING A VOCAL TECHNIQUE?

Learning to be a singer is different from learning to play any other instrument because you must build and develop your vocal instrument as you learn to "play" it. If you want to learn to play the piano, you purchase a well-built piano and find a teacher to teach you how to play it correctly. This is not the case for singers. Singing is a secondary function of the larynx, the physical function of which is to act as a valve to hold breath and to keep food from entering the lungs. The phonation process is something that humans have developed. Therefore, a would-be singer must work diligently to train the appropriate muscles to respond to mental commands consistently. This takes practice and patience. Good singing technique includes learning proper posture, breath support, resonance, articulation of vowels and consonants, projection, and more. Each aspect of vocal technique is initially taught separately and then all aspects must be coordinated as perfectly as possible. It is important to learn each aspect carefully and precisely; take time to be sure your voice is responding to your mental command and that you are concentrating fully on the task at all times. Once you have developed a solid and reliable vocal technique, you will know that every time you open your mouth to sing, your voice will do exactly as you command it. This takes time, patience, and perseverance. No one can develop a technique for you. You must do this yourself. Your teacher can guide you in the correct procedure and help you to correct your mistakes, but in many respects, you are your own best teacher. Practice what you learn in class, carefully and every day, to develop the best possible vocal technique.

IS THERE A SPECIFIC PROCESS FOR LEARNING A SONG?

There are many processes that can be utilized in learning vocal literature. The following process seems logical and helpful for the new singer. If you follow this procedure, you will "program" the song into your memory and muscles correctly and at the same time. Thus, there will be no problem with memorization later on—the work will have been done in the learning process. Use this process now and modify it as you become more proficient as a singer.

1. Learn the Poem Separately

Translate the poem *literally* (word for word) if it is in a language with which you are not familiar. Write the English translation for each individual word beneath its corresponding foreign language word, using a literal translation—learn the exact meaning of each word. Check every syllable for correct pronunciation, and for accurate vowel sounds until you are able to imagine and produce precisely every speech sound involved. After you have learned to use the *International Phonetic Alphabet (IPA)*, you will be able to write the IPA transcription into your musical score so that your pronunciation will be exact. Practice speaking the text aloud until it seems phonetically perfect, and you can speak it without any hesitation or strain. Then, learn to recite the text as a piece of poetry so that the sense of it may be

immediately grasped by anyone familiar with the language. Search for the right inflection in each sentence. Do not begin learning the music until you have mastered the verbal content of the song.

2. Learn the Rhythmic Pattern of the Vocal Line

Learn the rhythmic pattern separately from the pitch pattern by tapping it out or by using some syllable such as "la" to indicate the rhythm while singing a monotone pitch. Your metronome will be a great help to you in this endeavor. Be sure to set the metronome at a slow enough tempo so that you can maintain a steady pulse, and learn the rhythm correctly.

3. Synchronize the Poem and the Rhythmic Pattern

Synchronize the poetic text with the rhythmic pattern to which it has been set by the composer by learning to recite the poem in strict and precise time. A metronome will be of great help here as well.

4. Learn the Pitches of the Vocal Line

The only way to learn the pitches and rhythms of a vocal line is to learn to hear them. If your eye and ear coordination is inefficient, it should not be strained by an attempt to learn to sight-sing on the song you eventually wish to perform. It would be much more realistic to learn to hear the vocal line of a song by playing it slowly in strict time on the piano and by repeating this process until you can mentally hear each phrase with utmost precision. If you are fairly proficient in the use of *sòlfege* (the use of designated syllables associated with pitches as a mnemonic device for indicating melodic intervals), this may be a good alternative for you. You should not attempt to sing the vocal line in any fashion until you can hear it mentally, precisely on pitch and in rhythm, note for note.

5. Vocalize the Melody on One Vowel at a Time

After the speech sounds, rhythms, and pitches of the vocal line have been thoroughly absorbed, you may *vocalize* (a textless vocal exercise to help the singer achieve excellent vocal production) the melody on any vowel most comfortable for you. The vocalization should be metronomically precise. Eventually, all vowel sounds should be vocalized for greatest results. This procedure will aid in developing a *legato* line in the voice. By legato, we mean singing smoothly from one note to the next, so there is a connection of breath. We call this having "line" in the voice.

6. Vocalize the Song Using the Vowels Found in Each of the Words of the Song

Singing in strict time and with correct notes and rhythms, vocalize the song on the vowels contained in each word of the song, omitting the consonants completely. Be careful to sustain the sound from vowel to vowel without an interruption in the flow of the tone or breath. This too will aid in developing a legato line. For example, using the first line of text from *Long, Long Ago* by Thomas Haynes Bayly, the singer would vocalize on the vowels represented in IPA beneath the words as follows: (Be sure to sustain the vowels for the full rhythmic value as in the song.)

> Tell me the tales that to me were so dear
> [ɛ   i   ə   e   æ   u   i   ɣ   o   ɪː ə]

7. Sing the Song Using the Correct Words and Notes of the Music

Be sure you are in strict time, and work carefully to continue the flow of the breath. Continue working toward effortless flow of the sound and consistent breath support throughout every phrase. Let the consonants be gently applied at first, being careful not to disturb the legato line. Finally, work for absolute clarity of text. Use your recording device to check for accuracy and clarity of text pronunciation as well as effortless legato line.

8. Put the Song Away for a Few Hours

Overworking a song, or practicing when your concentration is poor is not helpful. After studying a song thoroughly and then allowing yourself to rest a bit, you will be able to practice without doing damage to the song or to your voice. When you begin your practicing again, check to make sure all notes, rhythms, and pronunciations are accurate, and begin to work for even clearer tone quality and excellent breath support. Slow tempos and patience are the keys to quality learning. Only after the technical skills of a song have been practiced carefully should you begin to work on the interpretation of the song.

IMPORTANT TERMS TO DEFINE AND UNDERSTAND

Vocal technique

Phonation

Respiration

Resonation

Articulation

Vocal artistry

Vocal technician

Intonation

Singing flat

Singing sharp

Straight tone

Tremolo (wobble)

Vibrato

Visualization technique

Literal translation

Metronome

Other terms which are new to you:

REFERENCES

Dance, Jr., M. (1999). *The Milton J. Dance, Jr. Head and Neck Rehabilitation Center at Greater Baltimore Medical Center*. Retrieved February 18, 2007 from http://www.gbmc.org/voice/vocalwarmups.cfm

Lehmann, L. (1985). *More than singing the interpretation of songs*. New York: Dover.

Miller, R., (1996). *The structure of singing—system and art in vocal technique*. New York: Schirmer Books.

Mish, F. C. (Ed.). (2005). *Merriam-Webster's collegiate dictionary*. Springfield, MA: Merriam-Webster.

Vennard, W. (1967). *Singing, the mechanism and the technic*. New York: Carl Fischer.

Chapter 2

ANATOMY OF THE SINGER'S INSTRUMENT: DESIGN AND FUNCTION

Because you are your instrument, it is important that you understand not only how your instrument is constructed, but also how it functions normally on a day-to-day basis, and especially how it functions for speaking and singing. Later on in this book you will find information regarding appropriate health concepts and concerns that will add to your knowledge of the proper care and development of your vocal instrument. The process of phonation is not limited to the action of the vocal folds or larynx. All the body musculature, bones, ligaments, additional tissues, and cavities are involved in producing beautiful vocal quality. A general understanding of human anatomy is necessary knowledge for anyone wishing to become a singer.

Referring frequently to the illustrations which follow as well as to your own body, become familiar with the anatomy of your instrument so that you are not only comfortable with the terminology, but understand how each part of the human anatomy relates to the function of human voice production. If you have this information, you will find that it is easier to develop a strong vocal technique and to determine what is not functioning well when the technique is not operating at its best. With this introductory information you will be on your way to becoming very knowledgeable about your instrument so that you can learn to use it to best advantage.

In this chapter we study the skeletal and muscular systems as well as some organs and cavities that are important to the functioning of the singer's instrument. We begin with the bone structure of the neck and chest cavity as it relates to the singing and speaking process. There are 206 bones in the human body and each is alive and changing continuously, providing mobility, support, and protection for your body. The bones are the supporting structure for the human body and each is acted upon in certain ways by muscles, ligaments, and tendons in the phonation process. Let us look at some of the most important anatomic skeletal parts separately.

THE SPINE (Figure 2-1)

The *spine* or backbone is made up of 24 vertebrae, each of which rests on the one below with a cushion of supportive connective tissue in between. The spinal cord, a large cable of nerve fibers descending from the brain, passes through a loop behind each vertebra. From this spinal cord, nerve "endings" branch out to all parts of the body. The smallest vertebrae are in the neck and the largest are in the small of the back; each vertebra gradually increases in size. There are seven *cervical vertebrae* in the

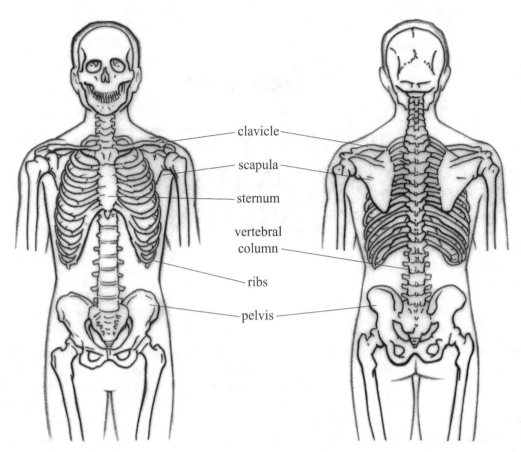

Figure 2–1. Major bones of the human skeletal system anterior and posterior views. Figure 2–1 shows specific bones of the human body important for singers to identify for the purposes of posture and breath management in singing.

neck, twelve *thoracic vertebrae* in the chest or thoracic cavity, and five *lumbar vertebrae* below, in the lower back, for a total of 24 vertebrae in the human body. The spinal cord (the central nervous system) and its connected nerve endings allow the human being to send signals from the brain directly to particular muscles in order to control physical actions as well as to receive signals from the tactile sensory areas (skin, ears, eyes, nose, and tongue) and return them to the brain for appropriate muscular responses.

THE RIB CAGE OR THORAX
(Figure 2-2)

The rib cage or *thorax* is the housing or protection for the lungs and heart. This is one of the most important parts of the human anatomy for the singer,

as the act of singing requires the use and control of air pressure, which is established in the lungs and thoracic cavity. Each of the rib(s) or *costa(e)* is hinged to a vertebra in the back. The upper seven thoracic or chest costae are joined in the front directly to the *sternum* or breastbone. These seven ribs form a sort of circle around the body, protecting the heart and lungs contained within. Each rib is composed primarily of bone with a small section of cartilage joining it to the sternum. This cartilage cushions the joining of the two bones, absorbing shock and weight during body movement. Thoracic ribs 8, 9, and 10 do not connect directly to the sternum, but are joined with the cartilage above and are known as *false ribs* or *abdominal ribs*. The eleventh and twelfth thoracic or chest ribs are quite short and have very little cartilage. They are known as *floating ribs* because they do not connect in any way to the sternum.

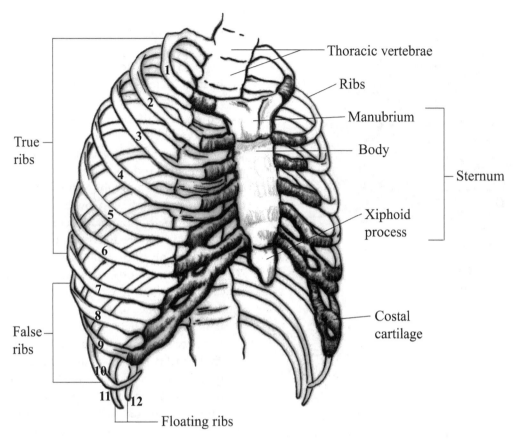

Figure 2–2. The rib cage or thorax. Figure 2–2 will aid the singer in identifying the important parts of the thorax, including the three parts of the sternum or breast bone, the true (1–7), false (8–10), and floating (11–12) ribs, and the rib cartilage (costal cartilage) which secures the true and false ribs to the sternum.

THE INTERCOSTAL MUSCLES (Figure 2-3)

It is important to note that nearly all human body muscles are found in pairs; each muscle coordinates with its paired muscle to cause motion. Although there are many muscles in the chest area, the most important muscles of the rib cage, as far as singing is concerned, are the *intercostal muscles*, so called because they are found between the ribs (the prefix *inter* meaning between and costa[e] meaning rib[s]). There are two pairs of intercostal muscles. The *external intercostal muscles* which are positioned diagonally downward and away from the backbone are the primary muscles of inhalation as they are responsible for pulling the ribs upward and increasing the size of the thorax or chest cavity. The second

pair or *internal intercostal muscles* are an inner layer of muscles running at right angles to the external intercostals, upward and outward from the backbone. These internal intercostal muscles are the primary muscles of exhalation as they pull the ribs downward. Working together, the two pairs of muscles coordinate in a sort of bellows action, expanding and contracting the rib cage, inhaling and exhaling.

There are many other chest muscles which may or may not come into action during singing, but it is sufficient for our purposes to understand the action of these primary and essential intercostal muscles for now. Later, in the chapter on breathing for singing, you will learn how the intercostal muscles can be developed for maximum inhalation as well as carefully controlled exhalation during the phonation process. Increasing your knowledge of the functioning of this musculature will help you as you

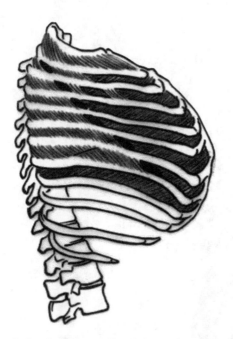

Figure 2–3. Action of the internal and external intercostal muscles in singing. Figure 2–3 demonstrates the lifting and opening of the rib cage upon inhalation by the external intercostal muscles. As a singer exhales, the external intercostal muscles continue to be engaged so that the rib cage remains open and the diaphragm and abdominal muscles take on the work of exhalation in the singer's phonation process. Note that the rib cage should already be elevated comfortably prior to the inhalation process, and should remain lifted and open throughout the full inhalation/phonation process.

continue your study of singing following this class. In the meantime, if you are interested in finding out more, there are many excellent books on anatomy, physiology, and vocal pedagogy. Many of these resources are mentioned in the Bibliography at the end of this book.

THE DIAPHRAGM
(Figures 2-4 and 2-5)

The *diaphragm* may be thought of as the floor of the rib cage. It is a large double-dome-shaped muscle, which separates the upper body cavity (thoracic cavity—containing lungs and heart) from the

lower body cavity (abdominal cavity—containing the remaining internal organs known collectively as the *viscera*). The diaphragm is attached at its highest point to the *pericardium* or the sac containing the heart muscle and at its lowest points to the lowest ribs. In its relaxed position, the diaphragm is arched high in the thoracic cavity. When the diaphragm contracts, it flattens out and lowers toward the abdominal area; consequently, the floor of the rib cage is lowered so that the space inside the rib cage is increased and lung volume is expanded. On inhalation, the diaphragm lowers and flattens, pressing against the abdominal viscera in a downward and forward motion and pulling the lungs downward causing air to flow into them.

The abdomen responds to this action by moving forward or outward to make way for the descending diaphragm. As the air is used or exhaled, the diaphragm slowly returns to its high arch within the chest cavity reverting to its dome-shaped form as it is pushed up by the contents of the abdominal cavity. This action causes a push against the lungs as well, causing them to expel the air, which has become compressed. The muscles of the lower abdomen aid in this process, especially when maximum air capacity is required as it is for singing. This process is involuntary in day-to-day life, but in singing we learn to carefully and consciously control certain abdominal and thoracic muscles in order to "support" the singing voice through a controlled exhalation process. Learning to breathe correctly (both the inhalation and exhalation process) is a very important part of developing a strong vocal technique. Please note the diaphragmatic action on inhalation/exhalation as demonstrated in Figure 2–4, so that you will know what to look and feel for when you begin the process of learning to breathe correctly for singing.

ADDITIONAL MUSCLES OF
RESPIRATION (Figure 2-5)

Remember that muscles generally operate in pairs using a principle known as *muscular antagonism*. Each muscle is opposed and steadied by one or more additional muscles. Having noted the motion of the diaphragm into the abdominal cavity on

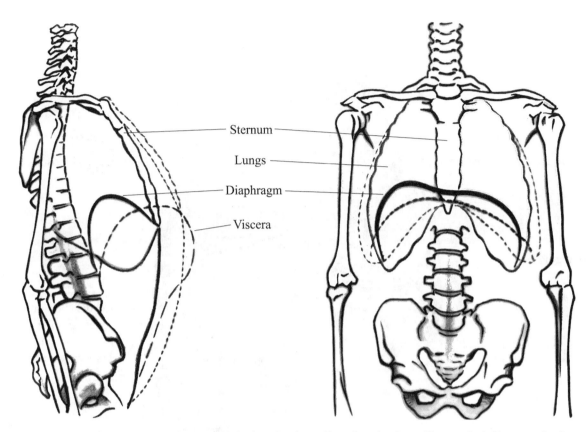

Sternum
Lungs
Diaphragm
Viscera

Figure 2-4. Diaphragmatic and abdominal motion for singing. Figure 2–4 demonstrates the downward motion of the diaphragm, and the forward motion of the abdominal contents (viscera) on inhalation. As the diaphragm descends, the abdomen moves forward to make room for the descending lungs. Notice there is no motion in the area of the clavicle bones or scapula, but the sternum is slightly elevated throughout the process.

inhalation, it follows that excellent muscular coordination between the muscles of the torso and the abdomen must be achieved in order for the inhalation and exhalation process to be controlled appropriately for the phonation process, especially for singing. The upper torso and abdominal muscles are mutually supportive and interactive throughout the respiration process.

Muscular movement in the abdomen may be achieved in two ways. The abdominal muscles may simply respond to the downward motion initiated by the lungs and diaphragm on inhalation as they do when they move down and outward, or the abdominal muscles may initiate motion; acting upon the organs and muscles of respiration by pushing them upward, as they do in the exhalation process. There are four pairs of abdominal muscles in the human body: the *external oblique, internal oblique, rectus*

abdominis, and the *transversus abdominis*. These muscles are both postural (they help to maintain proper positioning of the internal organs), and expiratory (they help the diaphragm and thoracic muscles to empty the lungs). In his *Professional Voice, The Science and Art of Clinical Care* (2005), Dr. Robert T. Sataloff gives a clear description of each of these important pairs of muscles, which will help us in our effort to visualize the muscles. Be sure to have Figure 2-5 in front of you as you read Dr. Sataloff's words.

The external oblique is a flat broad muscle located on the side and front of the lower chest and abdomen. Upon contraction, it pulls the lower ribs down and raises the abdominal pressure by displacing the abdominal contents inward. It is an important muscle for support of singing and

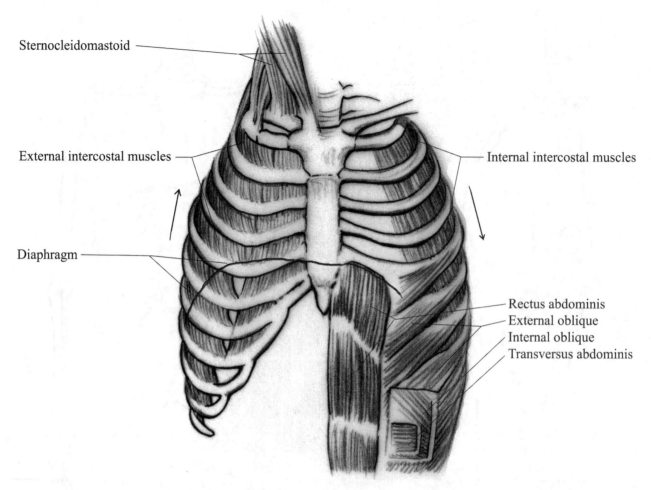

Sternocleidomastoid

External intercostal muscles

Internal intercostal muscles

Diaphragm

Rectus abdominis
External oblique
Internal oblique
Transversus abdominis

Figure 2–5. The muscles of inhalation and phonation. Figure 2–5 shows the muscles involved in inhalation and phonation for a singer. Note the position and direction of motion of the internal and external intercostal muscles, the position of the sternocleidomastoid muscle (aids in elevating the sternum), and the four abdominal muscle layers (rectus abdominis, external and internal oblique, and the transversus abdominis muscles). All are involved in the breath management process for singing.

acting voice tasks . . . the internal oblique is a flat muscle in the side and front wall of the abdomen. It lies deep to the external oblique. When contracted, the internal oblique drives the abdominal wall inward and lowers the lower ribs . . . The rectus abdominis runs parallel to the midline of the abdomen originating from the xiphoid process of the sternum and fifth, sixth and seventh costal (rib) cartilages. It inserts into the pubic bone . . . Contraction of the rectus abdominis also forces the abdominal contents inward and lowers the sternum and ribs . . . The transversus abdominis is a broad muscle located under the internal oblique on the side and front

of the abdomen. Its fibers run horizontally around the abdomen. Contraction of the transverse abdominis compresses the abdominal contents, elevating abdominal pressure (p. 126).

As breath control is so important in achieving a strong reliable vocal technique, voice lessons and practice time will include exercises for the development of the abdominal muscles. This can be done through singing vocalises as well as performing general exercises, which will strengthen these muscles and help the singer to gain conscious control over their use. Leg lifts and similar exercises are a good way to gain strength and flexibility of these muscles according to Dr. Sataloff. Traditional sit-ups or "curls" do not seem to develop the appropriate strength, flexibility or coordination needed in these muscles for singing (Sataloff, 2005). In fact, these exercises may cause the abdominal musculature to become too stiff for appropriate use in singing. Much more will be said about the development and use of the abdominal muscles in the chapter on breathing for singing.

THE LUNGS (Figure 2-6)

The lungs are the primary organs of respiration and are housed in the thoracic cavity immediately behind the twelve thoracic ribs and enclosed in the pleural sacs. It is important to remember that breathing is only one aspect of respiration, which also includes supplying oxygen to body cells as well as expelling the carbon dioxide given off by those cells. The act of filling the lungs with air can be called either inspiration or inhalation. The act of breathing out is called expiration or exhalation.

The lungs are most simply described as cone-shaped structures (organs) of a spongy, porous texture, possessing an abundance of resilient elastic fibers. The surface of the lungs follows the contours of the ribs and organs found in the thoracic cavity. Both lungs rest on the top surface of the diaphragm from which they extend upward, one on each side, to almost fill the thoracic cavity. The lungs are enclosed within a pleural membrane, the outer portion of which adheres closely to the walls of the thoracic cavity and diaphragm. The inner portion is

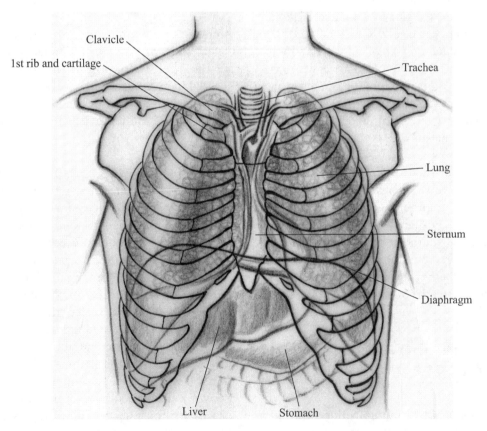

Figure 2-6. The lungs and their position in the body. Figure 2–6 will help the singer to identify the positioning of the lungs within the human body in relation to other organs and bones. Each rib is numbered, and the sternum and diaphragm are made evident in this drawing. Note also the positioning of the liver and stomach in relation to the lungs.

fused to the lungs. Only a thin film of fluid separates these two layers. As their movement is dependent on the action of the musculature around them, the lungs and thorax work together as a unit.

In his book entitled *The Science of the Singing Voice* (1987), well-known vocal scientist Johan Sundberg makes the following explanatory statement regarding the lungs which may be helpful in understanding the process of breathing as it relates to anatomic function:

> The lungs consist of spongy structure. If a lung is taken out of the body and suspended in free air, it shrinks drastically; it assumes a volume that is actually about as small as the smallest possible volume it may assume within the rib cage. This means that the lungs are always attempting to shrink when hanging inside the rib cage. However, they are prevented from shrinking by the fact that they are hanging in a vacuum. In this respect, the lungs can be said to be similar to rubber balloons. When they are filled with air, they attempt to exhaust this air with a force, which is determined, by the amount of air contained in them. This means that the lungs exert an entirely passive expiratory force that increases with the amount of air inhaled (p. 27).

It is a fact that singing demands the full range and vital capacity of the lungs, a fact untrue of the everyday breathing process. Singers spend years developing full lung capacity and attempting to gain conscious control over the inspiratory and expiratory muscles of the thoracic and abdominal cavities. Much more will be said about the breathing process itself in Chapter 4—Breath Management for Singers.

THE SHOULDERS
(Figures 2-1 and 2-4)

The shoulders consist of the collarbones or *clavicles*, which are attached to the top of the sternum by ligaments and to the two shoulder blades or *scapulae*. It is important to note that the shoulders are connected to the ribs by muscles, which influence breathing when they pull on the ribs. The

shoulder muscles are primarily inspiratory, and when used in the phonation process, especially in singing, leave the exhalation process completely uncontrolled. "Heaving" the shoulders is a sign of exhausted and uncontrolled breathing, which is inappropriate for singing. Shoulder motion during the singing and breathing process is considered to be a sign of poor vocal technique and uncontrolled exhalation.

THE NECK, HEAD, AND NASAL
CAVITIES (Figure 2-7)

The neck is the supporting structure for the head and houses the *larynx* or *voice box*. Its structure consists of layers of muscles which are involved in both speech and singing and which aid in the support of the movements of the larynx itself. One set of muscles, the *sternocleidomastoids* (sometimes called *sternomastoids*), provides postural support for the head. These postural muscles may be easily viewed by turning the head sharply to the side. The exposed muscle will be seen to run from behind the ear down to the clavicle and on to the sternum. In between this strong pair of muscles is located the larynx.

Also contained here are the structures of *articulation* (those concerned with producing vowels and consonants necessary for speech and singing) and include the tongue, lips, and teeth as well as the spaces used for resonating the tones produced in the larynx. The spaces or cavities used for resonating vocal tones include the mouth or *oro* cavity, the *pharynx* (area from the top of the voice box to the nasal cavities and between the back wall of the throat and the uvula) and the nasal cavities (the cavities behind the nose and above the hard and soft palate), all of which are involved in voice production to some degree. The tongue, lips, and teeth are known as the articulators of the voice whereas the oro cavity, the pharynx, and the nasal cavities are known as the resonators. The muscles of the head are divided into those used for creating facial expression (very important for emotional communication during singing and speaking) and those used in chewing. The development of conscious awareness

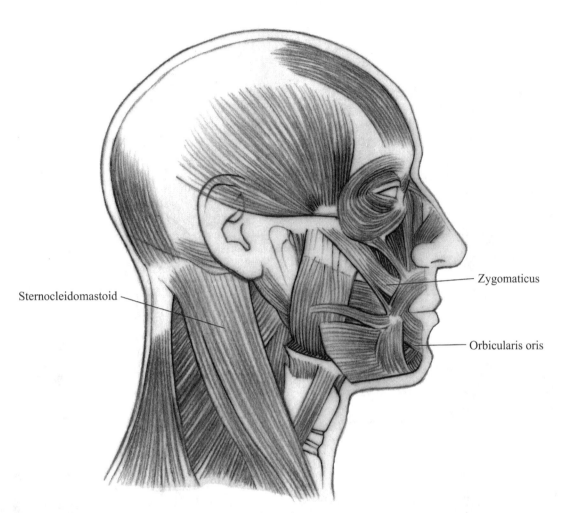

Figure 2-7. Important muscles of the human head and neck. Figure 2–7 locates three important muscles involved in the singing process, the sternocleidomastoid, a large muscle involved in posture for singing, the orbicularis oris muscle, surrounding the mouth opening, and which aids in the focus of tone and diction, as well as the zygomaticus muscle so important in creating resonance for singers and speakers.

and control over the way in which these structures, cavities, and muscles interact is an important part of the vocal technical skills building process.

THE LARYNX OR VOICE BOX (Figures 2-8 and 2-9)

The human body has evolved substantially over time allowing for many physical changes in the anatomy toward the purpose of human development. The function of the larynx itself has evolved in the human body from a purely biological function—acting as a valve at the top of the trachea; allowing the passage of air into and out of the respiratory system—to one which allows a secondary and specialized activity: the production of vocal sounds in order to communicate.

In his book *The Structure of Singing* (1986), Richard Miller quotes two important speech scientists regarding this evolutionary process (Sir Victor E. Negus, *The Mechanism of the Larynx* [1928] and W. R. Zemlin *Speech and Hearing Science: Anatomy and Physiology* [1981]). It seems appropriate to quote some of this material here to gain a better

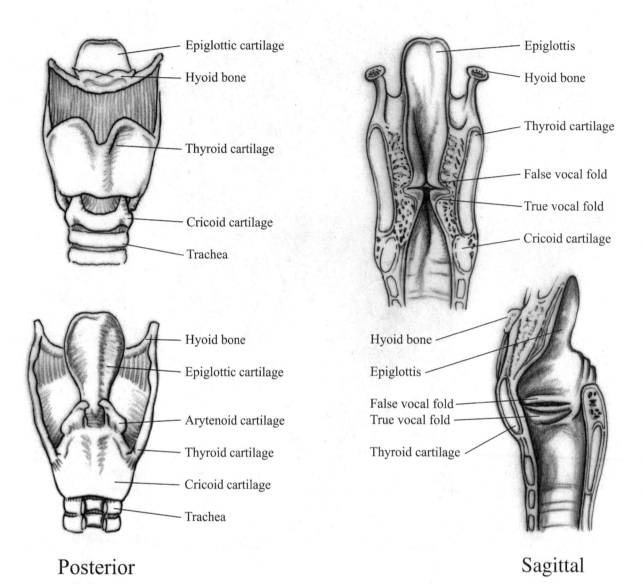

Figure 2–8. Structure of the larynx. Figure 2–8 shows both the anterior (from the front) and posterior (from the back) view of the larynx. This diagram will help the singer to identify the important parts of the larynx as they relate to sound production. The "sliced" view will help the singer to identify the vocal folds, both true and false, as well as the spatial relationship within the body of the larynx.

understanding of this process and development of the phonatory system of the human body.

There is no doubt that a simple larynx, such as that of the cat tribe, would be sufficient for the needs of Man in mere speech; his more highly

evolved organ, with its secondary valvular fold (usually called the vocal cord or vocal fold), is of advantage for purposes of song because of its greater flexibility and is of value in allowing modulation of the speaking voice . . . The vocal tones of Man are of a more mellow quality than those

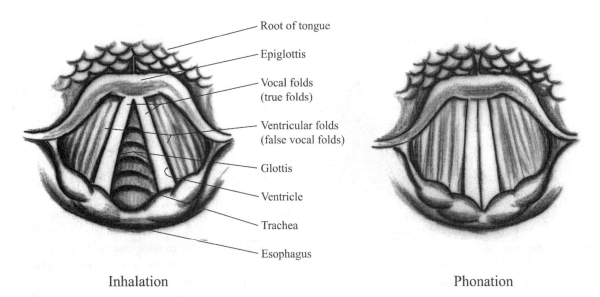

Root of tongue
Epiglottis
Vocal folds (true folds)
Ventricular folds (false vocal folds)
Glottis
Ventricle
Trachea
Esophagus

Inhalation   Phonation

Figure 2–9. The vocal folds on inhalation and phonation. Figure 2–9 is drawn from a position above the vocal folds looking down. This is what an otolaryngologist sees when looking through a scope at the singer's vocal folds. The top of each drawing represents the anterior view of the singer. On the Inhalation drawing, note the exact position of the epiglottis and the root of the tongue (at the top of the drawing), the true and false vocal folds and the trachea, by looking through the glottis (space between the vocal folds). Note, too, the esophagus (at the bottom of the drawing). The view on the right demonstrates the phonation process, closing the vocal folds almost completely over the top of the trachea.

of a Gibbon or a Chimpanzee, because the vocal cords have less sharp edges; this change to a less efficient type of valve is consequent upon the abandonment of a purely arboreal existence, as the complete valvular closure of Lemurs, Monkeys and Apes is not required (Negus, 1962, p. 194).

Later on in this section of Richard Miller's book, he quotes W. R. Zemlin (1981):

. . . Indeed, speech is so much a part of human behavior; it might well be considered a "second order" biological function. Regardless of the stand one may take, there is no debating that the larynx functions as a sound generator only when it is not fulfilling the vital biological functions . . . The human larynx is especially well-equipped for sound production. The vocal folds are long, smoothly rounded bands of muscle tissue which may be lengthened and shortened, tensed and

relaxed, and abducted and adducted . . . Compared with less well-developed animals, the human arytenoid cartilages are quite small with respect to the total length of the valvular mechanism. This means that the muscular, vibrating portion of the vocal fold is quite long and well suited for sound production (p. 127).

It is important that singers understand the basic anatomy and function of the larynx in order to learn to sing. If you go on to study singing in a university degree program and beyond, you will undoubtedly take a course in *vocal pedagogy*—the art of teaching vocal technique. In this vocal pedagogy course you will study and gain an in-depth understanding of the function of the anatomic parts involved in respiration and phonation. The following description of the larynx and its components will be helpful in beginning to understand the basic function of the larynx and its many intricate interactions as required for phonation.

The larynx or voice box is found at the top of the trachea or windpipe, and consists of a total of nine rings of cartilage connected by ligaments and membranes and one bone—the *hyoid bone*. Its shape resembles that of a vacuum cleaner hose except that the rings are not complete in the back; they are filled with muscular or membranous tissue. The "Adam's apple," found at the front of the neck, is actually the thyroid cartilage and is the most physically obvious or prominent part of the external laryngeal structure.

Internally, an additional cartilage—the *epiglottis*—is a somewhat leaf-shaped structure, which is attached to the anterior portion of the thyroid cartilage, hanging free and swinging in an upward direction. The epiglottis folds down over the larynx when we swallow to keep food and drink from passing into the trachea. When not swallowing, the epiglottis stands vertically, allowing the passage of air in and out of the trachea. There are additional cartilages which are important in the production of sound and which include the *cricoid* cartilage and two *arytenoid* cartilages (see Figure 2–8).

Within the larynx can be found the "valve" which helps to retain air in the lungs as needed. This valve is constructed of paired ligament and muscle groups lying horizontally and which stretch front to back along the laryngeal cavity. The two upper folds are called the *false vocal folds* and are used primarily to assist the *true vocal folds* found immediately beneath them in closing the valve tightly. They are not generally used in speaking or singing except when whispering as they assist the true vocal folds and occasionally do make sound. The lower set of folds are commonly known as the true *vocal cords* although they do not resemble cords in any way, nor do they function like the strings of a guitar or violin. They more closely resemble the sides of a balloon neck and are equally pliable in stretching over the trachea. When phonating, the false vocal folds relax and only the true vocal folds are brought together. As they close over the trachea, they offer resistance to the flow of breath, which is sent from the lungs. As the abdominal and intercostal muscles coordinate with the diaphragm to send the air upward through the folds, they vibrate and vocal tone is produced. The space between the true vocal folds is called the *glottis* and is quite wide during the inhalation process and quite narrow during phonation.

There are a number of muscles, both external and internal, which are important in the correct positioning and function of the larynx as well as the vocal folds during the phonation process. The physiologic structure of the larynx is complex and includes four anatomic parts: the *mucosa*—five layers of fiber, muscle, and cartilage which allow the smooth action of the vocal folds on vibration, the *intrinsic muscles*—a group of muscles which help to open, close, shorten, lengthen, thicken, and thin the vocal folds in the process of phonation, the *extrinsic muscles*—a group of muscles which connect from the larynx to the sternum, clavicle, and other portions of the upper body in order to coordinate the positioning of the larynx in phonation, and the skeleton—specifically the hyoid bone. The precise interaction and coordination of all these muscles, ligaments, membranes, bone, and various other living materials combined with the energy of the breath is what has been developed in the human being as the phonation process—whether the process results in speech or song. The development of this coordination and interaction is the process known as vocal technique.

THE MOUTH AND PHARYNX CAVITY (Figures 2–10 and 2–11)

The space above the larynx, including the mouth, pharynx, and nasal cavities helps to shape and resonate the vocal tones produced by the vocal folds. The mouth or oro cavity and its articulator components are used to shape tone into words, theoretically without diminishing the beauty of the tone quality generated in the larynx and resonated in the pharynx cavity. The size of the mouth can be greatly affected by the position of the jaw. Many changes in vocal quality will relate directly to the pronunciation or articulation of vowels and consonants in the mouth cavity.

The adult pharynx cavity is a tubelike structure approximately five inches long, which can be divided

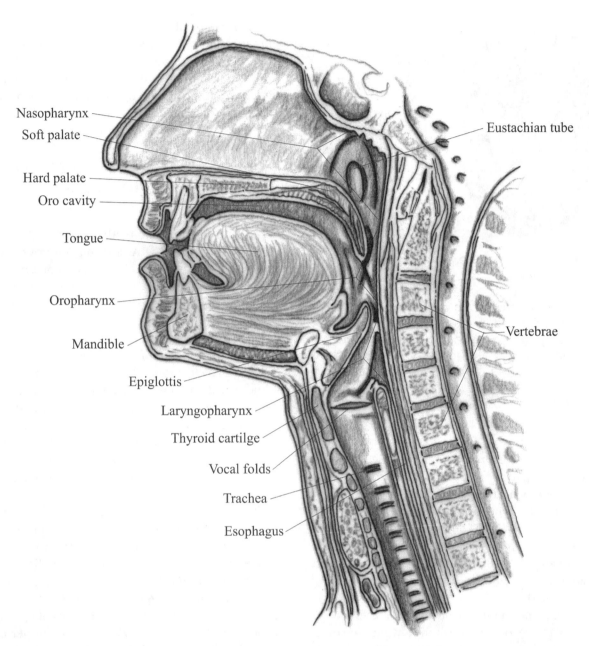

Nasopharynx

Soft palate

Hard palate

Oro cavity

Tongue

Oropharynx

Mandible

Epiglottis

Laryngopharynx

Thyroid cartilge

Vocal folds

Trachea

Esophagus

Eustachian tube

Vertebrae

Figure 2-10. An open view of the human head and neck musculature, bone, and cavities. Figure 2–10 is a clear view of the important muscles, spaces, and bones involved in the singing process. Locate the full pharynx cavity, so important in resonating vocal tone. Starting at the larynx, find the laryngopharynx, oropharynx, and nasopharynx cavities. Looking at the oro or mouth cavity, locate the large musculature of the tongue, the hard and soft palates, and the lower jaw or mandible. At the base of the tongue can be seen the thyroid cartilage, vocal folds, trachea, and esophagus. Note the eustachian tube connection to the oro cavity, and the position of the vertebrae in relation to the pharynx space.

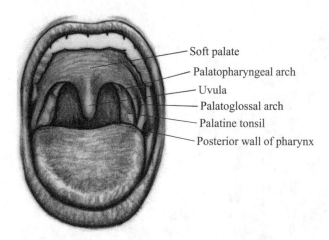

Soft palate
Palatopharyngeal arch
Uvula
Palatoglossal arch
Palatine tonsil
Posterior wall of pharynx

Figure 2–11. What the otolaryngologist sees in the oro cavity. Figure 2–11 is a drawing of the open mouth of a singer. Note the position of the velum or soft palate (in a lowered position in the mouth), and the uvula hanging from it. When singing, the uvula may almost disappear from view because of the elevation of the soft palate. Note the position of the palatopharyngeal arch and tonsils, as well as the back wall of the oropharynx, and the tongue muscle.

into three parts. The *nasopharynx*, which connects to the nose space, is at the top. The *oropharynx* is immediately beneath and connects to the mouth or oro cavity. The *laryngopharynx* is the lower third and extends downward and behind the larynx. The muscles of the three-part pharynx allow the space to be changed in size, thus varying the resonance capabilities as well as the actual tone produced by the vocal folds.

Within the mouth or oro cavity are found the hard palate or "roof" of the mouth, which separates the mouth from the nasal cavities. This is a bony structure covered with a mucous membrane. Behind the hard palate and *uvula* (a small projection at the back of the roof of the mouth) can be seen the *velum* or soft palate which is connected directly to the walls of the pharynx. The soft palate may be raised or lowered by muscles to open or close the space between the oropharynx and the nasopharynx. This action is an important part of the resonating aspect of vocal technique. Within the oropharynx space may also be seen the tonsils on both right and left sides of the pharynx if they have

not been surgically removed. The tonsils consist of lymphoid tissue covered by a mucous membrane and play a role in protecting the body from disease. They have nothing to do with singing unless they have become enlarged and are closing off needed resonance space within the pharynx.

TONGUE, JAW, LIPS, AND TEETH (Figures 2-10 and 2-11)

The tongue, jaw, lips, and teeth are considered to be articulators of the voice. As a singer, it is not enough to be able to produce beautiful vocal sounds, because these do not effectively communicate language. It should be mentioned, however, that there are some very effective "concert vocalises" written by various composers specifically to convey particular emotions and thus to communicate without the use of text as well as to show off the beauty and flexibility of the vocal instrument. Generally, however, the singing musician must make beautiful sounds and coordinate them with effective communication of language; whether that language is one's own, or a foreign language. The articulators, in coordination with the brain, are responsible for making this process successful.

The tongue is a mass of muscles covered by mucous membrane. Motion of the tongue is controlled by extrinsic (external) and intrinsic (internal) muscle groups. The shape and position of the tongue not only affects enunciation of vowels and consonants, but also resonance of the vocal tone. The *mandible* or lower jaw is the only movable portion of the skull. The two *maxilla*s form the upper jaw. Through the motion of the lower jaw, resonance and articulation as well as resonance space can be changed in the oro cavity and pharynx. Thus, motion must be carefully controlled and deliberate for the singer to have both excellent diction and beautiful tone quality.

The lips are both articulators and muscles of facial expression. They not only help the singer to enunciate, but also to convey the emotional content of the text. The lips are actually composed of skin, muscle, glands, and an internal mucosal layer. The principal muscle involved in controlling the motion of the lips is the *orbicularis oris*, which forms a circle around the mouth opening. This muscle is used to close and focus the lips. A number of other muscles interact with various facial muscles for additional movement capability. The singer learns to use and control the interaction of these muscles for expression as well as articulation and resonance. The 32 teeth found in both upper and lower jaw are used primarily for eating, but are also important to speech production as they interact with the motion of the tongue, lips, and airflow to produce consonants. In addition, as hard surfaces within the oro cavity, they create certain resonance properties through vibration.

By moving the jaw up or down to open or close the mouth, by placing the tongue quite flat on the floor of the mouth, or allowing it to bulge up and forward or up and back, by bringing the tongue into contact with the teeth or the ridge behind the teeth, by opening, closing, focusing, spreading or constricting the lips, as well as utilizing many combinations of these motions, the singer can create or articulate particular language sounds in order to communicate with an audience. The particular way in which these motions are achieved and coordinated will either give the singer excellent *diction* (the intelligible pronunciation and enunciation of language) or not. In creating artistic vocal music, the singer has the opportunity to express through the production of musical tone as well as through the delivery of the text of a poet or librettist. The two tasks must merge equally and vibrantly for the most successful vocal performance. Thus, the singer must learn to use the vocal production methods best suited to this coordination of beautiful vocal tone and delivery of text.

There are many additional physiologic and psychologic components of the human body involved in the singing process. For our purposes, it is necessary to understand that all the body parts discussed so far must carefully coordinate together to give the best possible vocal production. Learning the function of each individual part and then learning to coordinate each with all the others will be one of the goals of a voice class. This may seem to be an impossible task, but with patience and perseverance, you will bring all the correct muscular actions under control and learn to sing easily and freely. Review this chapter frequently as you continue your study of singing technique to become familiar with the location and purpose of particular musculature and coordination of the individual parts of the anatomy.

IMPORTANT TERMS TO DEFINE AND UNDERSTAND

Spine

Cervical vertebrae

Thoracic vertebrae

Lumbar vertebrae

Thorax

Sternum

Costa(e)

Internal intercostal muscles

External intercostal muscles

Diaphragm

Muscular antagonism

Abdominal muscles

    External oblique

    Internal oblique

    Rectus abdominis

    Transversus abdominis

Lungs

Sternocleidomastoids (sternomastoids)

Organs of articulation

    Tongue

    Lips

    Teeth

    Oro cavity

    Articulators

    Resonators

    Larynx

False vocal folds

True vocal folds (cords)

Epiglottis

Pharynx

    Nasopharynx

    Oropharynx

    Laryngopharynx

Diction

Additional terms that are new to you:

REFERENCES

Miller, R. (1986). *The structure of singing system and art in vocal technique*. New York: Schirmer Books.

Negus, V. E. (1962). *The comparative anatomy and physiology of the larynx*. New York: Hafner. (Reprint)

Sataloff, R. (2005). *Professional voice, the science and art of clinical care* (3rd ed). San Diego, CA: Plural.

Sundberg, J. (1987). *The science of the singing voice*. DeKalb, IL: Northern Illinois University Press.

Zemlin, W. R. (1981). *Speech and hearing science: Anatomy and physiology* (2nd ed.). Englewood Cliffs, NJ: Prentice-Hall.

Chapter 3

ESTABLISHING CORRECT POSTURE FOR SINGING

Correct singing posture is not a difficult concept to understand or establish, but learning to maintain this posture consistently while singing will take practice and perseverance on your part. In order to be the best you can be as a singer you must develop this most important foundation principle fully. Without correct posture, your breathing and support mechanisms will not function at their maximum potential and therefore your singing voice will not improve as quickly as it should. Be sure to practice the exercises consistently as given throughout this chapter to help maintain correct balance and posture even when you are not singing. This will strengthen the muscles necessary for maintenance of correct posture for singing.

Your posture for singing must never be stiff or rigid, but should always feel buoyant and flexible as if you are being supported by a flotation device on a smooth lake. To be sure, there are many positions in which singers are asked to sing, but you will find that maintaining a "lift" in the rib cage and an erect head; allowing the jaw to be free, will give you the freedom to sit, stand, kneel, or lie down to sing eventually. For now, you will learn to sing in a standing position and transfer all of this knowledge to other positions in which you may be asked to sing at a later time.

Many students have unwanted tension in the neck and shoulder area as well as in other parts of the body. The following relaxation and stretching exercises should be done prior to attempting any

vocal exercises to ensure that muscles are relaxed and flexible at the onset of singing. These exercises will allow you to warm up the muscles needed for correct posture and breathing for singing, but they are also good exercises to do even when you are not planning on singing. Prior to beginning any exercise program, it would be wise to check with your physician regarding your general health and physical conditioning. Be sure to ask the physician about the exercises which follow if you are worried about them in regard to a personal physical or medical condition. Always alert your voice teacher to any medical or physical problems, which might make it difficult for you to perform any of the following exercises prior to attempting them.

WARM-UP EXERCISES

The Head Roll (Figure 3–1)

In a standing position with your shoulders comfortably down, back, and relaxed, drop your head forward so that your chin rests on or as close to your sternum as possible. Roll your head slowly in a smooth and gentle motion as far to the left as you can go without rolling your head over your spine, and then back to the front, being sure that your chin stays low. Now, roll your head slowly and gently to the right in the same fashion and then return to the

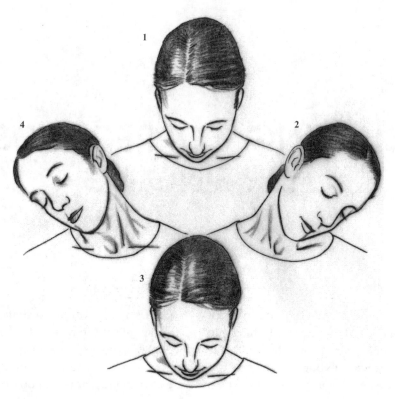

Figure 3-1. Relaxation and stretching exercises—head roll. In order to relax and stretch the muscles of the neck and shoulder areas prior to vocalization, a singer should perform head rolls as pictured above. Drop the head forward gently but fully, and then roll (with your chin as close to your body as possible) to one side, and back. Do not roll across your spine. Then, return to the center and roll in the opposite direction, again keeping the chin close to your body. Do this several times, very slowly, and smoothly for best results.

front. It is important to remember not to roll your head over your cervical vertebrae. Keep breathing regularly, deeply, and comfortably throughout the complete exercise for best possible results. Closing your eyes will allow you to concentrate fully on relaxing the muscles of the shoulders and neck as you perform the exercise. This exercise should be performed at least three times completely. When completed, you should feel much calmer, and the shoulder and neck muscles should feel less tense. Be sure to roll the head slowly and smoothly in both directions; never force your head in any direction to the point of causing pain. This is not necessary and may actually cause more harm than good. Again, do not allow the head to roll across the cervical verte-

brae of the spinal column. This can be damaging to the vertebrae and may cause wear and tear on the spinal structure itself.

This exercise may also be performed in a seated position, but be sure to sit up straight with both feet firmly planted on the floor in front of you; allow your arms to hang free at your sides or to lie comfortably in your lap. Do not be frightened by "cracking" and/or "popping" noises you may hear as you perform the head roll. In most cases, this means your neck muscles and/or tendons and ligaments are tight and lack flexibility. You are now loosening them. Of course, if you are a person with arthritis or any similar condition, you will want to notify your voice teacher about your condition before performing any exercises and check with your physician regarding exercises which might be inappropriate to that condition.

Simultaneous Shoulder Rolls (Figure 3–2)

Working gently and keeping in mind that these exercises are intended to relax and stretch the muscles rather than to strengthen them, continue to breathe deeply, and allow your arms to hang freely at your sides. Now, simultaneously roll both shoulders slowly upward and forward in a circular motion approximately five times. Then, reverse the action so that the shoulders are rolling in an upward and backward motion five times. Bring your shoulders up as close to your ears as you can without creating any sensation of pain or overstretching the muscles. Work slowly and gently with every stretch.

Individual Shoulder Rolls

Allowing the left shoulder to lie quietly down and back, roll the right shoulder up and forward in a circular motion, then down into its normal position. Now, allow the right shoulder to remain quietly down and back, and roll the left shoulder up and forward in a circular motion and then back into normal position. Continue to alternate between the shoulders for five complete rotations each. Next, do the single shoulder rolls in the opposite direction; rolling upward and back for five complete rotations, alternating between the two shoulders. Remember at all times to move the muscles slowly and gently, loosening and lubricating rather than forcing.

Rag Doll (Figure 3–3A)

Continue to breathe slowly and deeply throughout this exercise. Take a comfortably wide stance, with knees unlocked or even slightly bent, and allow your upper body to fall over forward gently from the waist; hands and arms should hang loosely from the shoulders. Gently shake any tension from your hands, arms, shoulders, and the neck area. It is not neces-

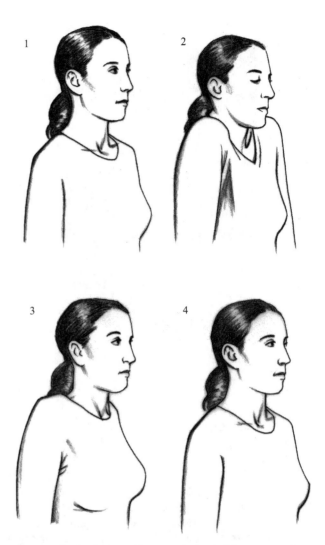

Figure 3–2. Relaxation and stretching exercises —shoulder rolls. First, establish a comfortable, but correct posture, and simultaneously raise both shoulders toward your ears. Bring the shoulders up as high as they will go, comfortably, feeling the stretch in your torso. Then, move both shoulders toward the back, and finally down again into your original resting position. Do the same exercise again in the opposite direction (up, forward, and down). It is also beneficial to do this exercise with one shoulder at a time. Do several repetitions of this exercise in each direction for best results.

sary or recommended that you bounce the torso up and down while in this position. While thinking about placing one vertebra on top of the other, bring your torso back up slowly, beginning with the

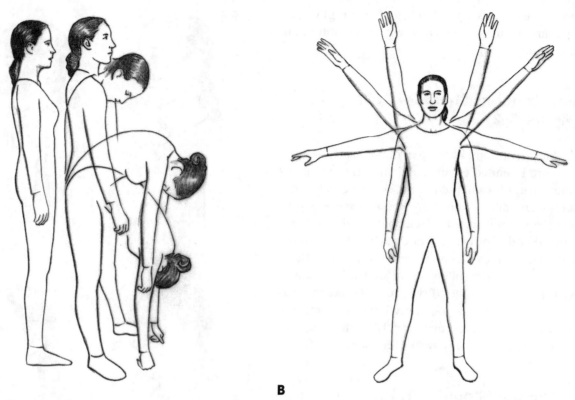

A   **B**

Figure 3–3. Relaxation and stretching exercises. **A.** Rag doll. Be sure you are wearing comfortably loose clothing, particularly around the waist and upper body for this exercise. Allow your upper body to fall over forward, slowly and gently, reaching with your arms as low as you can comfortably. Allow your arms to hang freely, and do not "bounce" in this lowered position. After holding this stretch for a moment or two, gradually return to an upright position, feeling each vertebrae align correctly in the spine until you are fully upright. You should feel an elongated stretch in your spine all the way to the crown of your head. **B.** Rib cage stretch. This exercise should follow the rag doll exercise. Begin with a comfortably upright body position, then, lift your hands and arms as high into the air as possible without overstretching any muscles. Feel the stretch along the sides, front, and back of the rib cage and abdomen. Maintaining this stretch in the torso, allow your arms to return to your sides. This lifted and stretched torso position is essential to proper breath management for singing.

lumbar spine, and moving one vertebra at a time up through the thoracic and cervical vertebrae; allow the arms and hands to hang freely from the shoulders, and keep the neck stretched long in the back. Your head should be the very last part of your body to regain an upright position. Bring your head finally to an erect position so that when you finish, your chin is parallel to the floor and the highest point of your head is at the top and back (the crown of the head) rather than above the forehead. Your shoulders establish a relaxed, slightly back and down-

ward position, allowing your arms and hands to fall comfortably at your sides with the palms facing in toward the thighs.

Rib Cage Stretch (Figure 3–3B)

Standing in the position you have just achieved through the rag doll exercise, reach your hands and arms as high into the air as possible without overstretching any muscles. Continue to breathe deeply and comfortably throughout the full exercise. You will be surprised how far you can stretch in an upward direction now that you have relaxed the shoulder and neck muscles. Reach as high as you can comfortably and feel the wonderful stretch along the side, back and front muscles of the rib cage and abdomen. This feeling of "lift" in the muscles of the rib cage will be an essential part of your posture for singing, so attempt to memorize the feeling as you stretch. Now, slowly lower your arms to your sides while attempting to maintain this feeling of lift in the rib cage. Be sure to allow the shoulder muscles to return to a relaxed position, allowing the hands and arms to hang freely at the sides of the body.

Now you are ready to begin a typical session of vocal exercises in order to prepare you for singing song literature or for continuing the development of your vocal technique. As your body is energized and ready to go, let us set the correct posture for good singing technique.

CORRECT POSTURE FOR SINGING (Figure 3-4)

Correct posture for singing is easy to establish and has some very definite sensations with which you can identify. We start with the position of the feet and move up from there.

Correct Position of the Feet

A singer's foot position should be similar to that of the athletic boxer; feet slightly apart (approximately 10 to 12 inches, or shoulder width) with the right foot slightly more forward than the left. Toes should be slightly turned out rather than pointing straight forward or being at thirty-degree angles. If you are left-handed, you may feel more comfortable with the left foot more forward and the right foot back. Either way is acceptable as long as you are comfortable and you feel your legs are flexible. Always keep the weight of your body forward on the "balls" of your feet and never rock back on your heels. This will help you to maintain the strength and balance

Incorrect Posture   Correct Posture

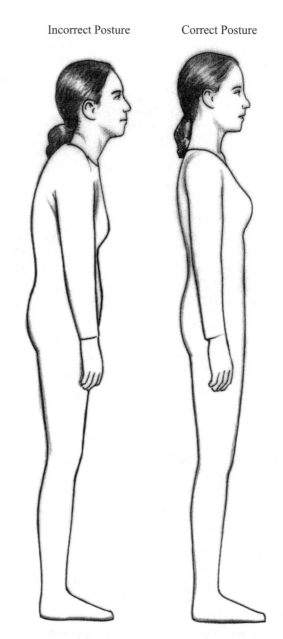

Figure 3-4. Correct posture for singing. The correct posture for singing includes a comfortably wide stance, unlocked knees, slightly tucked hips, an upward lift in the sternum and rib cage overall, shoulders comfortably down and back, and the upper most portion of the body should be the crown of the head (not the forehead). Your earlobes should be directly over your shoulders in order to align the head on the body correctly. Note the difference here between the poor posture on the left, and the correct posture on the right.

necessary for standing and singing for long periods of time. In addition, when the body is aligned correctly, the respiration process will work most efficiently. Body weight should be evenly distributed between the two feet and should not be carried completely on one foot or the other.

Correct Placement of the Knees and Legs (Figure 3-4)

It is important to remember flexibility at all times. Never lock your knees when you sing. This cuts off the circulation to your lower legs. Knee joints must never become rigid, inflexible, or uncomfortable, and should always be free of tension, even if you have to actually "flex" them back and forth slightly at times during your singing. Rigidity in any part of the body is unacceptable for a good singing posture, but it is especially important to avoid rigidity in the knees. A misaligned body is a body lacking in energy and coordination; both energy and coordination are necessary for good singing.

Correct Placement of the Hips and Pelvis (Figure 3-4)

Your hips and pelvis (see Figure 2-1) should be in proper alignment when the spine is stretched up and the weight is distributed equally over both feet. You should have the feeling that your hips are pulled under or rolled slightly down and in from the back, as in "posting" when riding a horse in English riding style. There should not be a large inward curve at the small of your back. You may find it helpful to stand with your feet slightly away from the base of a wall while allowing your hips, back, shoulders, and head to touch the wall. Feel the stretch in the spine and the upward stretch of the torso that is required to stay in this position. Be sure the highest point of your head is closest to the wall. Now, step away from the wall while maintaining this same stretch.

Correct Spinal Posture (Figure 3-4)

This is one of the most important areas of study in posture for the singer. If the spine and rib cage are not properly positioned, overall correct posture and breathing principles will be very difficult to establish. If necessary, reread the section in Chapter Two dealing with the anatomy of the spine and rib cage, and check the illustrations pertaining to these two areas, noting the connection of the spine to both pelvis and head, as well as rib connection to the spine (see Figure 2-1). For singing, it is necessary to establish a feeling of upward "stretch" in the spine and "lift" in the rib cage.

Balanced Posture for Singing (Figure 3-5)

Balanced posture combines a coordination of many muscles and may take some time to develop, but it is nonetheless essential for excellent singing technique. Here is a simple way to check both your body alignment and your balance. Set the posture of your feet, legs, and hips as described above, and continue to maintain the lift or stretch, which was obtained in the rib cage stretch exercise. When you feel comfortable in this position, shift your weight to one leg and lift the opposite leg in front of you, bending it at the knee until your thigh is parallel with the floor. You should be able to balance easily on one foot and leg if the body is aligned correctly. If alignment is still incorrect and you are unable to balance in this position, continue reading and perhaps you will be able to achieve this balance through appropriate alignment of the upper torso, or go back and review material already presented. It is important to achieve a balanced posture for strong vocal technique. The following positioning exercise for correct head and spinal posture should be a help to you in finding this lifted position.

Exercise for Correct Head and Spinal Column Posture (Figure 3–6)

With your feet, knees, legs, and hips in the position previously described and your shoulders down, back, and relaxed, imagine a string stretched from the top of the back of your head (the crown), down through the center of your spinal column and continuing to your tail bone. Tilt your head back very gently, but completely on your shoulders. Now, place your fingertips on your chin. Without letting your chin

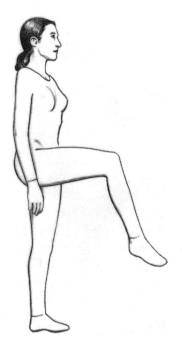

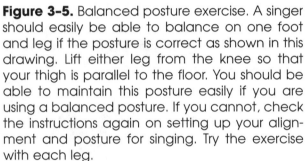

Figure 3-5. Balanced posture exercise. A singer should easily be able to balance on one foot and leg if the posture is correct as shown in this drawing. Lift either leg from the knee so that your thigh is parallel to the floor. You should be able to maintain this posture easily if you are using a balanced posture. If you cannot, check the instructions again on setting up your alignment and posture for singing. Try the exercise with each leg.

move any farther forward than it is in this tipped back position, lift your head from the crown, stretching toward the ceiling as though using the imaginary string to pull yourself up. Allow this lifting of your head to stretch your spine, which will in turn lift the rib cage as well. As your head gradually rotates forward to a normal position, the exercise should conclude with your chin parallel to the floor, and the crown of your head should be the highest point of your body. There should be a sensation of stretch in the back of the neck. Throughout the exercise, the shoulders should remain down, back, and relaxed, uninvolved in the entire process. You should now be in the correct position for singing.

You will know you have done the exercise correctly if you are aware of the sensation of stretch from your lower abdomen to the bottom of the sternum and you feel the same lift in the rib cage which

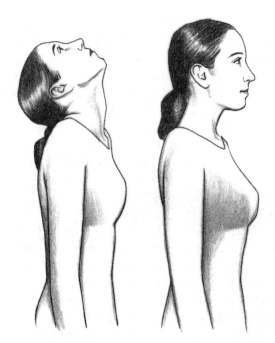

Figure 3-6. Exercise for correct head and spinal column posture. To find the correct posture for singing, begin with feet comfortably apart, and one foot slightly forward of the other, toes slightly turned away from the body, abdomen and shoulders should be very relaxed. Very gently and carefully, drop your head back on your spine as far as it will go comfortably. Now, begin to lift (rotate) your head up from the crown, without allowing your chin to move forward. Lift your head until you feel a good stretch in the spine and torso as you complete the exercise. Do not be afraid to stretch in the back of the neck, but never stretch in the front of the neck for singing. If you are performing the exercise correctly, you should feel the rib cage open and the sternum lift as well.

you felt in the "rib cage stretch" exercise performed previously. Even if you begin this exercise with very poor posture, if the exercise is performed correctly, the spine, shoulders, neck, head, rib cage, and abdomen will all pull into the correct posture and body alignment for singing. It will feel as though you have grown an inch or so due to the stretch in the spinal column and lift in the rib cage. Use the exercise often and always before you begin your vocal warm-ups to be sure you are in the correct posture for singing at all times. Especially check yourself at the ends of phrases prior to inhalation to see if the stretch is still part of your posture. The spinal column and rib cage should feel stretched from your tailbone to the top of your head in the back and from the navel to the sternum in the front. Please be aware that the chin should be parallel to the floor and the highest point of your body must be at the crown of your head and not the area above your forehead.

In this lifted position, you may be aware of the engagement of some muscles you have not felt before, or at least, for a while. Don't be concerned if you are a bit muscle sore after keeping yourself in this lifted and stretched position for only a short time. This is a natural and good sign, letting you know you are using the correct muscles. You may only be able to maintain this position for a short period of time until you develop the necessary muscle strength and coordination to sustain the posture. If you practice carefully and regularly, you will soon be able to increase the strength of these muscles to maintain the lift and stretch throughout an entire practice session and eventually a full performance, and throughout your everyday life. Development of these muscles and the ability to maintain this stretch are essential to a solid and reliable vocal technique, and will enable the respiratory system to function at its maximum efficiency. Practice this exercise in both a standing and a seated position. When you try it in the seated position, be sure to sit forward on the edge of the chair with both feet on the floor. The weight of your body should be forward and on the balls of your feet when sitting just as it is in a good standing posture. If you are in the correct seated posture for singing, you should be able to stand up from a chair without bending your torso forward! You will be balanced equally on three points, your feet, and hips, with the weight of your body primarily on your feet. The seat is for balance. Do not relax the torso down onto the pelvis when seated for singing.

Correct Posture for the Chest and Sternum

You are already aware from the exercises just performed, that the chest (thorax or rib cage) is lifted because of the attachment of the ribs to the spine. Let us add one more imaginary "string" to help lift

the sternum into the proper position as well. This will ensure an open and lifted chest cavity, which is absolutely essential for good singing.

Exercise to Lift the Sternum (Figure 3–7)

Imagine a string being attached to your sternum about midway (approximately 5 to 6 inches downward from your collar bone). This imaginary string will attach to an imaginary pulley on the ceiling about six feet in front of you. Now, as if pulling that string, lift the sternum as well as the rib cage gently up and forward toward the audience. Please note that it is unnecessary to fill the lungs with air in order to lift and open the rib cage. This entire process can and should be a muscular one. The illustration will help you to visualize the position of the rib cage when the spinal column is stretched and the sternum is lifted gently up and slightly forward. It is the proper torso position for singing. Maintaining this posture will require practice and perseverance as it utilizes the coordination of a number of muscles

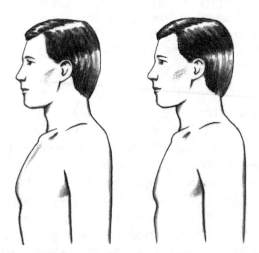

Figure 3–7. Exercise to lift the sternum. This exercise should follow the exercise performed in Figure 3–6. Imagine a string tied to the body of the sternum, and attached to a pulley a few feet in front of you on the ceiling. As if someone is pulling on the end of the string, lift the sternum slightly up and toward the audience to gain maximum space in the thoracic cavity for breathing. This lift of the sternum should be maintained throughout the singing process.

of the front, back, and side chest walls. (For further clarification, see Figure 2–3—Action of the internal and external intercostal muscles in singing).

Correct Position for the Shoulders

The shoulders should always remain relaxed in a comfortably back and downward position. The lifted sternum should help to emphasize this position as it pulls the sternum away from the shoulders slightly. A good singer never raises the shoulders during the breathing or singing process!

Correct Position for the Neck and Head

The neck has already been correctly positioned by the exercise to stretch the spine as the seven cervical vertebrae control the posture for the neck. The neck should feel long and gently stretched in the back, as it is the uppermost portion of the spine. The front of the neck must remain relaxed and comfortable. No feeling of stretch in the front of the neck is desirable. It is possible to check for correctly aligned shoulder and neck position by gently turning the head from side to side. When the head and neck are aligned properly, the head turns freely as though on an axis, allowing for a great deal of freedom in the area of the larynx. If the head does not turn easily or turns with difficulty, check to be sure the head is lifted from the crown and not the forehead. Repeating the exercise for establishing a lifted rib cage and stretched spine may help you to find this "floating head" posture which is so necessary to excellent singing technique.

Get used to having your eyes looking out at a level just above the heads of your audience rather than at the floor or ceiling. Initially, at least, correct

eye position will help to secure correct head position. The head should be in a position directly above the spine rather than forward from the shoulders. Check your posture against the wall to be sure your head is back far enough and correctly aligned on your spine and shoulders.

Correct Position for Arms and Hands (Figure 3–8)

Allow your arms to hang freely from the shoulders at your sides with the palms facing in toward the body. If the shoulders are rolled forward, the arms

Figure 3–8. Correct position for sitting and using a music stand. The correct seated posture for singing utilizes the chair as a third contact point for balance only. The singer's feet should be in the same position as for standing, with your body weight placed primarily on your feet while seated. A singer should be able to stand up from this position without leaning forward. Maintain the upper body stretch as established in previous exercises, and hold your music so that the bottom of the score is at the bottom of your sternum, with arms slightly stretched and away from the body. When using a music stand, be sure the stand height allows you to see the music without dropping your head, and that the audience can easily see your face.

The head position has also been established by the exercise to stretch the spine. Remember that the highest point of a singer's head must be at the back of the head (the crown), as a continuation of the spinal stretch, and never the front of the head (forehead). The chin should take a position in which it is parallel to the floor, with no tension in the muscles of the lower jaw.

will hang too far forward with the hands lying in front of the thighs. This is an indication that the shoulders need to be rotated down and back. If your arms and hands tend to hang stiffly and away from your body, you are probably tensing shoulder, back, and/or arm muscles. Using a mirror during practice will enable you to visualize tension in this area and to consciously relax these muscles so your hands and arms will hang freely, and without tension at the sides of your body. Eventually, you will develop a great deal of conscious control over these muscles so that you may use your arms and hands for interpretive gestures while singing without dropping your lifted posture. Initially, try to be aware of muscle tension, and release it whenever you are able. If you have "nervous hands" or "walking fingers," it may be helpful to gently touch your thumb to your third or ring finger. Let your other fingers hang loosely. This will stop your fingers from "walking" or fidgeting at your sides and actually looks quite natural to the audience.

CORRECT POSITION FOR SINGING WITH MUSIC (FIGURE 3-8)

When holding music, always keep the music comfortably high and directly in front of you. The choral folder or musical score should be placed at approximately sternum level and should never be so high that it hides your face. Keep your elbows away from your body and lifted slightly so they are not adding weight to the rib cage. Supporting the weight of the book or folder with the palm of either your right or left hand will allow the other hand to be free to turn pages or to balance the book as necessary. Never allow your arms to collapse onto your body as this will be a detriment to lifting the rib cage and will cause tension in your torso in addition to looking quite sloppy to the audience.

Using a music stand to support your music allows your arms and hands more freedom, as well as freeing the upper torso, and should be utilized when possible. The position of the music stand should be approximately the same as if you were holding the music in your hands. You should not have to drop your head to see the music. Place the stand high enough and far enough away from you that you can

see the music with a downward glance and no perceptible motion of the head. One mistake that young singers make is to place the music stand off to one side rather than directly in front of them. This forces the singer to place either the head or the entire body in an awkward position when it is necessary to consult the music. Even when the music is used only as a memory check, it is appropriate to place the music stand directly in front of you. This allows for more comfortable visualization and page turns.

Standing Versus Sitting for Singing (Figure 3-8)

In general, standing is the preferred posture for singing, and especially for learning to sing properly, because it allows a more complete coordination of the musculature, more efficient respiration, and gives the singer greater flexibility and endurance of muscle strength. However, this is not always possible. When sitting to sing, as in a choral rehearsal, sit quite far forward on the chair, supporting the weight of your body on the balls of both feet equally as much as on the hips. Be sure that the same stretched spinal posture is maintained when sitting as when standing; stretch in the spine and lift of the sternum and rib cage must always be present, whether standing, sitting, kneeling, or reclining if vocal technique is to be strong. You will know you are sitting in a balanced and correct manner when you can stand up from a seated position without bending forward. Try this test to check your posture when seated. If you cannot stand up from a seated position without bending forward, you are probably seated too far back on the chair. Move forward and place the weight of your body more on your feet than on your hips.

Practice carefully all the postural exercises given and be aware of your posture when you are singing at all times. Initially, it may seem that there are too many muscles to consciously control, but eventually you will find the muscles become accustomed to these positions and you no longer need to consciously control them—good posture becomes a habit. Practicing in front of a mirror helps to create a visual awareness on your part, but you should also work toward the understanding of what good posture sensations are. Practice good posture in your daily activities so that postural muscles become strong and responsive. This will help you to maintain balance and strength in your vocal technique.

In her recent book, entitled *Singing and Teaching Singing: A Holistic Approach to Classical Voice* (2006), Janice Chapman discusses the importance of posture and core stability in the following excerpt.

> Posture is important in many different forms of artistic expression but the rules for specific art forms differ according to their particular disciplines. Good core stability, that is, an underlying tonus in the abdominal and other torso muscles, is essential for the singer. Traditional classical dance training maintains a tight abdominal set in order to elevate the upper body, but this sort of postural alignment is counterproductive in the singer who needs flexibility in the abdominal wall in order to use the body's own elastic recoil action for breathing. Tonicity in the core stabilizers is crucial to the maintenance of high-energy singing tasks. Such systems as yoga, Pilates, and Tai Chi can assist in developing and maintaining core stability below the belt. In singers, this is very important as too much muscularity above the belt can interfere with the breath flow required for efficient vocalization. Singers need to have muscular tonus in the abdominal wall but the rectus abdominis muscles in particular should not be overdeveloped. The six-pack so desired by "gym junkies" is not useful for singers because it does not allow for the required flexibility in the abdominal wall (p. 29).

She later states:

> The rectus abdominis is also cited in some literature as contributing to expiration, but in my experience as a singer and singing teacher I have increasingly found that deactivation of this "6-pack" is essential in freeing up the supported air stream and the voice itself. Indeed, I forbid students to do stomach crunchers and to lift weights which would strengthen this pair of muscles (p. 46).

I could not agree more! There must be freedom of motion in the abdominal wall for proper support and posture during the singing process, and the overdevelopment of the rectus abdominis muscles

particularly will cause the singer to have difficulty in achieving the low and full breath so necessary for projection and beauty of vocal tone. It also interferes with the proper exhalation of the breath to be turned into vocal tone. Singers must be careful to know the difference between toned muscles, and muscles which are too tight for the classical singing process.

REVIEW OF EXERCISES FOR DEVELOPING PROPER SINGING POSTURE

Exercise to Establish Lift in the Spine and Rib Cage (Figure 3-6)

With your feet, knees, legs, and hips in the proper position, and your shoulders relaxed, imagine a string stretched from the top of the back of your head (the crown), down through the center of your spinal column and continuing to the tail bone. Tilt your head back gently, but completely, on your shoulders. Now place your fingertips on your chin. Without letting your chin move any further forward than it is in this tipped back position, lift your head from the back, stretching toward the ceiling as though using the imaginary string. Allow this lifting and rotation of your head to stretch your spine so that it lifts the rib cage as well. As your head gradually rotates back to a normal position, the exercise should conclude with your chin parallel to the floor, and the crown of your head becoming the highest point of your body. Throughout the exercise, the shoulders should remain down, back, and relaxed, uninvolved in the entire process. This is the correct position for singing. You will know you have done the exercise correctly if you are aware of the sensation of stretch from your lower abdomen to the sternum and you feel the same lift in the rib cage which you felt in the "rib cage stretch" exercise (see Figure 3–3B).

Exercise to Lift the Sternum (Figure 3-7)

Imagine a string attached to your sternum about midway (approximately 5 to 6 inches downward from your collarbone). This imaginary string will attach to an imaginary pulley on the ceiling about six feet in front of you. Now, as if pulling that string, lift the sternum as well as the rib cage, up and forward toward the audience. Please note that it is unnecessary to fill the lungs with air in order to lift and open the rib cage. This entire process can and should be a muscular one.

EXERCISES TO DEVELOP POSTURAL MUSCLES WHILE EXPELLING AIR FROM THE LUNGS

The "S" or "Hissing" Exercise

After having set the proper singing posture with a lifted sternum and stretched spine, take a deep breath into the lowest part of your lungs, slowly and quietly. Place the tip of your tongue low and forward in your mouth in order to make a very small space for air to move through so that you can make a "hissing" or "S" sound. Blow the air out without dropping the lifted and expanded rib cage or losing the stretch in the spine. Be sure to blow hard, as if trying to get as much air as possible through this small space. This will give you the feeling of creating "air pressure" in the chest cavity, a feeling that is important for singing. Attempt to keep the sternum lifted up and forward at all times, even when your lung capacity has been exhausted. Inhale again when you have exhausted your breath capacity, but do not drop your lifted sternum or the expanded rib cage. It is important not to drop and relax the muscles of posture at the end of your breath so that you will develop strength and coordination in the use of these postural muscles. Leaving the rib cage lifted will allow you to get a full breath quickly as you will not have to move the ribs with the air filling the lungs. Much more about the inhalation and exhalation process is found in the following chapter.

The Counting Exercise

Pretend you are standing on the stage of a very large auditorium and wish to project your voice to the last row. Do not yell. Rather, allow your voice to enter the nasal, mouth, and pharynx cavities for resonance and amplification. In this way, you will use resonance rather than muscle power to project your voice. If you attempt to lift your soft palate or velum as in the beginning of a yawn, you will feel the space available in the pharynx for resonating your voice. Using numbers from one to ten, begin counting sequentially, keeping track of how far you can count on one breath while projecting your voice as follows: 1,2,3,4,5,6,7,8,9,*10*; 1,2,3,4,5,6,7,8,9,*20*; 1, 2,3,4,5,6,7,8,9,*30*; 1,2,3,4,5,6,7,8,9,*40*, and so on until you have exhausted your breath capacity. Project your voice to the last row, and count as far as you can on one breath. At the end of your breath, and without dropping your rib cage or losing the stretch in your spine, breathe deeply and quietly and start over again: 1 to 10; 1 to 20; 1 to 30, 1 to 40, 1 to 50, and so on. Try to go further this time than the last, still using only one breath per cycle. Follow the same procedure a third time: 1 to 10; 1 to 20; 1 to 30, 1 to 40, 1 to 50, 1 to 60, and so on.

By placing your hands on the side walls of your rib cage at approximately thoracic rib numbers eight, nine, and ten, you will be able to feel the lift and expansion of the rib cage more easily. When you feel the rib cage beginning to collapse as you use the air in your lungs, try to work against that collapse both mentally and physically. This will help you to develop the intercostal and abdominal muscle strength and coordination needed to sustain the lifted and open posture of the chest cavity, and eventually will help you to expand your breath capacity as well as to control the exhalation process completely—a very necessary component of a strong vocal technique.

IMPORTANT CONCEPTS TO IDENTIFY AND UNDERSTAND

Correct singing posture (standing and seated)

Flexibility versus rigidity

Buoyancy in posture

Spinal stretch

Lifted sternum and rib cage

Balanced posture

EACH OF YOUR VOCAL PRACTICE SESSIONS SHOULD NOW INCLUDE:

1. *Head Roll* for muscle relaxation and flexibility development
2. *Simultaneous and Individual Shoulder Rolls*
3. *Rag Doll Exercise* for muscle relaxation and posture development
4. *Spinal and Rib Cage Stretch*
5. *Exercise to Lift the Sternum*
6. *"Hissing" or "S" Exercise* for maintenance of stretch and lift in the rib cage, ability to identify with sensations of breath pressure, and help build breath capacity
7. *Counting Exercise* for maintenance of stretch and lift in the rib cage, ability to identify with the sensations of breath pressure, build breath capacity, control exhalation, and projection of the voice.

Please Note: Regarding Exercises 6 and 7

Performing the complete exercise once means taking one breath, doing the exercise, taking a second breath and starting again, taking a third breath and starting again. Three repetitions should be completed at a minimum.

REFERENCES

Chapman, J. L. (2006). *Singing and teaching singing: A holistic approach to classical voice*. San Diego, CA: Plural.

Chapter 4

BREATH MANAGEMENT FOR SINGERS

No matter how well a person sings, if his breathing can be improved his singing can also.

—William Vennard

So says the late William Vennard, noted vocal pedagogue and author of the book *Singing, the Mechanism and the Technic* (1967, p. 18). Learning to breathe properly for singing is perhaps one of the less exciting aspects of vocal study, but a very necessary one. If the breathing process is incorrect, the vocal production will suffer.

BREATHING FOR SINGING

At this point, you may be thinking, "Why do I need to learn how to breathe when it is obvious that I have been breathing since birth?" The answer to this question is that singing requires maximum lung capacity as well as complete and conscious control over the dual process of inhalation and exhalation. "Everyday breathing" is primarily an unconscious process, which requires much less than the full capacity of the lungs. In order to learn to use the full vital capacity of the lungs and to gain control of the musculature involved in the breathing process the student of singing must concentrate carefully on this new and more efficient process and practice utilizing it on a regular basis. The breathing process, like correct posture, can be practiced in a manner

totally separate from singing as well as in combination with *vocalises* (vocal exercises designed to strengthen and develop the vocal production) and vocal literature study. The more you practice both correct posture and breathing, the more quickly you will be able to develop your true vocal potential.

In order for a singing tone to be produced at a specific pitch, a constant airflow through the *glottis* (the space between the vocal folds) must be maintained by the singer. This constant airflow is achieved through the maintenance of the air pressure beneath the vocal folds due to a concurrent control of the expansion of the rib cage. This is why the posture for singing presented in the preceding chapter is so important for singers. If the rib cage, including the sternum, is elevated comfortably prior to inhalation and maintained in this open position, both inhalation and exhalation can be efficiently controlled through the careful interaction of the intercostal and abdominal muscles. This entire process is controlled by the central nervous system and should become a learned habitual form of breath management for singers. Although everyday breathing requires little or no physical or mental effort for most of us, breathing for singing will require the use of both physical effort and superior mental concentration.

You will notice that the muscles used for singing purposes combine both *voluntary* and *involuntary* as well as *voluntary/involuntary* muscles. In other words, some muscles can be controlled consciously, some function automatically, and some can either be allowed to function unconsciously or can be consciously controlled; like the movement of your eyelids. You can control your breathing, or allow it to function totally automatically, as it does during sleep. Obviously, for singing, it is important to learn to control consciously all the breathing functions we are physically capable of controlling.

It is very important that you have a thorough understanding of the human anatomy involved in the breathing and phonation process, especially the articulation and resonance structures, the thorax, muscles of the rib cage, diaphragm, abdominal muscles, and the lungs. If you have questions regarding the anatomy or physiology of any of these areas, please ask your teacher to review the areas in question and/or return to Chapter 2 and review the information yourself. Understanding the human anatomy and its normal physiologic process will help you to understand the refinements necessary for developing a strong and reliable vocal technique. It may be helpful for you to refer back to the drawings in Chapter 2 as each of the methods of breathing is explained.

THREE INCOMPLETE METHODS OF BREATHING

There are many different types of breathing and support methods advocated by voice teachers and singers throughout the world. Some are more efficient than others and offer more vocal control for the singer. Among the most popular of these breathing methods are three which can be distinguished through an analysis of the use of various muscular processes and the effect exhibited on the respiration process in the human body. The three methods are *Clavicular*, *Costal*, and *Abdominal* Breathing. Each of the three methods is discussed separately and then a combination of two processes—*Diaphragmatic-Costal Breathing*—is discussed as the most efficient means of breathing for singers. As you read about the three methods of breathing, please refer to Figures 2–1 (Major bones of the human skeletal system), 2–4 (Diaphragmatic and abdominal motion for singing), 2–5 (The muscles of inhalation and phonation), and 2–6 (The lungs and their position in the body), or others you find helpful, as found in Chapter 2. Be sure to attempt the exercises illustrating each of the methods of breathing so that you will become aware of the sensations of each. It is important that a singer can identify muscular sensation during the breathing and singing process in order to analyze and critique vocal technical skill levels.

CLAVICULAR BREATHING (Figure 4-1)

Please note, using Figures 2–1 and 2–6, the anatomic placement of the clavicle or collarbone immediately above the first rib as well as the *scapula* or shoulder blade just beneath the clavicle bone. Note also the position of the lungs in relation to the clavicle bones and scapula. In Clavicular Breathing, the singer raises

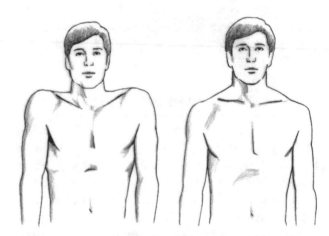

Figure 4–1. Clavicular breathing method. Figure 4–1 is a demonstration of this inappropriate method of breathing for singers. This is the breath of the exhausted athlete. Notice the rising clavicle bones (shoulders), which should never be a part of the singing process. On inhalation, the singer pulls the shoulders upward, causing tension in the neck and shoulders (*left figure*), whereas on phonation, the upper body shrinks back to a dropped position (*right figure*).

the clavicle bones and the shoulder blades on inhalation, causing oxygen to be drawn into the highest and smallest portion of the lungs. As the singer attempts to utilize this oxygen in the phonation process, the shoulders descend to a normal or sometimes slumped position, causing an uncontrolled exhalation process and appearance. This is the look of an athlete in the state of complete exhaustion, when breathing is uncontrolled and the athlete is struggling to get enough air into the lungs. In this case, the athlete is utilizing the attachment of shoulder muscles to the rib cage to aid the exhausted intercostal and abdominal muscles to bring air into the lungs.

For the singer, filling only this upper and smallest portion of the lungs with air gives little or no control over the exhalation process, and as vocal technique requires superior control over the exhalation process, the clavicular breathing method is not only extremely inefficient, but also completely inappropriate for singing. In addition, because of the muscular connections in this area of the body, clavicular breathing may cause tension in the throat as well.

Exercise to Feel Clavicular Breathing

Even though it is obvious that this method of breathing is inappropriate for singers, it is important to be able to identify the sensations of clavicular breathing so that you will be aware of utilizing the clavicular breathing process if it should appear spontaneously and unconsciously. In these instances, you will want to work extra carefully to re-establish correct posture and breathing habits before going on with a vocal warm-up or rehearsal. Working in front of a full length mirror will help you to be aware of the visual appearance of the clavicular breathing method, and each of the other breathing methods.

Inhale quickly and as fully as possible while raising the shoulders high. Physical sensations should include tightness or tension in the upper chest area as well as in the neck and shoulders. Visually, you will see the shoulders rise, perhaps the sternomastoids (see Figure 2-7) standing out, especially on exhalation of air, some tension in the upper abdominal area, and little or no expansion of the lower portion of the rib cage. You may even see the

abdominal area pulling in toward the spine. Now, expel the air with a "hissing" sound and notice the shoulders moving downward as the air is expelled. Be aware of how difficult it is to keep the airstream steady and also that your sternum and rib cage collapse as the air is expelled. There is no feeling of "support" or power behind this exhalation process because it is not under your conscious control.

Clavicular breathing is of no use to singers because it causes unwanted tension in the neck, upper chest, and shoulders, and therefore the exhalation process cannot be controlled. It is, rather, the breathing process used when a person is out of control, when breathing is difficult or labored for some reason. This is known as the "breath of exhaustion," because when the intercostal muscles are too tired to pull the ribs upward, the shoulders help in the respiration process. The shoulder muscles are inspiratory muscles. They cannot aid the intercostal muscles in the use of that air on exhalation, and thus force the rib cage to collapse upon exhalation, which we already know from our study of posture, is unacceptable. Because the singing process relies on the air of exhalation and demands excellent control of this process, clavicular breathing is totally inefficient and unacceptable for the singer. Become familiar with the sensation and "look" of clavicular breathing by doing the exercise above a few times in front of a mirror. Be aware, as you practice breathing and singing, of unwanted tension felt in the neck and shoulder area as well as the upper back and attempt to avoid it.

COSTAL OR RIB BREATHING (Figure 4-2)

Looking at Figures 2-2, 2-3, 2-5, and 2-6, remember that costa is the Greek term for rib, and thus this method of breathing has more to do with motion in the rib cage itself upon inhalation. This type of breathing is, in, fact characterized by a sideward expansion of the rib cage at the lowest portion of the thoracic cavity rather than at the shoulders due to the intentional filling of a lower portion of the lungs. Notice in Figure 2-6 that the lungs are somewhat tapered; the smallest portion is beneath the

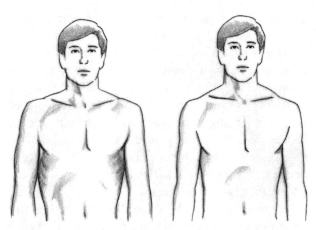

Figure 4–2. Costal or rib breathing method. Figure 4–2 demonstrates an incomplete method of breathing for singers. Here, we see only a small sideward expansion of the ribs, with no full descent of the diaphragm (*left figure*). Thus, it is not a full breath. The rib cage returns to a normal position upon full exhalation of the breath capacity (*right figure*).

upper three ribs, and the larger portion continues from ribs four through ten. Thus, it makes more sense to move air into the lowest part of the lungs in order to increase vital capacity. In addition, note in Figures 2-4 and 2-5, the attachment of the abdominal muscles onto the lower front and side portion of the ribs as well as the placement of the diaphragm well up into the rib cage at approximately the fifth rib. It seems logical that exhalation of air taken into this lower part of the lungs will be more easily controlled through a combination of intercostal, diaphragmatic, and abdominal muscles working together.

Exercise to Feel Costal or Rib Breathing

In order to allow the sideward expansion of the rib cage, air must be drawn into the lowest portion of the lungs. This requires the utilization of correct posture for singing as presented in the previous chapter. To feel the sideward expansion of the ribs, place your hands (without lifting your shoulders) on the left and right side of the rib cage at approximately the eighth to tenth ribs. Take a breath as

though drinking a thick milk shake through a slender straw, pulling or sucking the air in through tight lips. Although this "sucking in" of the air cannot be utilized for singing, it does allow for the easy filling of the lower lungs and enables the voice student to feel the sensation of inhaling air deeply into the lungs. As you are pulling this air into your lungs, feel the lower ribs expand as the air enters the lungs. Now, expel the air with a "hissing" sound, allowing the ribs to collapse back to their original position. There should be no movement in the shoulders or upper chest area during either inhalation or exhalation when practicing costal breathing.

The normal movement of the rib cage on costal breathing should be sideward, a bit forward, and very little, if any, upward. This can be seen clearly in Figure 4-2. If the rib cage pulls up on inhalation, it will coordinate with clavicular or shoulder breathing, which is undesirable for singing. When the posture is correct, the rib cage is already in a lifted position, allowing for some sideward expansion of the rib cage during the breathing process and the maintenance of the lifted rib cage even throughout exhalation. The sensations and visual appearance should include shoulders which are down, back, and relaxed, a lifted sternum and slightly expanded rib cage, air filling the lower part of the lungs, allowing sideward expansion on inhalation, and a return to the normal chest position on exhalation. There should be little or no movement in the upper chest or shoulder area during this costal breathing process. In proper breathing for singing, the intercostal muscles in combination with the abdominal muscles help to sustain the rib cage in an expanded position so that the diaphragm can work fully. In costal breathing, however, the rib cage is allowed to return to its relaxed and somewhat collapsed position. You will soon see that proper breath control depends on resisting the tendency to allow the rib cage to collapse as the breath is exhaled or used in the singing process. Remember that lung tissue is not muscle and will not pick the ribs up again after they have collapsed. If the rib cage collapses on the lungs as the air is expelled, a quick and full breath is very difficult, if not impossible, to attain. If the intercostal muscles hold the ribs open throughout the entire inhalation and exhalation process, the "quick" and full breath will be much easier.

DIAPHRAGMATIC, OR ABDOMINAL BREATHING (Figure 4-3)

The diaphragm is one of the most powerful muscles in the body. Note in Figure 2-4 that the diaphragm separates the upper body cavity, containing the heart and lungs, from the lower body cavity, containing the other internal organs, the viscera. In Figure 2-4, it can be seen that when the diaphragm contracts on inhalation, it flattens, lowering the floor of the thoracic or chest cavity, pulling down on the lungs, and drawing air deeply into them. This contraction of the diaphragm and subsequent lengthening and filling of the lungs forces the viscera to move forward to make room for the lung expansion on inhalation and causing a forward expansion of the abdomen. This is the process known as abdominal or diaphragmatic breathing.

It is important to note two things about this process for singers. First, looking at Figure 2-6, note that the stomach is immediately beneath the diaphragm. If the stomach is full or partially full of food or liquid, the diaphragmatic breathing process will

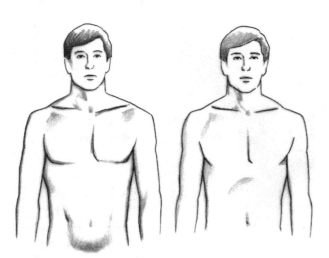

Figure 4-3. Diaphragmatic breathing method. Figure 4-3 demonstrates an incomplete breathing method in which the diaphragm descends without appropriate expansion of the lower ribs, or lift in the sternum. This is sometimes known as a "belly breath" because the lower abdomen is distended on inhalation, while the upper chest is concave. Upon full exhalation, the rib cage remains lowered.

not function well as the diaphragm will not be able to descend as it would normally. Second, the process requires that the abdominal muscles be relaxed on inhalation so they will allow the forward motion necessary to accommodate the viscera. It follows then, that singers should not eat during the two hours prior to singing and they should wear clothing that is comfortably loose around the waist and abdomen. These two things are very important for achieving good results in achieving the diaphragmatic breathing process.

Exercise to Feel Diaphragmatic Breathing

In order to allow expansion into the lower lungs, be sure to utilize the appropriate singing posture for this exercise. Put the palm of your hand gently against your abdomen with the little finger at the navel or "belly button," and the thumb at the "V" of the rib cage, just below the sternum. Take breath in as though drinking a thick milk shake through a slender straw. Feel the expansion under your hand—this region is known as the *epigastrium*. When the diaphragm lowers, the epigastrium involuntarily moves forward. Be sure that you allow the abdominal wall to be relaxed enough to move forward. The abdomen should not be flaccid, but must be relaxed enough to allow the diaphragm to contract in a downward direction. There is no need to push out on the lower abdomen when inhaling. The singer need only think about allowing the muscles of the abdomen to relax, they will move forward as necessary. Pushing the muscles of the lower abdomen out puts excess pressure on internal organs and is unnecessary to the breathing and singing process! After you have completely filled your lungs, expel the breath with a hissing sound, leaving the palm of your hand on the epigastric area. You should feel the upper abdominal area pull in again as the diaphragm rises and the carbon dioxide is sent out of your lungs. You have now felt the complete action of the diaphragm on inhalation/exhalation: a movement down and forward on inhalation and up and inward on exhalation.

Another way to gain the sensation of expansion of the abdomen on inhalation is to lie on your back on a hard surface and place a fairly weighty book or another object on your abdomen just below the waist. As you inhale deeply into your lungs, the abdomen and consequently the book should rise slowly. During the exhalation process, the book should slowly and smoothly descend. In attempting this exercise, do not push your abdomen upward as you inhale. The abdomen should rise due to the descent of the diaphragm, not because you are forcing the abdominal muscles upward.

THE CORRECT BREATHING METHOD FOR SINGING— THE DIAPHRAGMATIC-COSTAL BREATHING METHOD (Figure 4–4)

Diaphragmatic-Costal Breathing is the most efficient method of breathing for the singer, and combines the two methods of breathing just discussed. Thus, it utilizes an energized and lifted posture, sideward expansion of the rib cage, contraction and conse-

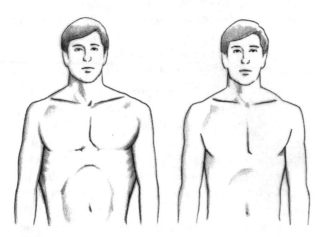

Figure 4-4. Diaphragmatic-costal breathing method. Figure 4–4 demonstrates the correct method of breath management for singers— the Diaphragmatic-Costal Breathing Method. This is the most efficient method of breathing for singers, and includes a lifted sternum prior to inhalation. The rib cage expands sideward, and the diaphragm lowers upon inhalation. On exhalation (phonation), the sternum remains lifted, the rib cage remains expanded, and the diaphragm returns to its high arched position in the thoracic cavity. There is a slight forward motion of the abdomen upon inhalation.

quent descent of the diaphragm, and a relaxed abdominal area which moves forward to make way for the viscera during inhalation. On exhalation, the singer maintains the lifted rib cage and sternum, allowing the diaphragm to return to its normal arch within the lower rib cage. The abdominal muscles contract in order to aid the process of exhalation and maintenance of the rib cage expansion.

It is important that the initial singing posture be maintained throughout the entire inhalation, exhalation/phonation of the singing process. There should be no involvement or motion of the shoulder musculature in this method of breathing. It is vital that the chest and sternum be set and maintained in a comfortably high position, that there be sideward expansion of the rib cage on inhalation, and that the abdominal muscles be relaxed so that forward motion is possible as the breath is drawn deeply into the lungs. As the breath is expelled, the sternum should remain lifted and the sideward expansion of the rib cage should be retained as long as possible without causing muscle tension. The lower abdominal muscles will begin to contract to aid the diaphragm's ascent into the upper body cavity as the air is expelled from the lungs. This is natural and helpful to the process and gives the feeling that is known as "support" to the voice, sending air up through the trachea so there is plenty of air with which to vibrate the vocal folds.

Exercise for Learning Correct Diaphragmatic-Costal Breathing

Be sure to utilize the appropriate singing posture for this exercise. When your posture is set, place your left hand on the left side of the rib cage approximately at the eighth, ninth, and tenth ribs (without raising your shoulders) and your right palm against your abdomen with the little finger at the navel and thumb at the "V" of the rib cage, just below the sternum. Inhale as if drinking a thick milk shake through a slender straw, feeling sideward expansion of the lower ribs, gentle forward motion of the abdominal area, allowing room for the descent of the diaphragm. Once the lungs are completely filled, exhale using the "hissing" sound while attempting to keep the rib cage expanded at the lower ribs, and the sternum lifted up and slightly forward (toward your audience). Notice that the lower abdomen draws in as the air is expelled in order to aid the diaphragm in its ascent into the rib cage.

If this process is difficult for you, try bending over forward so that your upper body is parallel to the floor. Place your hands on your knees, but do not allow tension to creep into your shoulders. Inhale through pursed lips as though drinking the thick milkshake through a slender straw. It should be easier to allow your abdominal muscles to relax as you inhale in this position. Now, you should be able to feel the air go deeply into your lungs, and even cause a little rise in the small of the back near the lumbar vertebrae as well as expanding the rib cage sideward. Once you have felt the sensation in this position, return to an upright position and inhale again, allowing the same feeling to accompany the breath.

The Sensations of Correct Diaphragmatic-Costal Breathing Are:

Inhalation
1. Buoyant and energetic posture
2. Comfortably lifted sternum and expanded rib cage
3. Sideward expansion of the lower ribs on inhalation deep into the lungs
4. Slightly forward motion of the abdomen as the diaphragm descends, and the lungs are filled to a comfortably full level
5. A slight forward motion in the region of the epigastrium as the lungs are filled completely
6. No upward motion or tension in the neck, upper chest, or shoulder area should occur.

Exhalation
1. Retain the buoyant and energetic posture
2. Maintain a lifted sternum and expanded rib cage
3. Maintain the sideward expansion of the rib cage achieved on inhalation
4. Slight muscular tension and inward pull on the lower abdominal muscles as the air is expelled from the lungs through the trachea and mouth
5. A slight sensation of outward pressure under the body of the sternum (see Figure 2–2) as air is expelled from the lungs
6. A definite feeling of muscular effort from the intercostal muscles as the singer attempts to maintain the outward expansion of the rib cage for as long as possible

7. No motion or tension in the neck, upper chest, or shoulder area should occur.

It is a good idea to check yourself often as you practice, through sensation and the use of a full length mirror, to be sure you are using the diaphragmatic-costal method of breathing at all times. In doing so, be sure that:

1. You are not raising your shoulders to lift the rib cage
2. You are not using air to set the proper position of the rib cage
3. You are keeping your sternum lifted gently up and forward throughout the process
4. You are relaxing the abdominal muscles when inhaling
5. You are retaining the sideward expansion of the rib cage on exhalation.

Do not be frustrated by a collapsing rib cage when you are doing your best to keep it expanded and lifted. Just keep practicing and remember you are working with muscles, which need time and consistent practice to develop the strength necessary to maintain this position. A singer must train muscles in the same way an athlete does to be sure that the signals from the brain to the muscles are clear and that the muscles are actually responding to those signals. This process takes time, patience, and perseverance.

BREATH CONTROL IN SINGING

Breath control as it relates to singing is primarily concerned with the process of exhalation, and assumes the diaphragmatic-costal method of breathing. Being able to sustain long phrases on a single breath takes practice. The "hissing" or "S" exercise will aid you with this as will the Counting Exercise. Do not be overly concerned with being able to sing long phrases initially. Rather, work for control over the rib cage musculature and keeping its sideward expansion as well as relaxing the lower abdomen on inhalation. This will help you to build lung capacity as well as control over the exhalation process, which is so important for singing.

Exercise for Sustaining Lower Rib Expansion on Exhalation

This exercise may be helpful as you attempt to strengthen the intercostal and abdominal muscles in order to maintain the lift and expansion of the rib cage. As with any exercise, do not overdo. You can overuse and injure muscles in the rib cage and abdomen as you can anywhere on your body. Exert effort, but not to the point of causing pain.

After finding the lifted sternum, stretched spine, and expanded rib cage for singing, put a leather belt around the rib cage at approximately the seventh ribs. Now, fill the lungs completely with air and fasten the belt so that it is loosely touching the rib cage. Expel the air with a "hissing" sound allowing the abdominal muscles to draw in, while the intercostal muscles hold the sideward rib expansion. You should be able to feel the intercostal muscles as well as the abdominal muscles working. Don't overdo. It is better to build muscle strength slowly and steadily than to push muscles too hard and have to stop practicing because they need rest from overexertion. As you exhale, attempt to maintain the expansion of the ribs by working against the belt. If the rib cage collapses, you will feel the belt fall. Working out against the belt as you exhale will help you to feel the intercostal and abdominal muscles working, will strengthen them, and will give you an idea of how much muscular effort is needed to keep the rib cage expanded throughout the exhalation process.

Your breath control will increase quickly if practiced regularly. Do not expect immediate results; although just the initial posture corrections will allow you to take a fuller breath and to have more control over it. Patience and perseverance will be the key.

TWO PURPOSES FOR BREATHING IN SINGING

There are two purposes for breathing in singing. The first is obvious—we must breathe to sustain life. Thus, the inhalation/exhalation process continues to fulfill the requirements of respiration, which includes not only breathing, but also cellular respiration, ridding the body of carbon dioxide, and the exchange of gases between blood and tissue fluid. In addition, the phonation process, whether speaking or singing, requires the use of breath pressure to vibrate the vocal folds. Singers and professional voice users must also consider a second purpose and benefit in the breathing process, and that is to open and relax the articulation and resonance structures of the voice. This second purpose is at least as important as the first. As the singer inhales he or she must imagine the air coming in through both mouth and nose, opening the passageways of the nasal cavities, mouth, pharynx, and larynx, and then dropping down into the lowest regions of the lungs. When inhalation is completed, the air is immediately turned around and sent back through the same spaces where it entered; up through the lungs, through the trachea and vocal folds where it is turned into sound and then carried up through the pharynx cavity, into the mouth and nasal cavities and far beyond the lips and nose out to a point well beyond the singer. The vocal resonance process requires that all of these articulation and resonance structures be controlled just as the breathing mechanism is controlled. Much more about the process is presented later in this book. Imagining or visualizing this process of opening all the resonance areas as you inhale will be a great deal of help to you not only in improving your breath control, but in adding resonance or "ring" to your voice. It will also help you to achieve an open and relaxed throat, which is a necessity for a long and successful career as a singer.

WHERE TO BREATHE IN AN EXERCISE OR SONG

Vocal development exercises, or vocalises, as they are called, are usually designed to be sung on one breath. If an exercise or vocalise was written or designed with more than one breath intended, this will be marked with an apostrophe ['] or a check mark [✓]. Breaths that are meant to be taken only if absolutely necessary are usually marked with an apostrophe in parentheses (') above the vocal line. In a song, it is best to breathe where rests are provided when possible, not breaking text that belongs together in order to make sense to the listener. Obviously, this is not always possible. When it is not, the singer should follow these rules:

1. Breathe only where the breath will not disturb the meaning of the text and do not take a breath in the middle of a word.

In some 17th century vocal music, such as that of J. S. Bach and G. F. Handel, some exceptions may be made for long, melismatic passages written in a more instrumental style. In these cases, it is often necessary for the contemporary singer to breathe in the middle of a word, which has been extended for many measures. Please see an example from Handel's *Messiah* in Figure 4–5.

2. Always breathe taking time away from the end of the last phrase so as not to be late for the beginning of the next phrase.

This is particularly true where the composer has not indicated a rest in the music in order to allow time for the breath. Please note the example from *Caro mio ben* by Giuseppe Giordano in Figure 4-6. In this example, if the singer wishes to breathe after "almen," the time value of the half note must be shortened so that the third beat of the measure will be exactly in time.

3. Be sure to end one word completely before tak-ing your breath. Put final consonants on care-fully and deliberately so that the breath will not interrupt the diction of the text.

4. Establish regular breathing places in your music and mark them clearly so that you consistently rehearse the same breaths in practice situations. Never leave breathing places to "chance." Practice them until they are quite comfortable and begin to be an unconscious habit.

5. Plan "extra" breaths where they might be necessary when performing "under pressure," or in a situation where you feel you might have less breath than needed.

Do not attempt to perform phrases which are too long for you in practice or which you can "just barely make" in the practice situation. Under the stress of performance, your breath control may not be as strong as in practice sessions.

6. Practice different tempos so that you find one which is not only suitable for the music and text, but which is comfortable for you technically.

At times, varying the tempo only slightly will help the breath management for the entire song. You will find that a faster tempo leaves less time for breathing and a slower tempo more. Therefore, it is sometimes wise to slow a tempo down in order to have more time to take a fuller breath and therefore to achieve longer phrases in the singing of the particular song or aria.

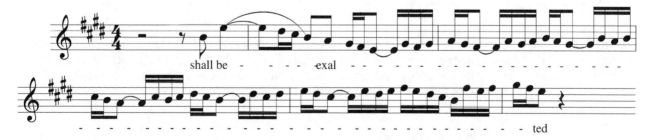

Figure 4–5. Example of music allowing a singer to breathe in the middle of a word. Figure 4–5 is an example of an aria from Handel's *Messiah*. In this example, the melisma is longer than a young singer's normal breath line, and it is therefore up to the singer to determine an appropriate breath place during the melisma as needed.

Figure 4–6. *Caro mio ben* selection. In this example of an early Italian song by Giuseppe Giordano, check marks have been placed where it might be appropriate for a singer to breathe in order not to interrupt the continuity of the song text and music. Only, if absolutely necessary, should a singer breathe where a comma has been inserted above the musical line.

EXERCISES FOR DEVELOPING BREATH CONTROL

Two exercises from the previous chapter are extremely helpful in developing breath control. Please return to Chapter 3 and review and utilize the "Hissing" or "S" exercises as well as the "Counting Exercise." In addition, the following exercise will help you to apply the appropriate breath pressure to phonation and will help to build air pressure.

The Card Buzzing Exercise Process

You will need a 3 × 5 index card for this exercise.

1. Sing an "ooh" vowel with well-shaped lips, and using the shorter of the two exercises that follow in Figure 4–7.

2. Now, sing the same "ooh," but close the lips into a "pucker" allowing the sound to come far forward, making the lips feel as if they are "buzzing." Allow enough air pressure to travel through the lips so that you feel air rushing past them. The process will produce a "whirring" sound.

1. Shorter Version

2. Longer Version

Figure 4–7. Buzzing the Card Exercise. This exercise should be performed as outlined in the text, and all on one breath. The singer holds the 3 × 5 index card vertically at the lips and buzzing the lips with air and tone, uses the card like a kazoo. This exercise helps the singer to realize how much air and air pressure is required to project a tone. Both a short and a longer version of the exercise are contained here. If it is easy to do the short exercise, you should be using the longer one. If it is easy to do the long exercise, do it twice on one breath in order to expand your lung capacity and ability to use all the air in your lungs.

3. Holding the 3 × 5 index card vertically between your thumb and first finger at a lower outside corner let one of the five-inch edges touch your lips. (Do not press the card against your lips as it may cause a paper cut!) Make the same sort of "whirring" sound, allowing the air and sound to rush toward the edge of the card. If done correctly, and with a strong stream of air, the card will pick up the vibrations of your voice and will "buzz," making a sound similar to a kazoo. Try "buzzing" the notes of the shorter vocal exercise shown in Figure 4-7.

Be sure to keep the card buzzing all the way through the entire exercise, which should be performed on one breath. More air will be required for the top notes than for the bottom notes just as it is in singing. Try to maintain the rib cage expansion and feel the lower abdominal muscles drawing in as you come to the end of your breath. Do this exercise a few times to get the feel of how much air is required to "support" and project the voice. There are two different versions (short and long) to try. Start with the shortest one and move up to the lengthier one as you gain more control over your exhalation process.

4. Now, sing the exercise as outlined on the vowel [i] as in "me" attempting to use the same type of "support." The feeling should be much the same, with the air carrying and supporting the voice well beyond the mouth opening.

This exercise will help you learn to use air pressure in the correct manner for singing. Try the exercise as shown in Figure 4-7 as a "sequence" exercise to develop control over the exhalation process alone and then combining it with phonation. You may use either the short or longer version as it suits your breath management skills at this time.

Sequence Exercise

1. Perform the "hissing" or "S" exercise; being sure to inhale deeply and attempting to completely empty your lungs as you exhale. Be sure to maintain a lifted and expanded rib cage, and remember to relax the abdominal muscles on the inhalation process.
2. Next, perform the "card buzzing exercise" using the exercise as shown in Figure 4-7.
3. Sing the same exercise as outlined on the vowel [i] as in "me" or [ɑ] as in father.

Repeat this sequence three or four times, being sure to maintain the lift and expansion of the rib cage, and moving from the end of one exercise right into the beginning of the next. It is important that you do not stop and rest in between each of the exercises. If the exercise does not fully empty your lungs, you may lengthen it until it fully exhausts your air capacity.

SUMMARY OF EXERCISES FOR DEVELOPMENT OF BREATH MANAGEMENT FOR SINGING

1. Exercise for feeling costal or rib expansion (See page 46)
2. Exercise for feeling and developing correct abdominal motion in breathing (See page 47)
3. Exercise for learning correct Diaphragmatic-Costal Breathing (See page 48)
4. Exercise for sustaining rib expansion as air is expelled (See page 50)
5. Hissing or "S" Exercise for building breath capacity and controlling exhalation (See page 40)
6. Counting Exercise for developing control of exhalation combined with phonation (speaking) (See page 40)
7. The Card Buzzing Exercise for developing control of exhalation combined with phonation (See page 53)

IMPORTANT TERMS AND CONCEPTS TO DEFINE AND UNDERSTAND

Clavicular breathing

Costal breathing

Diaphragmatic breathing (Abdominal breathing)

Diaphragmatic-costal breathing

Breath control

Two purposes for breathing in singing

EACH PRACTICE SESSION SHOULD NOW INCLUDE:

1. Head Roll for muscle relaxation and flexibility development
2. Simultaneous and Individual shoulder rolls
3. Rag Doll exercise for muscle relaxation and posture development
4. Spinal and Rib Cage Stretch
5. Exercise to Lift the Sternum
6. "Hissing" or "S" exercise for maintenance of stretch and lift in the rib cage, and building breath capacity and exhalation control
7. Counting exercise for maintenance of stretch and lift in the rib cage, to build breath capacity, control of exhalation, and projection of the voice.
8. Exercise for correct diaphragmatic-costal breathing
9. Exercise for sustaining rib expansion
10. Card buzzing exercise for breath control
11. Sequence of exercises: "Hissing"—"Buzzing"—Singing on [i] and [ɑ].

REFERENCES

Vennard, W. (1967). *Singing, the mechanism and the technic.* New York: Carl Fischer.

Chapter 5

THE PHYSIOLOGY OF VOCAL TONE PRODUCTION

It is widely assumed by singers and singing teachers in this century that increased knowledge of how the vocal instrument functions will enable a singer to sing more beautifully both technically and interpretively. With this increased knowledge comes a greater understanding and appreciation of the singer's "art." The singer's instrument is inside his or her body and therefore requires great control mentally and physically. A careful study of how the vocal folds and resonators function in conjunction with the breathing mechanism will thus enable the singer to exert more control over how the instrument is used. Of course, there are some singers who sing quite well without this knowledge, but, in general, a student of vocal technique will improve more quickly with this knowledge than without it.

THE PHYSIOLOGY OF PHONATION (CREATING VOCAL TONE)

If you gently put your finger on your "Adam's apple" (the somewhat prominent protrusion in the front of your neck), you are touching the most physically obvious or prominent part of the external laryngeal structure—the *thyroid cartilage*. This is the largest of the three large cartilages, which comprise the voice box or larynx along with two pairs of smaller cartilages. Please refer to Figure 2–8 for illustrations of the larynx anatomy. Swallow and notice that the Adam's apple rises and then falls approximately three-quarters of an inch. The flexibility necessary for this motion is present in the larynx because it is made up primarily of cartilage-translucent elastic tissue. Hum or sing in the middle or lower part of your range as you touch your Adam's apple and you will notice both motion and vibrations being produced here. This is where the singing tone begins.

As we have already seen in the chapter on anatomy of the vocal instrument (Chapter 2), inside the larynx or voice box are two tiny muscles, which are attached front to back and on the sides of the voice box at the top of the windpipe (trachea). These are the *vocal folds* or vocal cords. When a person merely thinks about making sound, these two tiny vocal folds come together or close over the top of the windpipe. When air is allowed to pass from the lungs through the windpipe and against the vocal folds, they begin to vibrate producing the sounds we associate with speaking or singing. There is only a slight difference between singing and speaking. Singing is an extension of speech, which allows each vocal vibration to continue for a longer period of time. Speaking requires short "puffs" of air and perhaps less breath support than singing as singing requires the sustaining of tone for a longer period of time. Much of this process of *phonation* or tone production is below the level of consciousness. In learning to sing correctly, however, we learn to control more of the process than the average person will ever need for the act of speaking.

Both speaking and singing are learned functions of the larynx for which it was not originally intended. The larynx and particularly the vocal folds function as a valve to open and close the windpipe to allow air to pass in and out of the human body. When additional strength is needed for heavy lifting or pushing, the valve closes to help create pressure in the thoracic cavity and thus to enable the human body to utilize increased energy levels. Humans have learned to use this valve to create the advanced sounds of communication as well as for its intended purposes. For a review of the structure of the larynx, please read the section in Chapter 2 entitled *The Larynx or Voice Box*.

Making vocal sound within the human larynx is a complex function; much of which takes place below the level of consciousness. The action of the two matched pairs of muscle that make up the vocal folds causes the vibrations that produce what we know and define as vocal tone. Through a complex interworking of all the muscles connected to the larynx and breathing mechanism, the vocal folds are able to change length, thickness, and tension in order to create a wide variety of sounds which are thought of as pleasant to the human ear. The coordination of these muscles either bring the vocal folds together or allow them to lie back inactively against the sidewalls of the larynx. Add to the complex muscle coordination of the larynx a proper supply of breath pressure, and sound is produced. This entire process is referred to as phonation. The larynx is capable, through a complex coordination of musculature, cartilage, and bone to perform the various necessary functions of singing as follows:

1. Starting and stopping tones
2. Establishing particular pitches
3. Changing volume levels in varying degrees from soft to loud
4. Changing timbre or tone color of a particular pitch.

Each of these functions is discussed separately.

STARTING AND STOPPING A TONE

The initiation of a vocal tone is generally referred to as the *attack* or the *onset* of that tone. Ending or stopping the tone is referred to as the *release* of that tone. At the attack, the vocal folds come together almost completely across the top of the windpipe, stretching the muscles to form a nearly complete closure over the *glottis*—the space between the vocal folds. When the tone is released, the muscles are relaxed so that once again air may pass through the windpipe freely in an unobstructed manner. When the vocal folds are mentally prepared for the attack of the tone, they obstruct the flow of air by closing the passage through the windpipe. The air then moves against the vocal folds causing them to vibrate. It is this action that produces vocal tone. The process, although seemingly simple, must be very carefully and consciously coordinated (particularly in the learning stages of vocal technique) by the ear and brain in order for the best vocal tone quality to be produced. For a completely coordinated vocal attack to take place, the inhalation process must be complete and relaxed so that the breathing mechanism may also be properly coordinated with the phonation process.

WHAT HAPPENS IF THE COORDINATION IS NOT PRECISE?

If air goes through the vocal folds before they have been mentally prepared to vibrate, the sound produced will initially be breathy. This is known as an *aspirated attack*, and is undesirable for the singer because the tone will lack clarity and focus. An example of this type of attack can be experienced if the singer will attempt to sing any word beginning with the letter "h" (ha, ho, hey). The breathy quality is caused by air escaping before the glottis (the space between the open vocal folds) is closed. This type of uncoordinated attack can usually be adjusted by having the singer mentally hear himself or herself singing the tone before allowing the process to happen physically. This allows the brain and laryngeal musculature to consciously close the glottis before the onset of vocal vibrations.

If the glottis is tightly closed before the breath reaches the vocal folds, causing a buildup of *subglottal* (below the closed vocal folds or glottis) pressure, the vocal folds explode open, producing an undesirable "chif" or scraping sound. This is known as a *glottal attack*, and should generally be avoided by singers. Not only can a glottal attack be harmful to the vocal folds, but it also produces a rather ugly tone quality. True glottal attacks are used rarely by professional singers and then only in a text requiring a highly dramatic or emotional outcry. This type of attack can be experienced by preparing to sing an "ah" vowel but not letting go of the breath until after a feeling of pressure has built up in the voice box. The feeling is much the same as holding one's breath, and then letting go suddenly with a cry. There are different degrees of glottal attack, the lesser of which are used carefully and in a consciously controlled manner when singing in some foreign languages, such as German, as well as some Slavic languages. Even in these cases, the singer must take care to avoid unnecessary subglottal pressure at all times.

The *coordinated attack* is the desired and correct way to begin a tone. In this instance, the release of the breath and the closure of the glottis are perfectly coordinated following the deep and relaxed inhalation process. The result is a smooth and beautiful beginning to a tone and vowel sound, which is free of extraneous noises and muscular tension.

DEVELOPING A COORDINATED ATTACK

Developing a coordinated attack is a very important aspect of learning a vocal technique, which will serve you through many years of fine singing. It requires first, knowledge of what the feeling and sound of a coordinated attack ought to be and then a conscious and determined effort to produce each new tone in this way until the process becomes automatic. Experiment with each of the three types of attack so that you have a good "feel" for which is the correct one. Following is an exercise, which will help you learn to produce a coordinated attack each time you begin to produce a singing tone. Be aware of the use of *glottal attacks* and breathiness in your speaking voice as well, remembering that singing is an extension of your speech process.

USE OF THE INITIAL (l), (m), AND (n) TO ACHIEVE A COORDINATED ATTACK

Using the consonant [m] or [n] at the initiation of a tone, rather than beginning a tone on a pure vowel such as [ɑ] or [o] has generally proven helpful for singers attempting to produce a coordinated attack. Try speaking the syllable [nɑ] and be sure the [n] is produced by placing the tip of your tongue gently on the ridge behind your upper teeth. There should be no feeling of pressure against the ridge of the gum line. Allow the tone to resonate freely in your nose and feel how gently the tone begins. Now try singing a five-note downward scale on this syllable. Try to feel the same freedom of vibration as on the spoken example. Attempt to memorize this feeling of freedom and tonal vibration. Do this several times at different pitch levels to be sure of the correct feeling. See Figure 5-1A for appropriate scale patterns, which can be used for this exercise.

Now, imagine feeling and producing the [n], but do not physically speak or sing it to determine if the tone will start as gently and smoothly as before. This should help you to bring the vocal folds together in order to close the glottis and prepare the vocal folds for vibration before the breath begins to actually vibrate the vocal folds. Be sure to consciously take a deep and relaxed breath before trying to speak or sing the sound. The consonants [l] and [m] can be used in the same way. It is almost impossible to create a glottal attack when beginning with an [l], [m] or [n] consonant. Figures 5-1A and 5-1B contain a series of exercises to help you develop a coordinated attack. The development of a smoothly coordinated attack takes time and perseverance, but will pay off in more beautiful tone quality and a healthy set of vocal folds, which will serve you for a long and productive singing life.

DEVELOPING A COORDINATED RELEASE

The *release* of a tone is as important as the attack, and can be thought of in a similar way. Here also the singer must be careful to coordinate the action of the vocal folds with the breath pressure. Releasing the vocal folds before stopping the flow of breath will allow the tone to become breathy, just as it did in the aspirated attack, and will not give solid closure to a phrase. Stopping the breath flow before releasing the vocal fold closure will give a "choked" quality to the end of a phrase, which is similar to the "chif" heard on a glottal attack. You may find it

A

Figure 5–1A. Exercise for development of coordinated attack and release. The coordinated attack. Begin each new note with an (l), (m), or (n) as follows, being careful to be aware of the feeling at the start of each tone. It is very difficult, if not impossible, to begin a tone with an (l), (m), or (n) and have the tone be breathy or begin with a glottal attack. Choose pitches that are comfortable for you. Now, remove half of the (m)s and (n)s then all of the (m)s and (n)s as follows and noted. If you cannot sing each vowel smoothly and with a coordinated attack, put some of the (m)s and (n)s back on; keep working until you achieve the coordinated attack.

helpful to think of releasing the tone several feet in front of your body so that the breath and vocal fold vibrations have traveled away from you rather than being stopped inside. This will help you to establish the coordination of breath and musculature necessary for ending the vocal fold vibrations and the breath

[lu no mi la u no i la u o i a]

mI ni mum mI ni mum mI ni mum mI ni mum
[I i ə I i ə I i ə I i ə]

B

Figure 5-1B. Additional exercises to develop a coordinated attack.

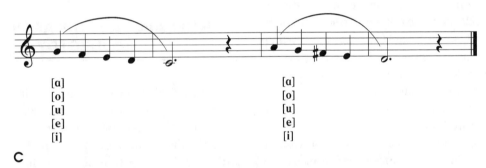

[ɑ]   [ɑ]
[o]   [o]
[u]   [u]
[e]   [e]
[i]   [i]

C

Figure 5-1C. The coordinated release. To practice a coordinated release, perform the following scale pattern, holding the last note for three full beats. On the fourth beat, stop the breath and sound at the same time, imagining that this process happens out in front of you rather than inside your throat or mouth. The ending of a tone should be just as smooth and quiet as the attack.

together. As in an appropriate attack, the release of the tone must be appropriate to the underlying meaning and emotional content of the text and music you are singing. Thus, on occasion, a breathy or dramatic opening or closure to a phrase might be appropriate, but generally, a smooth onset and release is desired. In a smooth release, the vocal folds relax at the same time the breath pressure is released and thus the tone quality remains consistent to the end of the phrase. It is not necessary to crescendo or decrescendo to the close of a phrase to achieve a good release. If this dynamic change is appropriate for musical and/or dramatic reasons, the singer must continue to work carefully to release the phrase endings at the new dynamic level without over or underusing the vocal musculature or breath pressure.

The singer must be aware that establishing a correct release of the final tone of a phrase will allow for a deep relaxed inhalation as well as a coordinated attack for the next phrase. Thus, the release of the tone at the end of one phrase physically prepares the singing mechanism for the attack of the next phrase. The same exercises used for practicing coordinated vocal attacks may be utilized for establishing coordinated vocal releases. The singer need only be aware of consciously controlling the release of the breath and vocal fold vibrations at the end of each phrase. Practice both long and short rhythmic durations in attempting to achieve coordinated attacks and releases.

ESTABLISHING PARTICULAR PITCHES

To create or change pitch, the vocal folds work in conjunction with breath pressure and the resonance process. Primarily, however, change of pitch is due to a change in the length, thickness, and tension of the vocal folds. This process is primarily subconscious and connected to the *auditory* or hearing process. It is a highly complex neurophysical process, which in simple terms might be explained as follows: the ear hears the specific pitch to be produced, sends a signal to the brain, which then sends the proper signal to the larynx to set the correct tension, length, and thickness of the vocal folds. When the air pressure sets the vocal folds in motion, they are already in the proper position to produce the desired pitch as heard. This is a subconscious process, which is almost impossible to control physically. In a few lucky individuals, this neurophysical process is so highly skilled that they are said to have *perfect pitch*. Each of these fortunate individuals is able to identify any pitch by letter name and then sing that pitch without having heard the pitch physically. This is quite rare and is considered a musical gift for those who have it. A student may acquire good *relative pitch* by memorizing certain pitch sensations and then relating all other pitches to those memorized. It is assumed to be nearly impossible to develop perfect pitch.

Musicians who have been fortunate enough to have had a strong musical foundation within their family life, or during their formal education, will have established a good sense of aural pitch memory before they come to a voice class. This means they have had the opportunity to listen to music and/or participate in musical organizations such as a school, community, or church choir, band, orchestra, or chamber ensemble. Those who have not been

so fortunate may have problems matching pitches, which are to be sung in class. This can be corrected, but requires concentration and development of good listening skills. The student who has not had a strong musical background may need to have extra help in the area of development of adequate listening skills. Classes in sight-singing and aural skill development are generally offered at most colleges and universities in the music department, and will aid greatly in this endeavor. Above all, the singing student who feels it is difficult to hear and produce pitches must remain relaxed and comfortable enough to be able to concentrate on hearing the pitches correctly. Experience is the best teacher in this instance and practice in matching pitches is essential to making progress in this area. Don't give up! It is possible for anyone with normally functioning ears and vocal folds to learn to sing.

HOW ARE PARTICULAR PITCHES PRODUCED?

The vocal folds have the ability to vibrate at several different lengths, thicknesses, and degrees of tension due to the flexibility of the entire vocal mechanism. This flexibility must be maintained at all times in order for the voice to function well. No stiffness or rigidity of musculature anywhere in the body can be acceptable for good vocal technique. Being careful to breathe in a deep and relaxed manner will help in establishing this flexibility in the throat as well as the chest cavity and the rest of the body. Stiffness in the vocal folds themselves will make it more difficult for them to vibrate and to produce appropriate pitches. Breath pressure is an important factor in pitch establishment and when the singer uses additional breath pressure to raise the dynamic level of a pitch, he or she must be careful not to use so much pressure that the pitch is also raised. Here again, the process requires a dynamic balance of breath pressure and muscular usage. We know the vocal folds must be brought together in order to produce sounds, or to phonate. The process of bringing the vocal folds together to close the glottis is known as *adduction*. This closure requires the use of musculature as well as breath pressure. The opposite action, separating the vocal folds, or opening the glottis is known by the term *abduction*. This process too requires the interaction of musculature with breath pressure. Figure 2-9 in Chapter 2 demonstrates both adduction (phonation) and abduction (inhalation).

An important principle of physics, which comes into play in the closure of the glottis as well as the vibration of the vocal folds in the process of phonation, is called the *Bernoulli principle*. The Bernoulli principle or effect states that when a gas or a liquid is in motion it exerts less than its normal pressure upon its surrounding environment. The air pressure exerted by the singer causes the vocal folds to open, as well as drawing them back together again through the physics of the Bernoulli effect. As air molecules move through the vocal folds causing them to vibrate, the space through which the air is passing becomes narrow. As the space through which the molecules pass is narrowed, the breath must pass through more quickly. This increased velocity of the airstream both opens the glottis, and after the molecules have moved through the glottis, actually forces the vocal folds together again, closing the glottis. Because the airway in the area of the glottis is narrower, the pressure within the glottis is much lower than that beneath (subglottal) and above the glottis (supraglottal). Please see Figure 5-2 for an illustration of these phenomena as presented by Dr. Robert Thayer Sataloff, M.D., D.M.A. in his book *Vocal Health and Pedagogy*.

The Bernoulli principle is important for singers to understand because it proves that a controlled and steady flow of breath is absolutely essential to the proper function of the vocal folds in the phonation process as demonstrated in singing. Allowing this aerodynamic process to function naturally will enable the singer to engage the breath for the primary work of singing rather than using too much muscle. For an additional exercise, as presented by William Vennard in his *Singing, the Mechanism and the Technic*, and to help you understand the concept of the Bernoulli principle, please see Figure 5-3. It is an act of muscle coordination, which initially brings the vocal folds to the center position, closing the glottis, but following the initial muscular closure the phonation process must become one of aerodynamic precision. Consistent breath flow must be achieved for a healthy and beautiful vocal production!

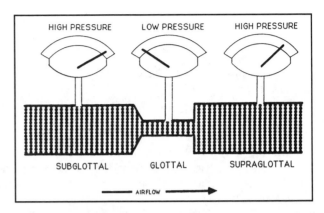

Figure 5-2. The Bernoulli effect demonstrated. Pressure changes in the laryngeal airway, showing the Bernoulli effect. Pressure is sensed by gauges connected to the region below the glottis (subglottal), to the glottal space, and to the area just above the glottis (supraglottal). Air pressure within the glottis is lower than in the spaces above or below it. From "An Overview of Laryngeal Function for Voice Production" by R. J. Baken in *Vocal Health and Pedagogy Science and Assessment*, 2nd ed., Sataloff, R. T., Vol. I, p. 69. Copyright 2006, Plural Publishing. Reproduced with permission.

CHANGING PITCHES

Changes in the length, tension, and thickness of the vocal folds will result in changes in pitch. Greater longitudinal tension of the vocal folds (front to back) combined with thinner musculature results in a higher pitch. It follows then, that if longitudinal tension is reduced, allowing the vocal fold musculature to be thickened, the pitch will be lower. The amount of air pressure supplied to the vocal folds affects the degree of tension and thickness of the muscles as well, and is also a factor in creating and changing pitch for the singer. It may be helpful to use a balloon as a simple example of this rather complex process. Blow the balloon up, then stretch the neck of the balloon, in varying degrees allowing air to escape and noting the rise and fall in pitch as well as volume. Relaxing the neck of the balloon not only creates a lower pitch quality, but allows more air to escape as well. Relaxing the neck of the balloon relates to relaxing the tension of the vocal folds and allowing thicker musculature, and thus a lower

---

Exercise:

1. Hold two sheets of standard typing paper vertically up to your lips—one sheet in each hand.

   Note: It does not matter if the two sheets fall apart.

2. Blow through the center of the two sheets of paper and note how they are sucked together and begin vibrating.

   Note: It is the Bernoulli principle, which brings the two sheets together, stopping the flow of air, which then allows them to be blown apart, only to be sucked together again immediately.

3. Continue blowing through the center of the two sheets of paper for as long as you can—the Bernoulli cycle will continue until you stop the flow of air.

Note: This is a good demonstration of how the vocal folds are blown apart and sucked together using the air pressure from the lungs and causing phonation in the human voice.

Figure 5–3. Vennard exercise demonstrating Bernouli effect. William Vennard's exercise in demonstrating aerodynamic vibration through the use of the Bernoulli principle. From *Singing, The Mechanism and the Technic* by W. Vennard, p. 42, paragraph 176. Copyright, 1967 Carl Fischer, LLC. Reproduced with permission.

pitch. Stretching the neck of the balloon relates to adding tension to the vocal folds by stretching them longitudinally and allowing for thinner musculature; thus a higher pitch is created. Notice that with both the balloon and the vocal mechanism, as the vibrating walls become more taut (greater longitudinal tension is achieved) and the pitch ascends, a smaller amount of air is utilized, whereas more air pressure is built up beneath the opening or glottis (subglottal). Lower pitches require more actual flow of air, and less subglottal air pressure. So, it follows that when singing higher pitches, where the vocal folds are offering more resistance to the breath, more subglottal air pressure is created than when singing lower pitches. Both pitch and volume (dynamic level) must be regulated through careful use of the singer's ear as coordinated by the brain.

Registration

The basic understanding of another aspect of vocal technique, known as *registration*, will also be valuable in learning to control the production and changing of particular pitches. Remember the terms *chest voice* and *head voice* from Chapter 1. These terms relate to the phenomena of registration for singers and have some very specific connotations for various types of vocal literature. For example, you may have heard the term *belter* being applied to some musical theater performers. This term refers to the use of chest voice as demonstrated by many singers of rock music and some other popular music genres as well. The term refers to the fact that the singer is utilizing a heavy registration, or a high degree of muscular action in the phonation process. Another term which is part of the registration phenomena in singing is *falsetto*, a term which refers to the very high "feigned" voice of male singers. The use of the term head voice indicates that the singer is utilizing a much less muscular approach to the phonation process, allowing the vocal folds to be thinner for the production of high notes than for low notes. One additional term may not be known to you, but is extremely important in the establishment of a solid vocal technique—*mixed voice*. This term refers to a mixing of the registers so that no *breaks* appear in the scale passage from the lowest to highest notes of a singer. This mixing of the chest register with the head register may take place constantly from note to note throughout the entire range of the voice, or only at particular places in the scale passage of the singer depending on the type of vocal technique taught by the voice teacher. Achieving one smooth and consistent vocal quality throughout the entire range of the singer is generally the goal of all voice teachers regardless of how that quality is achieved. The voice teacher will work carefully with each student to achieve the use of a full voice, which blends both the heavy and light mechanisms of vocal production throughout the full range of the singer.

Other common terms used in relation to registration include *middle voice, passaggio, lift*, and, of course, the voice classifications themselves. Female singers generally use the middle or mixed voice more than the outer most areas, whereas basses, baritones, and tenors utilize the chest register more often, bridging into the head voice for upper notes of the singing range. The Italian term *passaggio* refers to the place or passage where the registers naturally shift from heavier to lighter or the opposite. Learning to make this shift effortlessly as well as maintaining a consistent quality of voice throughout the phenomena is important to developing a solid vocal technique. Another term for this passaggio is lift. When this term is used, it refers generally to the fact that the breath is "lifted" when the register changes take place causing a change also in the place where the singer "feels" the resonance of the voice.

WHAT IS REGISTRATION?

Richard Miller gives a very helpful and concise explanation of the term registration in his *English, French, German and Italian Techniques of Singing —A Study in National Tonal Preferences and How They Relate to Functional Efficiency*:

The transition from one extreme of the vocal range to another, or from one neighboring note to the next, entails delicate instantaneous adjustments of the laryngeal mechanism which have no counterpart in any other musical instrument. In untrained voices, vocal quality will seldom be unified throughout the entire vocal compass, tending to display characteristic timbres in certain segments of the voice. To some extent, several distinct qualities of tone can be produced on

identical pitches, resulting from different kinds of muscular action within the larynx. These several qualities often are perceived by the singer as varying resonance sensations. The adjustments in muscular balances within the larynx which produce these sensations directly correspond to what singers term factors of registration (p. 101).

The interaction of several groups of muscles within the larynx is responsible for the longitudinal tension as well as the thickness demonstrated by the vocal folds themselves. It is the combination of this longitudinal tension and the changing thickness in the vocal folds that results in what we term *registration of the voice*. The control over these muscles is actually below the level of consciousness, and yet the muscles can be controlled somewhat through the use of imagery and the awareness of the sensations of resonance. In creating and changing pitches, the vocal folds as well as the entire laryngeal structure must be free to change shape, thickness, tension, and position. When this flexibility is present, we term the vocal function of the larynx as *active* or achieving a *dynamic balance* of the vocal musculature. It is similar to the body musculature of an athlete in that the muscles are strong and yet very flexible and free to move quickly or slowly as directed by the brain. When the vocal musculature is stiff and unwilling to change freely, we call this *passive* or *static balance* of the musculature. Obviously, for the singer with excellent technique, the adjustment should always be active or dynamic. The lowest possible notes of a singer are produced with very little longitudinal tension, and using relaxed and thickened vocal folds. As the singer ascends the scale upward, the vocal folds become thinner and the longitudinal tension is increased. If this happens very gradually so that the vocal muscles are gradually shifting muscular weight from the lowest tones to the highest, then there will be no "breaks" in the voice which might cause a change in the timbre or tone color of the singer; the singer will be able to sing a seamless scale from the lowest to the highest tones, using the same tone color and quality of voice. This "one register" ideal takes time and perseverance to achieve, however, and must be practiced carefully in the voice studio as well as the practice room.

When a singer (usually a female) attempts to use the muscular thickness and tension intended for the low notes while attempting to produce the higher pitches of the scale, this muscular action requires an extreme amount of air pressure and eventually the singer will get to a point in the scale where the vocal muscles can no longer sustain this thickness and muscular tension. This tension results in a *crack* or break in the voice, allowing the musculature to relax, and the vocal muscles to now produce sounds with a lighter muscular action. Thus, we talk about the voice having "cracked" into head voice or falsetto. At the opposite end of the spectrum, is the vocal student who does not use enough vocal muscular thickness, air pressure, or muscular tension. The result here is a very small, thin sound, which is quite light in timbre and lacking in focus. The vocal quality may even be breathy due to the fact that there is not enough breath pressure to close the vocal folds completely in order to produce optimal vibration. This is known as singing in pure head voice. Neither pure head voice nor pure chest voice should be utilized regularly in the phonation process of an excellent vocal technique. Rather, each of these registrations may be occasionally utilized to produce a special effect. The excellent singer will use a dynamic balance of muscles, which will ensure a smooth and free vocal production, a beautiful vocal timbre and just the right amount of muscular action along with a steady stream of air. A student singer will want to develop the dynamic balance of musculature necessary for good vocal production as well as for producing the dynamic levels and vocal timbres essential to professional singing. In the lower part of the range, the muscular adjustment will be somewhat heavier or thicker than in the upper range. The balance of muscle pull will gradually change throughout the full range of the singer so that no "breaks" are present and the vocal timbre remains consistent throughout the full range of the voice.

Resonance

Resonance also plays an important part in both the establishment of pitch as well as the variety of dynamics and tone colors that are available to singers. For singers, resonance is the quality imparted to voiced sounds by vibration in anatomic resonating chambers or cavities (as the mouth or the nasal cavity) (*Webster's Eleventh New Collegiate Dictionary*, 2005, p. 1061).

To experience this phenomenon in its simplest context, open your mouth as widely as possible, stretching the cheeks in a downward direction and making the space within the mouth cavity as large as possible. Now, tap lightly on the outer walls of your cheeks with your fingers. As you tap, change the size of the interior of your mouth cavity by allowing the lower jaw to close gradually. You will notice that the pitch can be varied and controlled enough to produce a diatonic scale if the ear is properly attuned. Thus, changing the shape and size of the resonating chambers of the head cavity will affect the pitches created in the larynx.

More is discussed regarding resonance in a subsequent chapter, but for now, be aware that the size of the mouth, nasal, and pharynx cavities as well as the vocal tract itself can and will affect pitch produced in the larynx as that pitch interacts with resonance spaces. Singers need to be aware of creating and controlling appropriate resonating spaces whenever possible when singing. If the resonance space is inappropriate to the pitch desired, the pitch may be affected either negatively or positively; making the pitch flat, sharp, or precisely in tune.

THE CLASSIFICATION OF VOICES

Obviously, the classification of voices into soprano, mezzo-soprano, contralto, tenor, baritone, or bass has much to do with the range of the voice, but voice classification is also concerned with the timbre of the voice as well as the singer's ability to sustain a particular tessitura. The vocal range of a singer encompasses all the notes from the lowest to the highest note that can be produced by the singer with an acceptable tone quality, and thus can be used on the performance stage. The term *tessitura* refers more generally to the particular area on the staff where the singer is most comfortable. We speak of song literature as having high, medium, or low tessitura. Obviously, the higher, lighter voice categories will be more comfortable in higher vocal tessitura than the lower, heavier voice categories.

Thus, when determining the voice category of a singer, not only the range will be considered, but the relative weight or lightness of the quality of the voice as well. Tessitura will also be an important factor in choosing appropriate vocal literature for each of the voice categories. Although a mezzo-soprano may be able to sing a high B flat, she would not be comfortable singing them over and over again in a piece of music, whereas a coloratura soprano might be perfectly happy to sing many notes above the staff within a song, including the high B flat.

WHEN SHOULD A SINGER'S VOICE BE CLASSIFIED?

Young singers are very anxious to know exactly what voice classification they belong in, but classifying a voice correctly is sometimes difficult. In order to classify a voice correctly, the breath support must be consistent and utilized well, the throat must be free of heavy muscular use, and the muscles must be developed somewhat so they are functioning well. Do not expect to have your voice classified immediately in a voice class. Allow yourself time to develop your technique, range, and muscular coordination so that you will not be limiting your learning by a label which may not fit later on when your technique is more fully developed. Perhaps the following general information about voice classifications in singers will be helpful to you as you continue to develop your technique.

VOICE CLASSIFICATIONS

The voice classification process will include an analysis of body size and type because this will very definitely affect the vocal category. A smaller, less muscular body type will generally be categorized as a lighter, and sometimes a higher vocal category. A larger, more muscular body type will generally achieve a heavier and lower vocal quality. Of course, this is not always the case, but it will frequently be found to be true. All the registers of the voice must be free and usable before the voice can be catego-

rized. For example, a female cannot be classified as a contralto simply because she has no high notes. It will be important to learn to utilize the head voice as well as the middle or mixed voice before attempting to classify a voice. A singer should generally be able to produce two octaves of pitches before trying to classify his or her voice. A professional singer will generally need to be able to produce a good quality tone over two and a half octaves or more. The extremes of range achieved by the bass voice at the low end, and the coloratura soprano at the high end, will be the most unusual and thus the least common vocal categories. The voice categories in the middle—mezzo-soprano and baritone—will be the more common categories identified among a group of new singers.

Voice categories can also be more carefully identified by the weight of the voice within particular categories. The lightest of all vocal categories is termed the *leggiero* voice. This term means light in Italian and can be applied to any voice type, although it is most appropriately applied to the young high soprano or tenor. Another descriptive term used in the classification of voices is *lyric*. This term indicates a voice that is a bit heavier than a leggiero voice, but still not of a heavy or weighty quality. When the muscularity of a lyric voice is pushed a bit further to create a heavier or weightier quality, the voice is termed a *lyrico-spinto*. The Italian verb *spíngere*, from which spinto comes, translates literally as "to push," and indicates that the singer will be able to push the muscles a bit harder to make a more dramatic sound in climactic sections of music.

The term *dramatic* is often used in categorizing heavy voices, which can be used in very dramatic situations on the operatic stage. This category would indicate quite a large voice, which is embodied by a singer who is a strong actor. A voice classified as dramatic is able to sing easily over a very large orchestra without the help of amplification. Sopranos, mezzo-sopranos, tenors, baritones, and basses can all be categorized as dramatic voice types, just as they might be categorized as leggiero or lyric voices. A special term utilized for the tenor voice, which is so important in the music dramas of the German composer Richard Wagner, is *Heldentenor*. The German noun *Held* literally means hero; thus, the Heldentenor category is used for a male singer with a high voice singing in a dramatic role requiring great heroism. This category is reserved for a very select few who have the power and brilliance required to project over the very large brass section used in Richard Wagner's orchestrations.

Some voice types cross over into others and thus a voice may be distinguished as a combination of two categories, such as the *bass-baritone*, the *mezzo-contralto*, or the *zwischenfach*. The term *zwischenfach* designates a voice type in between two categories. When a singer, generally a mezzo-soprano, is categorized as zwischenfach, it means the singer has the ability to sing in both categories with much success. The bass-baritone, and mezzo-contralto categories are similar. In these cases, the voice may have the power and timbre of one voice category, while also possessing the color and range generally attributed to the other voice category. Some composers may exploit the fact that these particular voice categories have both sets of attributes, thus creating an operatic role that may be suitable only for a very specific voice type. There are additional terms that apply to particular voice categories, such as the basso *cantante* or basso *cantabile*. We generally think of the bass voice as a heavier sound, but in this case, the singer will have the low range required of a bass but with a lighter or more lyrical quality. This type of bass voice can be very effective in the singing of sacred cantatas, and more lyric operatic roles on the dramatic stage. The *basso profundo*, or dramatic bass is the largest and darkest of all the vocal categories, and is quite rare. This bass will be able to sing a low C with the power to carry over the orchestra even in this very low tessitura.

The term *coloratura* may be applied to any vocal category, but in the 21st century is generally attached to the highest voice category—the soprano. The term itself indicates that the voice is very agile and able to sing florid passages (having many notes) easily and rapidly. There are *dramatic coloraturas* as well as *lyric coloraturas* in the soprano category, and other voice types may also be categorized as having the ability to sing coloratura. In order to sing light, fast moving passages, a singer must have excellent vocal technique with great agility and dynamic balance of the muscles involved in the phonation process. All singers should work to be able to sing at least some coloratura styles in their vocal repertoire.

A voice category that has come about through the development of the male falsetto is called the *countertenor*. In this case, the falsetto of the tenor or baritone singer is highly developed so that the voice is able to project over an orchestra. The countertenor category in the 21st century replaces the *castrati* category from a much earlier time, and has become an important new category for contemporary composers as well. In the early days of the Roman Catholic Church and Italian opera, women were not allowed to sing in the church or on the stage. But, composers were composing music containing many upper treble staff parts and also wished to use female characters on the stage. It was found that by castrating a young boy before achieving puberty, his high voice would be preserved throughout his adult life while his body continued to develop normally in size. This was common practice in the 17th century and beyond until women were allowed to sing on the stage and in the church. There were many music schools developed for this rather odd class of male singers, where they developed extremely fine vocal techniques. Through years of strenuous and disciplined study, they developed tremendous lungpower, were able to achieve extremes of range, had brilliant coloratura technique, and could execute very long phrases with powerful vocal projection. Today, of course, this is not the practice, and thoughts about the practice vary from historical interest to absolute disgust, but there is still the desire to perform the operas and sacred choral music written for and displayed by these unusual singers. Thus, came into being the category of the countertenor. These male singers study for years to achieve what we believe to be the same type of brilliance and power the castrati were capable of, and are able to sing the roles on the operatic stage or in the performance of sacred cantatas and oratorios in the church. It should be noted that, in the 21st century, these male singers are physically normal and are achieving their vocal effects through an exaggerated falsetto technique. They can generally also sing in their normal vocal category quite easily. Most countertenors begin as baritones.

In Supplements 5–A and 5–B of this chapter you will find a listing of the vocal categories with specific attributes for each category. Audio and video recorded examples of each of the vocal categories, as demonstrated by professional singers, are readily available in university and local libraries. Although it is not necessary that your voice be categorized at this point in your studies, it is important that you understand the reasons for categorizing a voice in a particular way as well as what a voice category should reveal about a particular voice. Listen and view as many of the examples as you can, and follow the printed materials carefully as you listen. You will learn to be able to hear a voice and identify the category to which it belongs by identifying the physical size of the singer, his or her range, tessitura, timbre, and dramatic power.

CHANGES IN VOLUME IN VARYING DEGREES FROM SOFT TO LOUD

The volume, loudness, or dynamic level of the vocal tone is primarily affected by three functions; air pressure, muscular use, and resonance. The loudness of vocal sound is affected proportionately by the amount of air pressure supplied to the vibrating vocal fold muscles. The greater the air pressure against the vocal folds, the louder the sound. Resonance, however, also influences volume by adding extra overtones or sympathetic vibrations to the primary tone produced in the larynx. This resonance factor is discussed more fully in the subsequent chapter on resonance.

It will suffice at this point to understand the concept of creating vocal dynamics as the amount and way in which air is being supplied to the vocal folds within an appropriate resonating space. For a louder tone, more air is allowed to vibrate the thicker vocal folds and for a softer tone, less air is supplied to the thinner and more relaxed vocal folds, whereas air pressure seems more important to the production of such a tone. The production of a variety of dynamic levels from pianissimo to fortissimo is a concept that takes much practice and control. This concept cannot be fully developed in a vocal technique class, but is the result of years of study and practice with a private voice teacher. The process of creating a variety of dynamic levels requires excellent ear training, and precise muscular coordination in combination with absolute control over the breathing and support systems. The ability to create a wide variety of dynamic levels for the

purpose of expressing both text and musical line is essential to the vocal artistry required for a professional career in vocal performance. Your studio voice teacher will work with you on exercises that will help you to achieve these dynamic levels. For now, please see Figure 5-4 for some examples of exercises to be used to begin creating a variety of dynamic levels and colors.

In regard to dynamics, singers just beginning to work on establishing a solid vocal technique must remember to sing only as loudly as they can sing beautifully, and as softly as they are able to produce a focused and pure tone quality that is free of breathiness. Let your ear, and your teacher's ear, be your guide as you begin to work on achieving a wide variety of dynamics. It is important for the student, attempting to establish a solid vocal technique, to know that it is difficult to sing high notes at soft dynamic levels because raising the pitch automatically requires more breath pressure and longitudinal tension which will naturally make the dynamic level louder. Do not be concerned about creating high soft sounds at this point. It is best to start your vocal work at a moderate dynamic level and work outward in both directions, attempting to increase both your loud and soft dynamic levels carefully and slowly as you develop the appropriate ear training skills and vocal musculature.

CHANGES IN TIMBRE OR TONE COLOR

Changes in tone color or *timbre* are primarily achieved through control of the resonance mechanism. However, it is believed that basic tone color does begin at the voice box. The shape of the vocal mechanism including the specific size of the larynx, pharynx, mouth, and nasal cavities as well as head and body structure all contribute to the timbre of vocal tone. This is why no two voices are exactly alike. Learning to guide the vocal tone produced in the voice box into different resonance areas as well as learning to use mental imagery in adjusting the size and quality of the resonance space will help you to learn to create a wide variety of interesting and beautiful tone colors. This concept is much too complex to be highly developed in a vocal technique class and requires years of listening and studying in

Figure 5–4. Exercises to help achieve a variety of dynamic colors.

a private studio. It is, among other things, the ability to achieve a wide variety of beautiful tone colors that makes a singer marketable in the professional world of music, enabling the singer to portray a multitude of emotions. If this were a skill easily acquired, there would certainly be more professional singers. In the voice class, we begin to experiment with the development of different tone colors through the use of imagery. Please see Figure 5–5 for some exercises as a beginning to experiment with the use of a variety of tone colors for your singing voice.

The emotions play a very large part in the creation of vocal timbre (tone color) for the singer. Because the vocal instrument is housed within the human body, appropriate stimuli from the brain are extremely important in the creation of timbre

[ɑ   ɔ iːɑ   ɛ   e   i iːɑe   ɛ   ɑ i   ɛ   ɑ wi ɛːi   ɔ - -]

Figure 5–5. Exercises to help achieve a variety of vocal timbres. Use the notes from the opening line of *Caro mio ben* by Giuseppe Giordano (*above*) while performing the following exercises.

1. Changing the breath energy to create a variety of tone colors
   Use the following imaginary frames of mind to allow you to change the quality of your voice. Utilize your imagination as you pretend you are:
   a. Exuberant
   b. Depressed
   c. Angry
   d. Lonely
   e. In love
   f. Extremely happy
   Notice how your state of mind can alter the quality and texture of your voice.

2. Change the resonance space in the following ways, noting how the vocal quality is changed for each muscular change in your anatomy.
   a. Allow your jaw to be overly open—stretch the jaw downward
   b. Close your mouth tightly, feeling some tension in the muscles of your jaw
   c. Close your mouth loosely; leave the jaw muscles loose and relaxed
   d. Tighten your lip muscles
   e. Sing with the lips very loose and the vowels unarticulated

3. Change your thoughts only for the following:
   a. You have just won the lottery!
   b. You have just demolished your brand new car!
   c. You have just failed an important examination!
   d. You are completely calm and relaxed on a Bahamas vacation!
   Notice how all of the physical and mental changes have or have not altered your tone quality—think about how the imagination could be used in this way to add a variety of colors to your art songs and arias.

changes in the voice. Of course, the text will play a big part in the correct establishment of a variety of timbres for a particular song or aria. This is why it is so important for a singer to understand every aspect of the text being studied and prepared for performance. Generally, vocal music composers expend a great deal of time and thought in choosing exactly the right pitches, rhythms, and dynamic levels to effectively set a poetic work to music. The singing performer's responsibility then is to attempt to be true to the poet and the composer in the delivery of both text and music. Certainly an important part of the final performance effect is achieved through the use of appropriate vocal timbres to best exemplify the text as well as the music.

SUMMARY

The overall phonation process is an extremely complicated one about which even medical doctors disagree. Singers, voice teachers, vocal scientists, laryngologists, speech pathologists, and others continually study this process. It seems, the more we study, the more we have to learn. The knowledge we have gained to date tells us that the phonation process requires excellent coordination of all muscle, ligament, and bony structures in conjunction with conscious and precise control over the inhalation and exhalation process. For the most part, this coordination and control can be learned by anyone with a physically healthy vocal mechanism and a positive mental attitude. Much of what takes place in the singing process requires a conscious relaxation of certain muscles, such as the swallowing muscles, keeping the throat free from tension. Understanding these concepts should be quite helpful in learning to avoid tension of any kind. Just as an athlete's musculature must remain flexible and ready for use at all times, a singer's musculature must have the same feeling of flexibility, never allowing body muscles to become rigid or tense. In addition to the necessary anatomic understanding and control, the role of the emotions and their interaction in the process of interpretation will have a great deal to do with the overall production of sound for the singer in the act of performing as the vocal instrument is contained within the human body. Although the development and fine tuning of the phonation process itself will be our main concern in this class, the interpretive and emotional side should never be overlooked in the process and functioning of the human voice as used in singing.

IMPORTANT TERMS TO DEFINE AND UNDERSTAND

Phonation

Coordinated attack

Coordinated release

Aspirated attack

Glottal attack

Timbre (tone color)

Perfect pitch

Relative pitch

Adduction

Abduction

Bernoulli principle (effect)

Registration

Falsetto

Mixed voice

Passaggio

Active or dynamic balance

Static or passive balance

Range

Tessitura

Leggiero

Lyric

Lyrico-spinto

Dramatic (voice categorization)

Heldentenor

Cantante/cantabile

Coloratura

Countertenor

Castrati

REFERENCES

Boldrey, R. (1994). *Guide to operatic roles and arias.* Dallas, TX: Pst.

Miller, R. (1977). *English, French, German and Italian techniques of singing—a study in national tonal preferences and how they relate to functional efficiency.* Metuchen, NJ: The Scarecrow Press.

Mish, Frederick C. (Ed.). (2005). *Merriam-Webster's collegiate dictionary.* Springfield, MA: Merriam-Webster.

Sataloff, R. T. (1998). *Vocal health and pedagogy.* San Diego, CA: Singular.

Vennard, W. (1967). *Singing, the mechanism and the technic.* New York: Carl Fischer.

SUPPLEMENT 5–A

VOICE CLASSIFICATIONS

Following are a listing of the common voice classifications used in professional classical singing. Each voice type has a brief definition or description, which should be helpful in determining where you fit into the classifications and to your understanding of how professional voices are classified. However, remember that a voice can easily be misclassified due to improper use of vocal technique. A voice cannot be correctly categorized until the posture, breathing, support, and resonance mechanisms are comfortably in place and are being utilized in the singing process every time the singer opens his or her mouth. It is also necessary to consider that much of the categorization process is quite subjective, and dependent upon who is doing the classifying. Voices may be classified by voice teachers, singers, conductors, or even critics. The classification process includes an evaluation of range, comfortable tessitura, timbre, weight, agility, and physical presence as well as particular acting ability. Thus, many of the voice categories and singers themselves can cross from one category to another.

Even famous singers' voices have been classified incorrectly. For example, the great dramatic coloratura soprano Joan Sutherland was initially classified as a contralto due to improper vocal technique. Until she learned to sing correctly, she had many vocal problems and seemed destined to a career in the practice room. Let this be a lesson to us all. A voice must be free of muscular tension and produced as efficiently as possible before it can be categorized correctly. Do not let misclassification keep you from having the voice you could have.

Soprano

This is the highest category of the female voice, with a general range from b^b to c^3, and extending down to g and up to f^3, depending on the particular singer.

Coloratura Soprano: *Range: (a) c^1–f^3*

This is the highest and generally lightest voice type, capable of great agility and florid singing. The German term *Koloratur* refers to the "elaborate ornamentation" of a melody, and designates the singer's ability to sing quick runs, leaps, and embellishments within the vocal line. In Italian opera the term *fioritura* is interchangeable with the term coloratura. The dramatic type also has excellent low and middle notes. Typical composers would include Handel, Mozart, Rossini, Bellini, Donizetti, and Verdi. Examples of operatic roles would include:

Voice Category	Character	Opera	Composer
Light Lyric	Juliette	*Romeo et Juliette*	Gounod
Coloratura	Gilda	*Rigoletto*	Verdi
	Lucy	*The Telephone*	Menotti
	Olympia	*Les contes de Hoffmann*	Offenbach
	Adele	*Die Fledermaus*	J. Strauss
	Norina	*Don Pasquale*	Donizetti
	Oscar	*Un ballo in maschera*	Verdi

Voice Category	Character	Opera	Composer
Full Lyric	Juliette	*Romeo et Juliette*	Gounod
Coloratura	Rosalinde	*Die Fledermaus*	J. Strauss
	Adalgisa	*Norma*	Bellini
	Amina	*La Sonnambula*	Bellini
	Cleopatra	*Giulio Cesare in Egitto*	Handel
	Desdemona	*Otello*	Rossini
	Gilda	*Rigoletto*	Verdi
Dramatic	Donna Anna	*Don Giovanni*	Mozart
Coloratura	Queen of the Night	*Die Zauberflöte*	Mozart
	Konstanze	*Die Entführung aus dem Serail*	Mozart
	Fiordiligi	*Così fan tutte*	Mozart
	Norma	*Norma*	Bellini
	Lucia	*Lucia di Lammermoor*	Donizetti
	Violetta	*La Traviata*	Verdi

Soubrette: *Range: (b♭) c¹–c³*

This term originated in French comedy to describe a female character who is generally small in stature, young, and coquettish, flirting with everyone around her on stage. She is frequently the maidservant of another character, but upon whom the operatic drama turns. The vocal color is somewhat warmer than the coloratura soprano, particularly in the middle voice, and she frequently portrays a somewhat comic character. Typical composers would include Sullivan, J. Strauss, Mozart, Rossini, Humperdinck, and even Puccini. Examples of operatic roles would include:

Voice Category	Character	Opera	Composer
Soubrette	Papagena	*Die Zauberflöte*	Mozart
	Zerlina	*Don Giovanni*	Mozart
	Patience	*Patience*	Gilbert and Sullivan
	Yum-Yum	*The Mikado*	Gilbert and Sullivan
	Marzelline	*Fidelio*	Beethoven
	Barbarina	*Le nozze di Figaro*	Mozart
	Despina	*Così fan tutte*	Mozart
	Lauretta	*Gianni Schicchi*	Puccini

Lyric Soprano: *Range: c¹–c³*

This is the most common soprano type. The term "lyric" connotes a lighter voice quality and great beauty rather than dramatic power. Her dynamic range is quite impressive, including very big fortissimos, and incredibly soft pianissimos. This category divides into "light" and "full," with the light lyric soprano the younger of the two, as well as the more innocent. The full lyric soprano is generally a more mature character and vocal quality. Typical composers include Mozart, Massenet, Menotti, Floyd, Gounod, and even Bizet and Puccini. Examples of operatic roles would include:

Voice Category	Character	Opera	Composer
Light Lyric	Laetitia	*The Old Maid and the Thief*	Menotti
Soprano	Monica	*The Medium*	Menotti
	Sophie	*Werther*	Massenet
	Pamina	*Die Zauberflöte*	Mozart
	Susanna	*Le nozze di Figaro*	Mozart
Full Lyric	Susanna	*Le nozze di Figaro*	Mozart
Soprano	Susannah	*Susannah*	Floyd
	Marguerite	*Faust*	Gounod
	Macaëla	*Carmen*	Bizet
	Countess	*Le nozze di Figaro*	Mozart

Lyrico-Spinto Soprano: *Range: (a) c¹–b♭² (c³)*

The term spinto is an Italian term for "pushed," and is used to describe soprano and tenor voices that increase their power and brilliance at very dramatic points in the opera by using more muscular power in their vocal production. Usually shortened to *spinto* soprano, this is a heavier and darker quality voice than the lyric soprano. Typical composers for this vocal category include those of the *verismo* period of the late 19th century, a period of realism on the stage, such as Bizet, Puccini, Boito, and Mascagni among others. Examples of operatic roles would include:

Voice Category	Character	Opera	Composer
Lyrico-Spinto	Cio-Cio-San	*Madama Butterfly*	Puccini
Soprano	Carmen	*Carmen*	Bizet
	Leonore	*Fidelio*	Beethoven
	Margherita	*Mefistofele*	Boito
	Musetta	*La Boheme*	Puccini

Dramatic Soprano: *Range: (g) b–b♭² (c³)*

This is the largest and heaviest of the high female voices, with a vocal timbre more similar to the mezzo-soprano than the lyric soprano, but with a higher range and tessitura. Her body size may be as dramatic as her voice at times. This rather rare vocal category is not generally well developed until middle age, as the soprano must have the power to sing over very large orchestras such as those of Richard Wagner, Giuseppe Verdi, and Richard Strauss. This category is divided into a young dramatic soprano, and full mature dramatic soprano. Examples of operatic roles would include:

Voice Category	Character	Opera	Composer
Young Dramatic	Vanessa	*Vanessa*	Barber
Soprano	Agathe	*Der Freischütz*	Weber
	Elisabeth	*Tannhäuser*	Wagner
	Eva	*Die Meistersinger von Nürnberg*	Wagner
	Leonore	*Fidelio*	Beethoven
	Salome	*Salome*	Strauss
	Aïda	*Aïda*	Verdi

Voice Category	Character	Opera	Composer
Full Dramatic	Donna Anna	*Don Giovanni*	Mozart
Soprano	Leonore	*Fidelio*	Beethoven
	Brünhilde	*Die Walküre*	Wagner
	Brünhilde	*Götterdämmerung*	Wagner
	Brünhilde	*Siegfried*	Wagner
	Fricka	*Das Rheingold*	Wagner
	Isolde	*Tristan und Isolde*	Wagner
	Elektra	*Elektra*	R. Strauss

Mezzo-Soprano

The term *mezzo* literally means "middle" or "rich" and in combination with the term soprano, indicates a female singer with a general range from b^b–b^2, possessing a fuller, darker sound than that of the previously discussed soprano categorizations. The range is similar to the dramatic soprano, and some mezzo-sopranos can actually sing within both the soprano and mezzo-soprano categories. We categorize these singers as *Zwischenfach* (between categories) singers. The category is separated into light and full lyric mezzo-sopranos, dramatic mezzo-sopranos, and mezzo-contraltos. Each is discussed separately.

Lyric Mezzo-Soprano: *Range: (a) b–b² (c³)*

This is the lighter voice type within the mezzo category. Displaying a strong lower range, and more vocal weight than a lyric soprano, she is still able to move quickly in coloratura passages, but lacks the depth of tone color of the dramatic mezzo-soprano or the mezzo-contralto. This singer generally has a slender figure and is able to portray young male characters in what are termed *pants roles*. In these roles, the lyric mezzo portrays a young man such as Siebel in *Faust,* or Cherubino in *Le nozze di Figaro.* This category is separated into the light lyric mezzo, and the full lyric mezzo; the full lyric mezzo has a more mature vocal sound and characterization. Notice the wide variety of composers writing music for this category. Examples of operatic roles would include:

Voice Category	Character	Opera	Composer
Light Lyric	Erika	*Vanessa*	Barber
Mezzo-Soprano	Nancy	*Albert Herring*	Britten
	Frau Reich	*Die lustigen Weiber von Windsor*	Nicolai
	Marcellina	*Le nozze di Figaro*	Mozart
	Rosina	*Il barbiere di Siviglia*	Rossini
Pants Roles:	Cherubino	*Le nozze di Figaro*	Mozart
	Stephano	*Romeo et Juliette*	Gounod
	Hänsel	*Hänsel und Gretel*	Humperdinck
	Sesto	*La Clemenza di Tito*	Mozart
Full Lyric	Dido	*Dido and Aeneas*	Purcell
Mezzo-Soprano	Dinah	*Trouble in Tahiti*	Bernstein
	Mother	*Amahl and the Night Visitors*	Menotti
	Carmen	*Carmen*	Bizet
	3rd Lady	*Die Zauberflöte*	Mozart
	Dorabella	*Così fan tutte*	Mozart
	Maddalena	*Rigoletto*	Verdi

Voice Category	Character	Opera	Composer
Pants Roles:	Romeo	*I Capuleti e i Montecchi*	Bellini
	Orfeo	*Orfeo ed Euridice*	Gluck
	Count Orsini	*Lucrezia Borgia*	Donizetti

Dramatic Mezzo-Soprano: *Range: g–c²*

This voice is very large, heavy, and usually dark quality in the mezzo range. She is generally capable of generous volume, similar in quality to contralto, but with slightly higher range. This mezzo is cast in the more dramatic roles such as Carmen, and is a favorite voice type of the 19th century. The vocal quality is very similar to that of the dramatic soprano. Wagner and Verdi use this voice type frequently, in roles that require a mature, rich dark sound, and a strong character. Examples of operatic roles would include:

Voice Category	Character	Opera	Composer
Dramatic	Eboli	*Don Carlo*	Verdi
Mezzo-Soprano	Augusta	*The Ballad of Baby Doe*	D. Moore
	Elizabeth	*The Crucible*	Ward
	Secretary	*The Consul*	Menotti
	Carmen	*Carmen*	Bizet
	Dalila	*Samson et Dalila*	Saint-Saëns
	Brangäne	*Tristan und Isolde*	Wagner
	Fricka	*Das Rheingold*	Wagner
	Waltraute	*Götterdämmerung*	Wagner
	Amneris	*Aïda*	Verdi
	Maddalena	*Rigoletto*	Verdi
Pants roles:	Octavian	*Der Rosenkavalier*	R. Strauss
	Der Komponist	*Ariadne auf Naxos*	R. Strauss

Mezzo-Contralto: *Range f–g² (b²)*

This category recognizes the rare ability of the mezzo-soprano to extend her range in both directions, while maintaining the richness of the voice at the top, and the brilliance of the voice at the lower extremities of the range. An excellent example of a mezzo-contralto in the current time period is Marilyn Horne, who demonstrates a lower range comparable to a tenor, and is still able to sing high *b*'s and *c*'s with the sopranos. This is a rare instrument indeed. Examples of operatic roles would include:

Voice Category	Character	Opera	Composer
Mezzo-Contralto	Dalila	*Samson et Dalila*	Saint-Saëns
	Orlando	*Orlando furioso*	Vivaldi
	Waltraute	*Götterdämmerung*	Wagner
	Amneris	*Aïda*	Verdi
	Dame Quickly	*Falstaff*	Verdi

Contralto: *Range: f–g² (b²)*

This category usually reserved for the lowest, heaviest, and darkest female voices. She is able to sing down to a low *g*, but is rarely required to sing above *e²* at the top of the staff. This singer consistently utilizes a heavy mixture of "chest voice" when singing operatic roles. Because this voice takes much longer to mature, most contraltos singing on the opera stage today are older than their counterparts, and are able to take on roles such as the mother, witch, or a buffa (comic) character such as Katisha in *The Mikado*. Examples of operatic roles would include:

Voice Category	Character	Opera	Composer
Contralto	La Principessa	*Suor Angelica*	Puccini
	Ulrica	*Un ballo in Maschera*	Verdi
	Dame Quickly	*Falstaff*	Verdi
	Baba	*The Medium*	Menotti
	Katisha	*The Mikado*	Gilbert and Sullivan
	Miss Todd	*The Old Maid and the Thief*	Menotti
	Carmen	*Carmen*	Bizet
	Cenerentola	*La Cenerentola*	Rossini

SUPPLEMENT 5–B

Countertenor: Range: f-b^{b2} (c^3) (the male alto)

The countertenor is a 20th century phenomenon. This is a male voice singing in a female register, though not in a true falsetto, and is considered the replacement for the castrato roles of the 17th century. This is a highly strengthened falsetto, which gives the singer power and range very similar to that of the mezzo-soprano. In addition to singing roles that would have been performed by the castrati, there are some 20th century roles written specifically for the countertenor voice category. Contemporary composers writing for the countertenor voice include Philip Glass, Benjamin Britten, Michael Tippett, and György Ligeti, among others. Castrati roles were composed by Handel, Purcell, Rameau, Lully, Pergolesi, and many others. Examples of operatic roles would include:

Voice Category	Character	Opera	Composer
Countertenor	Chinese Man	*The Fairy Queen*	Purcell
substituting for	Acis	*Acis et Galatée*	Lully
a castrati	Adalberto	*Ottone*	Handel
	Giulio Cesare	*Giulio Cesare*	Handel
	Adriano	*Adriano in Siria*	Pergolesi
	Armindo	*Partenope*	Handel
	Ruggiero	*Orlando furioso*	Vivaldi
Countertenor	Akhnaten	*Akhnaten*	Glass
in contemporary	Apollo	*Death in Venice*	Britten
times	Oberon	*A Midsummer Night's Dream*	Britten
	Trinculo	*The Tempest*	Eaton
	Orfeo	*Orfeo ed Euridice*	Gluck

Tenor

This is the highest category of the male voice, with a general range from c to c^2, and extending down to G and up to e^{b2}, depending on the particular singer.

Comic or Buffo Tenor: *Range: (A) c-b^{b2} (b^2)*

This tenor has a fairly light voice, and may at times be more actor than singer. He is roughly comparable to the soubrette in the female categories, and frequently plays opposite her on the stage of the comic opera. Another term for a buffo tenor would be a *character tenor*, and would indicate an actor of some skill who sings well. Comic tenor roles can be separated into those with a light lyric tenor tessitura as in the role of Pedrillo in *Die Entführung aus dem Serail*, and those with a light lyric baritone tessitura, such as Monostatos in *Die Zauberflöte*. There are even occasions where composers write for comic tenors in "skirts," such as the role of the witch in Humperdinck's *Hänsel und Gretel*. A wide variety of composers write for this type of voice. Examples of operatic roles would include:

Voice Category	Character	Opera	Composer
Buffo, Comic, or Character Tenor	Pedrillo	*Die Entführung aus dem Serail*	Mozart
	Beppe	*Pagliacci*	Leoncavallo
	Albert Herring	*Albert Herring*	Britten
	Don Basilio	*Le nozze di Figaro*	Mozart
	Magician	*The Consul*	Menotti
	Monostatos	*Die Zauberflöte*	Mozart
	Sportin' Life	*Porgy and Bess*	Gershwin
	Remendado	*Carmen*	Bizet
	Don Curzio	*Le nozze di Figaro*	Mozart
	Goro	*Madama Butterfly*	Puccini
Skirt Role:	Witch	*Hänsel und Gretel*	Humperdinck

Lyric Tenor: *Range: c–c²*

Comparable to the lyric soprano, this tenor may possess a light, flexible, pretty voice, capable of coloratura, or a somewhat heavier voice, both of which must be able to express love, warmth, and passion. Like the lyric soprano, he must have a full range of dynamics and the ability to sing with ease over a full complement of strings in the orchestra. He must be able to sustain a fairly high tessitura, and have a strong high *c*. This singer must also be "good looking" in order to portray the leading love character in the opera. The category separates into "light" and "full" just as it did in the sopranos. The lighter voice is heard frequently in works that contain coloratura, by such composers as Mozart, Bellini, Rossini, and Donizetti. The larger of the two voices is heard in Puccini as well. Examples of operatic roles would include:

Voice Category	Character	Opera	Composer
Light Lyric Tenor	Tamino	*Die Zauberflöte*	Mozart
	Ferrando	*Cosí fan tutte*	Mozart
	Nemorino	*L'elisir d'amore*	Donizetti
	Le Dancaïre	*Carmen*	Bizet
	Orphée	*Orphée et Eurydice*	Gluck
	Fenton	*Die lustigen Weiber von Windsor*	Nicolai
	Ein Hirt	*Tristan und Isolde*	Wagner
	Count Almaviva	*Il barbiere di Siviglia*	Rossini
	Ernesto	*Don Pasquale*	Donizetti
	Little Bat	*Susannah*	Floyd
Full Lyric Tenor	Dr. Faust	*Faust*	Gounod
	Roméo	*Roméo et Juliette*	Gounod
	Werther	*Werther*	Massenet
	Des Grieux	*Manon*	Massenet
	Belmonte	*Die Entführung aus dem Serail*	Mozart
	Alfredo Germont	*La Traviata*	Verdi
	Rinuccio	*Gianni Schichi*	Puccini
	Rodolfo	*La Boheme*	Puccini
	Tom Rakewell	*The Rake's Progress*	Stravinsky

Lyrico Spinto Tenor: *Range: c–c²*

This is the male equivalent to the lyrico spinto soprano, and is basically a lyric tenor with the ability to push the voice a bit further muscularly, and dramatically. This tenor has more brilliance than the lyric and is more aggressive sounding. He is heard primarily in the works of the verismo composers of the late 19th century, specifically, Bizet, Leoncavallo, Mascagni, Boito, Puccini, and Verdi among others. You will find the spinto tenor singing with the spinto soprano in Italian opera generally. Examples of operatic roles would include:

Voice Category	Character	Opera	Composer
Lyrico Spinto Tenor	Des Grieux	*Manon Lescaut*	Puccini
	Cavaradossi	*Tosca*	Puccini
	Pinkerton	*Madama Butterfly*	Puccini
	Turiddu	*Cavalleria Rusticana*	Mascagni
	Canio	*Pagliacci*	Leoncavallo
	Faust	*Mefistofele*	Boito
	Don José	*Carmen*	Bizet
	Don Carlo	*Don Carlo*	Verdi
	Il Duca di Mantua	*Rigoletto*	Verdi

Dramatic Tenor: *Range: c–c²*

This is a stronger voice with more dramatic character than the spinto tenor. This tenor is known more for strength of tone rather than beauty, and for his vocal stamina, as he must frequently sustain a high tessitura for long periods of time. He is the hero of the opera dramatically, and this portrayal requires more weight in the voice and the physical presence of the man generally. This tenor is heard primarily in the operas of Verdi and Wagner as well as the verismo composers. Examples of operatic roles would include:

Voice Category	Character	Opera	Composer
Dramatic Tenor	Radames	*Aïda*	Verdi
	Don Carlo	*Don Carlo*	Verdi
	Otello	*Otello*	Verdi
	Canio	*Pagliacci*	Leoncavallo
	Hoffman	*Les contes d'Hoffman*	Offenbach
	Don José	*Carmen*	Bizet
	Max	*Der Freischütz*	Weber
	Lohengrin	*Lohengrin*	Wagner
	Peter Grimes	*Peter Grimes*	Britten
	Anatol	*Vanessa*	Barber

Heldentenor: *Range: c–b♭²*

The true "heroic tenor" with a dark baritone quality and the ability to sing over a large orchestra, this tenor is capable of great brilliance and power. Some heldentenors were baritones who learned to sing in this slightly higher tessitura. This voice requires a tremendous amount of physical strength and great stamina. The tessitura is similar to that of a baritone, rather than a lyric tenor, so, the high *c* is no longer an absolute requirement. This voice is heard primarily in the works of Richard Wagner, but also in the heavier tenor roles of Giuseppe Verdi. Examples of operatic roles would include:

Voice Category	Character	Opera	Composer
Heldentenor	Florestan	*Fidelio*	Beethoven
	Samson	*Samson et Dalila*	Saint-Saëns
	Siegmund	*Die Walküre*	Wagner
	Tristan	*Tristan und Isolde*	Wagner
	Tannhaüser	*Tannhaüser*	Wagner
	Lohengrin	*Lohengrin*	Wagner
	Parsifal	*Parsifal*	Wagner
	Rienzi	*Rienzi*	Wagner

Baritone: Range: (G) c–a^{b1} (a^1)

The term baritone comes from the Greek *barytonos*, which means "deep sounding," and indicates a middle category of the male voice similar to the mezzo-soprano in the female categories. You will note from the range indicated above that even if we are speaking of a light lyric baritone, the highest notes of the tenor range will not be present in this category. This is the generally preferred voice for the young lover in American Broadway theatre, and is also an important voice category for some leading roles, and secondary roles in opera. All composers of opera utilize this category, but it is a particularly important vocal category for Mozart.

Lyric Baritone:

Like the mezzo-soprano category, this category is divided into the light or young lyric baritone, and the full mature lyric baritone. The more mature lyric baritone is the preferred vocal category for the leading male character in 19th century French opera, where the tessitura is higher, but earlier French opera utilized the lighter lyric baritone. This baritone can sing nearly as high as tenor at times, but the overall vocal timbre is darker and warmer. Note, that like the lighter weight mezzo-sopranos, the lyric baritone must be able to execute coloratura passages, and should have the ability to sing with legato and a full complement of dynamic levels. Examples of operatic roles would include:

Voice Category	Character	Opera	Composer
Light Lyric Baritone Range: (G) c–a^b (a^1)	Papageno	*The Magic Flute*	Mozart
	Figaro	*Le nozze di Figaro*	Mozart
	Guglielmo	*Cosí fan tutte*	Mozart
	Leporello	*Don Giovanni*	Mozart
	Figaro	*Il barbiere di Siviglia*	Rossini
	Dandini	*La Cenerentola*	Rossini
	Dr. Falke	*Die Fledermaus*	J. Strauss
	Mercutio	*Roméo et Juliette*	Gounod
	Le Dancaïre	*Carmen*	Bizet
	Lescaut	*Manon*	Massenet
	Sportin' Life	*Porgy and Bess*	Gershwin
	Bob	*The Old Maid and the Thief*	Menotti
	Ben	*The Telephone*	Menotti

Voice Category	Character	Opera	Composer
Full Lyric Baritone	Count Almaviva	*Le nozze di Figaro*	Mozart
Range: (G) c–f# (Ab)	Figaro	*Le nozze di Figaro*	Mozart
	Valentin	*Faust*	Gounod
	Escamillo	*Carmen*	Bizet
	Morales	*Carmen*	Bizet
	Figaro	*Il barbiere di Siviglia*	Rossini
	Gianni Schicchi	*Gianni Schicchi*	Puccini
	Schaunard	*La Boheme*	Puccini
	Giorgio Germont	*La Traviata*	Verdi
	Melchior	*Amahl and the Night Visitors*	Menotti
	Mr. Gobineau	*The Medium*	Menotti

Dramatic *Baritone: Range: (G) c–f# (ab1)*

This is a weightier voice, with a dark quality with generous power. Because of the weight and timbre required, this is generally a more mature singer, and a larger physical presence. This voice is used frequently in the operas of Giuseppe Verdi, and one of the most popular roles for this category is the title role in Verdi's *Rigoletto*. Adding the descriptive term dramatic also adds the requirement for strong characterization and acting skills. Examples of operatic roles would include:

Voice Category	Character	Opera	Composer
Dramatic Baritone	Mephistopheles	*Faust*	Gounod
	Escamillo	*Carmen*	Bizet
	Don Pizarro	*Fidelio*	Beethoven
	Peter (Father)	*Hänsel und Gretel*	Humperdinck
	Alberich	*Götterdämmerung*	Wagner
	Alberich	*Siegfried*	Wagner
	Wozzeck	*Wozzeck*	Berg
	Lescaut	*Manon Lescaut*	Puccini
	Rigoletto	*Rigoletto*	Verdi
	Falstaff	*Falstaff*	Verdi
	Porgy	*Porgy and Bess*	Gershwin
	Daniel Webster	*The Devil and Daniel Webster*	Moore

Bass-Baritone: *Range: (E) Ab–f1 (g1)*

This voice combines the dark bass quality with ability to sing notes into the baritone range with a darker quality. The voice is deeper than most baritones, but higher than many basses. Although this singer's voice essentially encompasses the range of both categories, he prefers a lower tessitura. This voice category is similar to the mezzo-contralto category in the female voices. The number of composers writing for this voice type is smaller than the other baritone types, but includes a wide variety from Mozart, and Bizet, to Wagner and more contemporary composers. Examples of operatic roles would include:

Voice Category	Character	Opera	Composer
Bass-Baritone	Don Giovanni	*Don Giovanni*	Mozart
	Figaro	*Le nozze di Figaro*	Mozart
	Count Almaviva	*Le nozze di Figaro*	Mozart
	Escamillo	*Carmen*	Bizet
	Alberich	*Siegfried*	Wagner
	Wotan	*Siegfried*	Wagner
	Alberich	*Das Rheingold*	Wagner
	Wotan	*Das Rheingold*	Wagner
	Wotan	*Die Walküre*	Wagner
	Horace Tabor	*The Ballad of Baby Doe*	Moore

NOTE: The baritone categories are not as easily distinguished and separated as the previous categories. The boundaries of baritone types are crossed frequently in opera. The role of Figaro, for example, can be sung by a lyric baritone, a dramatic baritone, or a bass-baritone. The choice is up to the musical and theatrical directors of the opera theatre.

Bass: (C) E♭–f¹ (g¹)

The Italian term *basso* and the Latin term *bassus* both mean "low," and the bass is the lowest of all the human voice categories with a general range from *F* to *e¹*. Because the voice requires tremendous maturity to reach the extremes of the low range, a true bass will be more mature than his counterparts on the operatic stage. In early opera, this low voice was used to portray gods, kings, and mysterious figures. By the 18th century, Mozart had begun to use this voice category for more comic roles, and in the 19th century, the bass can be heard as the villain, or the person of authority. In the 20th and 21st centuries, the bass is used freely in any character or role. This category is divided into three parts according to range, dramatic ability and color of the voice.

Basso Buffo, or Comic Bass: *Range: (D) F–e¹ (f¹)*

This voice is used frequently in the 18th century in the operas of Haydn, and Mozart, as well as in the 19th century *bel canto* tradition in works of Rossini, Bellini, and Donizetti. This means, of course, that the singer must have the ability to sing coloratura as well as excellent acting skills. The acting ability of this singer is perhaps even more important than the singing technique. In this requirement, this is the male counterpart to the contralto, and the two are frequently paired on the operatic stage. Examples of operatic roles would include:

Voice Category	Character	Opera	Composer
Basso Buffo	Don Alfonso	*Così fan tutte*	Mozart
	Osmin	*Die Entführung aus dem Serail*	Mozart
	Bartolo	*Le nozze di Figaro*	Mozart
	Figaro	*Le nozze di Figaro*	Mozart
	Bartolo	*Il barbieri di Siviglia*	Rossini
	Basilio	*Il barbieri di Siviglia*	Rossini
	Don Magnifico	*La Cenerentola*	Rossini
	Don Pasquale	*Don Pasquale*	Donizetti
	Alcindoro	*La Bohème*	Puccini
	Sparafucile	*Rigoletto*	Verdi
	Dr. Caius & Falstaff	*Die lustigen Weiber von Windsor*	Nicolai
	Doktor	*Wozzeck*	Berg

Lyric Bass (Basso cantante or basso cantabile): *Range: (F) G–f¹*

Remembering that the term "lyric" refers to a moderately sized voice with a warm color, capable of singing long legato lines and portraying romantic characters, we can apply the term to this low male voice category. This singer generally has the most beautiful of the bass voices, and is heard not only on the operatic stage, but in the sacred tradition as well, in oratorio, cantata, and in frequent solos in choral music. This is a lighter weight voice than the dramatic baritone, and can be heard in the operas of Handel, Gluck, and Mozart. In the 19th century bel canto tradition, Rossini, Donizetti, and Bellini have written well for the lyric bass. It is essential that this singer have a beautiful vocal timbre. Examples of operatic roles would include:

Voice Category	Character	Opera	Composer
Lyric Bass	Sarastro	*Die Zauberflöte*	Mozart
	Figaro	*Le nozze di Figaro*	Mozart
	Friar	*Roméo et Juliette*	Gounod
	Capulet	*Roméo et Juliette*	Gounod
	Des Grieux	*Manon*	Massenet
	Escamillo	*Carmen*	Bizet
	Alidoro	*La Cenerentola*	Rossini
	Sparafucile	*Rigoletto*	Verdi
	Olin Blitch	*Susannah*	Floyd
	The Mikado	*The Mikado*	Gilbert and Sullivan

Dramatic Bass or Basso Profundo: *Range: (C) E♭–d¹ (f¹)*

This is the lowest and darkest of all the voices, and the voice darkens with age, so it is possible to hear a young dramatic bass who sounds more like a lyric until the voice has fully matured. Full maturity for this particular category can be as late as age 40. This voice is sometimes referred to as the *Schwarze Bass* (black bass) in Germany because of its dark rich timbre. When fully mature, this voice is used frequently in the operas of Richard Wagner. The voice has great power and can easily be heard over the large low brass section in Wagner's operas of "the Ring cycle." Examples of operatic roles would include:

Voice Category	Character	Opera	Composer
Basso Profundo	Commendatore	*Don Giovanni*	Mozart
	Mefistofele	*Mefistofele*	Boito
	Ramfis	*Aïda*	Verdi
	King of Egypt	*Aïda*	Verdi
	King Philip	*Don Carlo*	Verdi
	Boris Godunov	*Boris Godunov*	Musorgsky
	Baron Ochs	*Der Rosenkavalier*	R. Strauss
	Fafner	*Siegfried and Das Rheingold*	Wagner
	Fasolt	*Siegfried and Das Rheingold*	Wagner
	Hagen	*Götterdämmerung*	Wagner
	Hunding	*Die Walküre*	Wagner

Chapter 6

ARTICULATION FOR SINGERS
(THE INTERNATIONAL PHONETIC ALPHABET)

ARTICULATION

Merriam-Webster's Collegiate Dictionary, Eleventh edition defines the term "articulate" in several ways, including "expressing oneself readily, clearly, or effectively," and "to utter distinctly." (*Merriam-Webster*, 2005, p.70) In singing we refer to *articulation* as the act of singing the text in a manner, which allows the listener to hear every aspect of the text clearly, and to understand it through appropriate stressing of particular syllables. Excellent articulation skills for the singer also include the correct pronunciation of each vowel and consonant in every language in which we sing. When this happens we say that the singer has excellent *diction*.

There are many enunciation "traps" in attempting to pronounce even our own language when singing. First of all, the singer's mouth is open much further than it would be for speaking; second, the audience may be as much as a quarter of a mile away from the singer; and third, the singer is sustaining pitches, making the text even more difficult to comprehend than if the same text were spoken. Most professional singers learn to sing in at least five languages. The most common are: English, Italian, French, German, and Latin. Many singers also learn to sing in languages such as Russian, Polish, Spanish, and others. In order that the singer is able to pronounce correctly, and with the proper inflection, the many languages in which songs are written, a

phonetic alphabet system has been devised which allows singers the ability to learn these languages without necessarily studying in depth the languages of each of these countries. This pronunciation system is known as the *International Phonetic Alphabet*—a standardized pronunciation system of symbols, which represent sounds from nearly all spoken and sung languages. This alphabet is used not only by singers, but also by speech-language pathologists and others who deal regularly with languages or dialects, which are partially or totally foreign to them. The system allows for colloquialisms to be represented as well as "high classical" pronunciation of each language.

INTERNATIONAL PHONETIC ALPHABET (IPA)

IPA is a standardized system of symbols, which represent sounds from nearly all spoken and sung languages. This system will help you in attempting to pronounce or articulate correctly the components of a language that is not your own. It is a form of shorthand to help you gain control over the sounds you will be dealing with in English and Italian in this course. For most of us, English is our first language, so a student of singing may ask why it is necessary to use IPA when singing an English text. Think of the different "varieties," dialects, or *colloquialisms* found throughout the United States. The same word pronounced by persons from the North, South, East, and West portions of the United States would sound very different. In singing, we must attempt to remove all colloquial speech differences so we will be easily understood by everyone. Learning the IPA system and applying it to all sung languages, even your own, will help you to discover your own idiosyncratic pronunciations and help you to identify and modify any incorrectly produced speech sounds.

It will be most beneficial for you to memorize the symbols for sounds in IPA so that they are at your command. The IPA Vowel and Consonant charts found in Figures 6–1A and 6–1B will be helpful to you in studying and attempting to produce or artic-

International Phonetic Alphabet
Vowel Chart (Vowels are the carriers of Vocal Tone)

	I.P.A	Webster	English	Italian
Lip Vowels:	[ɑ]	å	father	casa
	[ɔ]	o	taught	morte
	[o]	ō	obey	dove
	[ʊ]	u	book	
	[u]	ü	moon	luna
(neutral) (Schwa)	[ə]	ə	about	
Tongue Vowels:	[i]	e	me	mi
	[e]	ā	chaotic	tempesta
	[ɪ]	i	it	
	[ɛ]	e	met	bello
	[æ]	a	cat	
Diphthongs:	[ɑː ɪ] [ɑː i]	i	my	mai
	[ɔː ɪ] [ɔː i]	ói	boy	poi
	[ɛː ɪ] [ɛː i]	ā	say	sei
	[oː ʊ]	ō	hoe	
	[ɑː ʊ] [ɑː u]	au	cow	causa
Triphthongs:	[ɑ ʊ ə]	auə	our	
	[ɑ ɪ ə]	iə	ire	
	[j ɛ i]			miei
	(There are others in other languages)			
Glides	[j]	yü	you	ieri
	[w]	w	witch	uomo
	[ʎ]		lute	gli

Figure 6–1A. IPA Vowel Chart.

Consonant Chart (Interrupters)

	I.P.A	Webster	English	Italian
Voiced Consonants	[b]	b	box	bene
	[d]	d	do	dente
	[g]	g	go	gondola
	[ʒ]	z	measure	
	[l]	l	long	lungo
	[m]	m	man	mamma
	[n]	n	no	naso
	[ŋ]	ng	ring	vengo
	[r]	r	red	rosso
	[v]	v	very	verde
	[z]	z	zebra	casa
	[ð]	th	there	
Unvoiced Consonants	[dʒ]	j	joy	gioia
	[dz]	dz	adds	azzura
	[f]	f	fine	forte
	[gz]	gz	exile	
	[h]	h	high	
	[k]	k (or) c	kick	caro
	[ʒd]	jd	edged	
	[ks]	ks	lax	
	[ɫ]	l	milk	
	[ɲ]	ny	onion	ognuno
	[p]	p	pan	padre
	[s]	s	sing	sangue
	[ʃ]	sh	show	sciocco
	[ʃt]	sht	rushed	
	[t]	t	too	tutto
	[ts]	ts	rats	zio
	[tʃ]	ch	church	cielo
	[θ]	th	thing	

Figure 6-1B. IPA Consonant Chart.

ulate correct sounds. Take a portion of some text in your own language and attempt to transcribe all the vowels and consonants into IPA symbols.

Notice that the chart is divided in several ways. Across the top, the chart is divided by categories, including the IPA symbols for the sounds, the Webster dictionary symbol for the sounds, and both English and Italian examples of words using the particular sounds. Figure 6-1A is the chart for vowels, and Figure 6-1B is the chart for consonants. On the

Vowel Chart (Figure 6-1A), there are further divisions, which have to do with the way in which a particular sound is produced or articulated. A brief discussion of these categories follows.

Vowels

Much time will be devoted to singing vowels as you study vocal technique, as it is "on the vowels" that we are able to make and sustain sound. As defined by William G. Moulton in his book *The Sounds of English and German* (Moulton, 1962), and quoted by John Moriarty (from *Diction*, Moriarty, 1975, p. 5): vowels are "sounds articulated in such a way that the breath stream flows essentially unhindered along the median line of the vocal tract." Thus, "the vocal cords are in vibration."

The Tongue Vowels

[i] [e] [ɪ] [ɛ] [æ]

As you have probably guessed, *tongue vowels* are produced by changing the shape of the airflow in the mouth by positioning the tongue in different ways. In vowels known as tongue vowels, the tongue is more active than the lips in the formation of the sound. In speaking your own language, you have learned to do this subconsciously. Learning to articulate tongue vowels correctly for singing requires a bit of conscious effort to be sure the tongue is in the correct position for each vowel. This too will become a subconscious activity after a short time of conscious practice. Be aware, as you practice and try each sound, of how the tongue and mouth positions "feel."

[i]   This is the designated symbol for the sound of the English language vowel in the word *me*. In English it can be spelled as: *ee*; *ea*; *ei*; *ie*; *y*; or just *e*. In pronouncing [i], the tip of the tongue should touch where the teeth meet the gums on the bottom jaw and the center of the tongue should arch upward. Acoustically, it takes a short, wide space to make this sound. Many untrained singers attempt to make this space by spreading the corners of the mouth,

which also spreads the tone, making it less "warm" and certainly less focused. Rather, let the corners of the mouth remain loose and relaxed, drop the jaw so there is approximately an index finger's space between the upper and lower teeth and let the tongue form the correct space by arching in the mouth. As you attempt to sing notes in the upper voice range on this vowel [i], you may drop your jaw lower and your tongue will retain its arch, thus giving good tone and vowel quality to the sound from lowest to highest pitches. Your mirror and tape recorder will be very helpful in achieving best results.

[e]   Allowing the tongue to drop very slightly lower, but retaining some arch, will move the sound into [e] as in the English words *date, bait*, or *gate*. This sound can be spelled in two different ways in the English language: *a*, *ai*. This sound is sometimes referred to as a *closed e*, which in no way refers to closing the throat but refers rather to the fact that the tongue is partially closing off the air space in the mouth by being close to the roof of the mouth. Try saying [i] and [e] back to back several times to feel the difference in tongue position. Remember to leave the lips in a loose and relaxed position. Do not spread the corners of the mouth. Try the exercises in Figure 6-2, and create some of your own exercises to be sure that you understand the concept.

[ɪ]   Allowing the tongue to drop slightly lower than the position for [e] will help you to find the sound [ɪ] as in *mitten, it, fit*. Again, be careful not to spread the corners of the mouth. Use the exercises in Figure 6-3 to help you with your own pronunciation of this sound.

[ɛ]   Dropping the tongue slightly lower than for the [ɪ] will help you to find the next sound [ɛ] as in *met, bed, dead*. This sound also has a variety of spellings in the English language: *e, ai, ae, ai* as in "*air*," *ae*, as in "*aesthetic*." This is not an easy vowel to pronounce or sing because it requires a much more relaxed tongue than you would expect. Work from the [i] through the [e] and [ɪ] and then to the pronunciation of [ɛ], so that you can feel the change

---

Exercise: Pronunciation practice for [i] [e]

Practice pronouncing the following words, using the new tongue position to guide your pronunciation. Sustain the vowels so that you can feel the appropriate sensation when singing.

[i]	[e]	[i]	[e]	[i]	[e]
me	made	we	grade	team	gate

[i]	[e]	[i]	[e]	[e]	[i]	[e]
We	made a	green	cake for	Jake's	sleek	snake.

[i]	[i]	[e]	[e]	[ɪ]	[i]	[i]	[i]
See	me	make a	date	with	mean	green	teens.

Now make up an exercise of your own using words which utilize the [i] and [e] tongue vowels. Be sure to use the correct IPA symbol above each appropriate vowel.

Figure 6-2. Exercise for [i] [e] pronunciation.

Exercise: [ɪ] [i] [e]

Try sustaining a comfortable pitch while pronouncing the following words. Get used to "feeling" the tongue position in your mouth so that you will know when it is correct as you are singing these same sounds.

[i]	[i]	[ɪ]	[ɪ][ɪ][ɪ] [ɪ]	[ɪ]	[ɪ]	[ɪ]
See	me	in	Mississippi	in	Rick's	Gym

[ɪ]	[i]	[e]	[i]	[i]
It	seems	baked	enough to	me

[e]	[ɪ]	[i]	[i]	[i]
Make	it	beep so	Pete can't	sleep

Now make up an exercise of your own using words which utilize the [ɪ], [i], and [e] tongue vowels. Be sure to use the correct IPA symbol above each appropriate vowel.

Figure 6-3. Exercise for [ɪ] [i] [e] pronunciation practice.

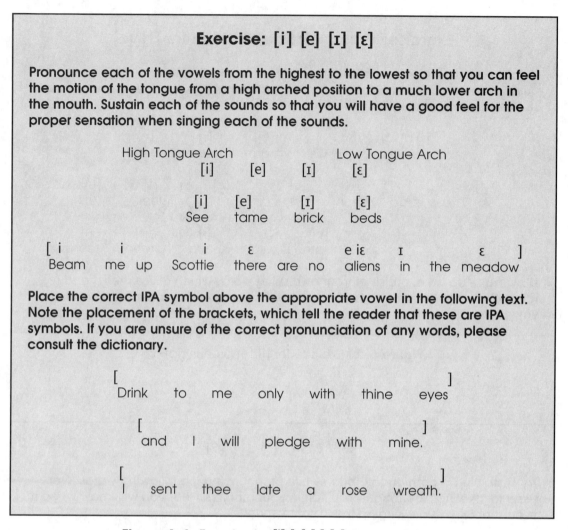

Figure 6-4. Exercise for [i] [e] [ɪ] [ɛ] pronunciation.

in the tongue position for each distinct vowel. Try the pronunciation exercises in Figure 6-4 to help you feel the position of the tongue and its formation changes.

[æ] This is the last and the lowest tongue position in formation of the tongue vowels. It is represented in the English language by the vowel "*a*" as in *cat*. For the articulation of this vowel, allow the tongue to drop even lower, almost flat and very wide in the back of the mouth. It is very important to remember not to spread the corners of the mouth as you sing

this vowel so the tone will stay forward and clear. See Figure 6-5 for exercises to help you with the formation of this difficult vowel.

If you have used the exercises provided in Figures 6-2 to 6-5, you should now have a good understanding of the articulation and "feel" of the tongue vowels. Be sure to put these IPA symbols into any vocal music you are working on so that you will have a practical application of the IPA in your day-to-day work. This would include choral music as well as solo or small ensemble music. IPA symbols are

Exercise: [i] [e] [ɪ] [ɛ] [æ]

Pronounce each of the vowels above from the highest to the lowest so that you can feel the motion of the tongue from a high arched position to a much lower arch in the mouth. Sustain each of the sounds so that you will have a good feel for the proper sensation when singing each of the sounds.

Sustain one single pitch (monotone) while pronouncing this phrase.

[i   ɪ   e   ɪ   æ   æ   æ]
See   him   make   dinner   for   that   fat   cat.

Place the IPA symbols [i], [e], [ɪ], [ɛ], [æ] above the appropriate vowels in the following phrases and then pronounce each phrase carefully and correctly.

[
As   long   as   he   needs   me   ]

[
The   afternoon   is   heavy   with   rain   ]

[
The   happiness   that   living   with   you   brings   me   ]

Now make up an exercise of your own using words which utilize the [i], [e], [ɪ], [ɛ], [æ] tongue vowels. Be sure to use the correct IPA symbol above each appropriate vowel.

Figure 6-5. Exercise for (i) (e) (ɪ) (ɛ) (æ) pronunciation.

always shown in brackets and are placed directly above or below the appropriate vowels. You need not bracket each word of the text. It is more precise to place a single bracket at the beginning of a musical line and at the end of that line. Please see Figure 6-6 for an example of a song text with IPA placed appropriately. Note placement of the brackets carefully.at the end of that line.

Example of IPA text placed appropriately for a song text without music:

[o   se   kæn   j u   si   baːɪ   ð ə   dɔ n z   əʳl ɪ   laːɪt]
Oh   say   can   you   see   by   the   dawn's   early   light

[hwət   so   praːʊ dlɪ   wi   hel d   æt   ð ə   twaːɪ laːɪ ts   læst]
What   so   prou dly   we   hailed   at   the   twi - light's   last

[gl i m ɪŋ]
gleaming

Note placement of the IPA brackets carefully!

Here is an example of IPA text placed appropriately for a song text with music:

(') = Breathe only if you must
(check) = You should breathe

Figure 6-6. Examples of IPA placed for Text and Song.

94

The Lip Vowels

[ɑ] [ɔ] [o] [u] [ʊ] [ɐ]

[ɑ] Can be spelled using "a" or "o" in the English language and has the most open and relaxed mouth shape of all the lip vowels. The jaw is dropped from the temporomandibular joint, and the tongue is flat and relaxed on the floor of the mouth. You should be able to feel the outside of your tongue on the inside of all your bottom teeth. Do not attempt to place your tongue flat in your mouth—allow it to go to this position on the intake of a relaxed breath and then be aware of where it is. The tongue should feel wide, especially across the front, bottom teeth. The lips should be loose and relaxed and never pulled or stretched at the corners of the mouth. When the mouth is open properly for singing, the lower jaw will feel as if it has dropped down and slightly back, leaving the lower jaw slightly behind the upper jaw. It has been said that Mortimer Snerd, the ventriloquist Edgar Bergen's "dummy" of old time radio fame, is the "patron saint" of all singers because his favorite saying ("Duh!") sets the lower jaw into an appropriate position for singing—down and slightly behind the upper jaw (Figure 6-7).

Using the exercises in Figure 6-8, be sure to pay close attention to the position of both lips and tongue for the correct pronunciation of the [ɑ] vowel.

Figure 6-7. Typical ventriloquist's "Dummy." Note the dropped down and back, relaxed mandible. All singers should emulate this relaxed lower jaw position.

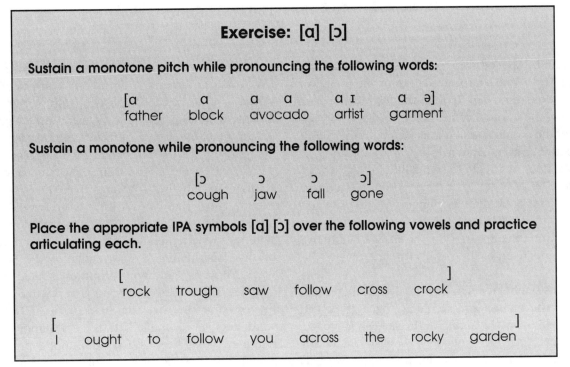

Exercise: [ɑ] [ɔ]

Sustain a monotone pitch while pronouncing the following words:

[ɑ	ɑ	ɑ ɑ	ɑ ɪ	ɑ ə]
father	block	avocado	artist	garment

Sustain a monotone while pronouncing the following words:

[ɔ	ɔ	ɔ	ɔ]
cough	jaw	fall	gone

Place the appropriate IPA symbols [ɑ] [ɔ] over the following vowels and practice articulating each.

[
rock   trough   saw   follow   cross   crock
]

[
I   ought   to   follow   you   across   the   rocky   garden
]

Figure 6-8. Exercise for [ɑ] [ɔ] pronunciation.

Exercise: [ɑ] [ɔ] [o]

Pronounce each of the vowels above from the most open to the most closed so that you can feel the motion of the lips from an open and relaxed position to one using more musculature in the lip formation. Sustain each of the sounds so that you will have a good feel for the proper sensation when singing the sounds.

Sustain one single pitch (monotone) while pronouncing this phrase. Be careful not to allow the diphthong [oːu] to occur.

[o   o   o   o   o   o o æ]

soap rope poke grow sew phonograph

Practice the following Italian words as there are few, if any, real closed o's [o] in the English language.

[vo tʃɛ ombra donɔ doloroza]

voce ombra dono dolorosa

Try to think of words, which would be appropriately pronounced with the closed o sound [o], and are frequently heard with the diphthong when pronounced in the United States. List those words here with the correct IPA for the [o] vowel as if you intended to sing the vowel.

Figure 6–9. Exercise for [ɑ] [ɔ] [o] pronunciation.

[ɔ] Can be spelled *ou, o,* or *aw* in the English language. The sound is produced by allowing the lower jaw to close very slightly from the [ɑ] position, and bringing the corners of the mouth in a bit. The corners of the mouth should never widen for the vowel. Keep the corners drawn in toward the center so that [ɔ] does not begin to sound like [ɑ]. [ɔ] is often referred to as "open o" because the lips are more relaxed and open than its counterpart [o], which is referred to as "closed o." This has to do with closing and opening the lips, not the throat. See Figure 6–8 for a comparison of the vowels [ɑ] and [ɔ].

[o] This symbol for "closed o" really exists "purely" only in the French and German languages. It can be spelled *o, oa, ow,* or *ew,* in the English language. However, American colloquial English frequently uses a *diphthong* [o: u] as in the word *row.* This diphthong can be highly exaggerated in some South-

ern U.S. dialects and can be almost nonexistent in Northeastern dialects. A diphthong consists of two vowel sounds voiced consecutively within one syllable with the stress of the syllable always placed on the first vowel; this elongates the first vowel in comparison with the second. For example, if the word "toy," were to be sung, the singer would want to sustain the "o" rather than the "y" vowel sound. Thus, the IPA for this word would look like this: [tɔ: ɪ]. The colon following the "open o" signifies the lengthening of this vowel and because of this lengthening, a shortening of the second vowel. More is said about diphthongs later in this chap-ter. The closed [o] sound is very close to the [u] position, in that the lips are quite far forward and very rounded. It is very important to remember that there be no diphthong produced after the [o]. See Figure 6–9 for exercises utilizing [ɑ], [ɔ], and [o].

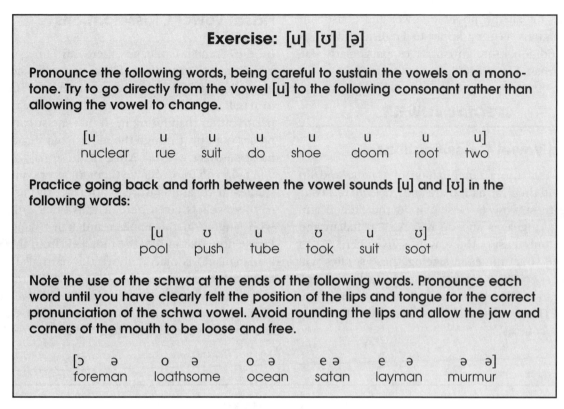

Figure 6-10. Exercise for [u] [ʊ] [ə] pronunciation.

[u]   The [u] vowel sound can be spelled in many ways in the English language, including: *u, ue, ui, o, oe, oo, ou,* and *wo.* To find the proper sound for [u], you should round your lips with a gentle pucker, drop the lower jaw slightly and let the vowel fall forward into the mouth at the lower front teeth. There is a slight diphthong toward the neutral vowel [ə] in the American pronunciation of the [u] at times. This is considered to be very colloquial and should be avoided when singing. See Figure 6-10 for exercises to practice pronouncing [u].

[ʊ]   Represents the more open "u" vowel as found in the word "foot." It occurs frequently in the English and German languages, and never appears in Italian or French. It can be spelled in the English language: *u,* or *oo.* To find the best position for the [ʊ], start with the position for [u], using well-rounded lips, then allow the lips to relax slightly, keeping the tip of the tongue resting against the back of the lower teeth or slightly lower. The back of the tongue should arch somewhat. See Figure 6-10 for exercises comparing [ʊ] and [u].

[ə]   Represents the neutral vowel, often known as *schwa.* In the English language this sound can be found at the ends of some words where the syllable is unstressed and is spelled *e, ea, ei, o, u,* or *a.* In this case the singer must avoid rounding the lips and allow the jaw and corners of the mouth to be loose and free. This vowel occurs in the English, French, and German languages, but never in Italian. See Figure 6-10 for exercises comparing [ʊ] [u] and [ə].

These are the basic vowels necessary for beginning study of correct articulation in the English and Italian languages. There are additional vowel sounds occurring in many languages, which we will refer to as "special vowels." These special vowels are discussed briefly in the following paragraphs. If you study voice in a college, conservatory, or a university, you will have the opportunity to register for courses in which you will learn the correct IPA symbols for all the possible vowel and consonant combinations as they apply to English as well as many additional foreign languages, particularly Italian, German, French, and perhaps Latin.

SPECIAL VOWELS

Mixed Vowel Classifications

Vowels that use a combination of tongue and lip motion in their formation are known as *mixed vowels*. As these vowels exist only in the French and German languages and do not exist in Italian and English, only a list of the vowels is given here. If you continue your studies in singing, these studies will include specialized courses in the correct pronunciation and articulation or diction of foreign languages. These vowels will be discussed extensively in those courses.

Nasal Vowel Classifications

In the French language, there are four vowels, which may be *nasalized*. These vowels do not exist in the English, Italian, or German languages. In order to nasalize a vowel, the singer must relax the soft palate rather than lifting it, so that the stream of air passes not only through the mouth, but through the nasal passages as well. A list of these nasal vowels will help you to recognize them for your continuing studies in vocal literature. No further discussion of nasal vowels is given here, as this book only deals with singing in the English and Italian languages. Please note that in IPA, the tilde [~] (from the Spanish language) is placed above the particular vowel to be nasalized. This is the singer's cue to relax the soft palate when singing the nasalized vowel. A list of the mixed and nasal vowels as used in German and French is found on Figure 6–11.

SPECIAL VOWELS

Mixed Vowels as used in German and French:

IPA Symbol	Spelled	Pronounced	German	French
[y]	ü, u	place lips in [u] & say [i]	✓	✓
[ø]	ö, eu	place lips in [o] & say [e]	✓	✓
[œ]	ö, oeu	place lips in [ɔ] & say [ɛ]	✓	✓
[ʏ]	ü	place lips in [ʊ] & say [ɪ]	✓	

Nasalized vowels used in the French language:

IPA Symbol	Spelled in French
[ɑ̃]	an, am, en, em, ean, aen, aon
[ɛ̃]	in, im, ein, eim, ain, aim, yn, ym
[õ]	on, om, eon
[œ̃]	un, um, eun

Figure 6–11. Special Vowels.

Diphthongs and Triphthongs

Combinations of vowels can be placed in two categories. When two vowels are sounded consecutively, one following the other within one syllable with the accent or emphasis on the first vowel, the combination is known as a *diphthong*. When three vowels are sounded one following the other within a single syllable, the combination is called a *triphthong*. The English language contains both. The Italian language contains only diphthongs and always spells out its vowel combinations, so they are rarely difficult to determine. The primary diphthongs in the English and Italian languages are: [ɑː i] [ɑː ɪ] [ɑː u] [ɑː ʊ] [ɛː i] [ɛː ɪ] [ɔː i] [ɔː ɪ] and [oː ʊ] Some examples of these from both the Italian and English languages are seen in Figure 6–12. When singing a diphthong, the first or primary vowel is sustained (remember this is the meaning of the colon following the first vowel) and the second vowel is treated almost as a consonant, moving away from it quickly.

In a triphthong, either the first or the middle vowel may be the primary vowel, and therefore the vowel to be sustained will vary when singing or speaking a triphthong. Be sure to check your dictionary for the correct emphasis. Examples of triphthongs are seen in Figure 6–12. The most common triphthongs in the English language are: [ɑː ɪə] and [ɑː uə].

Examples of Diphthongs and Triphthongs from the English and Italian Languages

DIPHTHONG	English	Italian
[ɑː ɪ] or [ɑː i]	my	mai
[ɑː ʊ] or [ɑː u]	loud	Laura
[ɛː ɪ] or [ɛː i]	say	sei
[ɔː ɪ] or [ɔː i]	annoy	noi
[oː ʊ]	no	n/a

TRIPHTHONG	English	Italian
[ɑ ɪ ə]	fire, choir, lyre	n/a
[ɑ ʊ ə]	our, hour, flower	n/a
[j ɛː i]	n/a	miei

(The final example in Italian [*miei*] is really a glide plus a diphthong.)

It is important to note the distinction between the English words *are*, and *our*! Pay close attention to the IPA for singing each word below.

[ɑʳ]	[ɑ ʊ ə]
are	our

Figure 6–12. Examples of Diphthongs and Triphthongs.

Glides

The combination of two vowels pronounced consecutively within one syllable can also produce what is known as a *glide*. In this instance, the unstressed or first vowel is pronounced quickly, and the singer or speaker proceeds quickly and smoothly to a following vowel, which is stressed and elongated. An example would be the word you. In this case, the semivowel "y" is considered a glide, and, thus, the second vowel, represented by the IPA symbol [u] is sustained when singing. In IPA, the word "you" would be transliterated or transcribed as follows: [ju]. Common English and Italian glides are represented in IPA symbols on the chart in Figure 6–13. Notice that vowels and consonants that are not sounded are not transliterated into IPA. As IPA is a language representing actual pronunciation of sounds, it is inappropriate to display vowels or consonants that are silent.

Four Glides Existing in the English and Italian Languages

IPA	Spelled	Pronounced	English	Italian
[j]	y, i	an intensified [i]	yacht, yes	fiero, miele
[w]	w	an intensified [u]	west	questo
[ʎ]	gli	compressed version of two sounds [l] & [j]	lute	gli, foglio, aglio consiglio
[ŋ]	gn, ne, nu	two sounds tightly compressed [n] & [j]	new nuisance	segno, bagno vigna

In singing the glides, the singer must be careful to sustain the vowel following the glide rather than sustaining the glide vowel itself. Thus, if singing the word "yacht," the singer would want to sustain the [ɑ] vowel rather than the y [j] as follows:

[j ɑ t]
yacht

Figure 6–13. Four Glides existing in the English and French languages.

CONSONANTS

Although singers consider vowels more important for carrying tone, without consonants, words would not exist and there would be no reason for singing with text. Composers and poets have argued for hundreds of years over which is more important—the music or the text. Although there may never be complete agreement, it would seem appropriate for singers to consider text and music to be of equal importance in the singing of a song in order to maintain the integrity of both the words of the poet and the music of the composer. Thus, as we consider pronunciation or diction in singing, the vowels are used to convey the beauty of the vocal tone and the consonants are used to give more powerful meaning to the text. Consonants may be grouped into two categories: *Voiced* and *Unvoiced*.

Voiced Consonants permit vibration of the vocal folds in order for correct pronunciation to take place. *Unvoiced Consonants* do not require

the use of the vocal folds and, as a matter of fact, it is impossible to make vocal sound while producing unvoiced consonants. Unvoiced consonants are not capable of carrying pitch whereas voiced consonants, by definition, must carry pitch. Figure 6–14 presents a list of voiced and unvoiced consonants as they exist in the English language. It is important for singers to recognize the difference between the two categories of consonants, as voiced consonants can carry pitch and thus aid in the creation of legato and vibration in the singing process, and unvoiced consonants are utilized for clarity of diction as well as dramatic delivery in the way that the singer produces them. The voiced consonants, to some degree, may be utilized in the singing process as if they were vowels.

Consonants may also be grouped according to how they are formed or articulated. In this case we refer to Plosive, Fricative, and Nasal consonants. *Plosive Consonants* are consonants articulated by stopping the flow of the breath in some way, either with the lips or tongue, before moving on to the

---

Voiced and Unvoiced Consonants as they appear in the English Language

Voiced Consonants	Unvoiced Consonants
b, d, g, j, l, m, n, r, v, w, y, z	c, f, h, k, p, s, t, x

PLEASE NOTE: Q = [k] + [w] as in *quick*—[k w ɪ k] is a combination of two consonants pronounced consecutively. The first consonant is unvoiced, but the second is voiced.

Figure 6-14. Voiced and Unvoiced Consonants.

next vowel. The plosive consonants are: "b, d, g, p, t, and k." In the following words, note which are the plosive consonants, and feel the stop of the breath for the plosive consonant as you sing the word on some comfortable pitch:

bite **d**ay **g**one **p**art **t**ake **k**ing a**c**ting

Fricative Consonants are consonants produced by interfering with the flow of breath in some way, but not stopping it completely. These may be voiced or unvoiced consonants. The fricative consonants are "f, v, s, and z." Again, sing the following words on some comfortable pitch, and feel what happens to the breath on a fricative consonant.

far **v**ictory **s**oul **Z**ion

Some consonants may be combined or have their roots in foreign languages to create other fricatives as follows:

[ʃ]	[ʒ]
shore	a**z**ure

In the following words, feel the interference with the flow of breath (fricative quality) as you articulate the consonant, singing the word on some comfortable pitch:

for **v**oice **s**ave **z**one A**s**ia **sh**ore

Nasal Consonants are articulated by allowing the sound to completely enter the nasal cavities. This may be done by closing the mouth with the lips [m] or by raising the tongue to touch the hard palate [n]. All nasal consonants are voiced due to the way they are formed. The nasal consonants are "m," "n," and the consonant combination *ng* [ŋ]. In the following words, sustain the nasal consonant to feel the tone entering the nasal cavities. Notice how the nasal consonants help to project the overall tone quality by aiding resonance.

mine **n**ight si**ng** hu**ng**

LEGATO SINGING (SINGING FROM VOWEL TO VOWEL)

To achieve excellent diction while retaining the beauty of "line" or legato in the voice, a singer must learn to sing from vowel to vowel while allowing the consonants to divide the vowels enough to make words. This requires careful practice and the use of what is known as *elision* of words. When a singer elides words together, he or she places the last consonant of the first word on the beginning of the next word, so that the vowel is sustained as long as possible and the consonants seem to occur at the beginning of words. As a matter of fact, if you listen

---

Singing Legato Phrases

An example of an IPA transcription which shows how ending consonants can be elided in order to connect the breath and tone of a phrase of music follows:

[ð ə   str i   mi͡   n͡ð ə   væl ɪ   r ə   nz͡di ͡]
The   stream   in   the   valley   runs   deep

[͡p æ   nd͡ rə   nz͡slo]
and   runs   slow.

Notice how the vowels are extended as long as possible and the final consonants are put on gently so as not to interrupt the legato line—thus, the singer sings from vowel to vowel.

Figure 6-15. Singing Legato Phrases.

to a recording of a fine singer singing in a language with which you are unfamiliar, and you attempt to transcribe what you hear, you will be writing down words which seem to have consonants at the beginning with very few ending consonants and very long sustained vowels on which the tone is carried. This beautiful legato or smooth line of vocal sound is the ultimate goal of the singer. Notice in Figure 6-15 how a line of words in English might be transcribed when sung with legato. The singer is careful to sustain the vowels for as long as possible, given the pitches of the song, and then puts the consonants on gently just before beginning the next word. Practice speaking and singing your texts in this way. Be careful to sustain the vowels for as long as the rhythmic value will allow before articulating the ending consonant, but be sure to leave room for the articulation of that consonant. This may take some practice to develop the coordination necessary for perfect diction.

IMPORTANT TERMS TO DEFINE AND UNDERSTAND

Articulation

International Phonetic Alphabet (IPA)

Diction

Tongue vowels

Lip vowels

Open vowel

Closed vowel

Schwa

Mixed vowels

Diphthong

Triphthong

Glide

Voiced consonant

Unvoiced consonant

Plosive consonant

Fricative consonant

Nasal consonant

Legato singing

Other terms which are new to you:

REFERENCES

Marshall, M. (1953). *The singer's manual of English diction.* New York: Schirmer Books, a division of Macmillan Publishing.

Mish, F. C. (Ed.). (2005). *Merriam-Webster's collegiate dictionary.* Springfield, MA: Merriam Webster.

Moriarty, J. (1975). *Diction.* Boston: E. C. Schirmer Music.

Chapter 7

DEVELOPING BEAUTIFUL TONE QUALITY, RESONANCE, AND FREEDOM

The production of beautiful vocal tone quality is achieved through the correct combination of breath support, tone initiation at the vocal folds (attack and phonation), careful articulation of vowels and consonants, and resonation (vibration) of that tone in and beyond the larynx. This process requires a careful balancing act of the appropriate muscles as well as a careful coordination of all the processes that have been discussed previously in this book.

The correct production of the vocal tone (phonation) is just the beginning of the singing process. The tone produced by the vocal folds must be appropriately shaped and resonated as it travels from the singer's larynx, through the pharynx, into the mouth, through the lips, and out to the audience. As the tone travels through this pathway, a kind of filtering process takes place, which gives the singer's voice the particular tone quality or timbre by which listeners recognize it. Some overtones are added, some removed, and the sound, if the vocal technique is learned well, is transformed through the resonance process into a beautiful vocal tone, capable of communicating all types of emotion.

WHAT IS RESONANCE?

An appropriate definition for resonance can be found in *Merriam-Webster's Collegiate Dictionary,*

Eleventh edition: "2a: the intensification and enriching of a musical tone by supplementary vibration, 2b: a quality imparted to voiced sounds by vibration in anatomical resonating chambers or cavities (as the mouth or the nasal cavity)" (*Merriam-Webster,* 2005, p. 1061). Although these words are helpful, they still do not tell us anything about the process of resonating for a singer.

HOW IS A TONE RESONATED?

In *English, French, German and Italian Techniques of Singing*, Richard Miller states: "Among most singers, the term resonance is seldom given a scientific usage, but loosely refers to vocal timbre. Sensations of resonance indicate the manner in which sound originating at the vocal bands is modified by the resonators" (Miller, 1977, p. 58). Miller goes on to discuss where the resonators are located, and how they may be combined to produce a resonant quality of timbre in the singer. He states:

> These resonating cavities include those in the chest (trachea and bronchi), the larynx itself (especially the ventricles of Morgagni, it is sometimes thought), the pharynx (which for purposes of further clarity in identifying resonance activity can be subdivided into the laryngopharynx, the

oropharynx and the nasopharynx), the mouth, the nose and the sinuses (which are probably mostly agitated by sympathetic resonance (p. 59).

Miller also states "the resonant quality of the voice (actually the timbre), although initially dependent upon laryngeal function, is further determined by the interrelationship of the combined resonators, responding to the laryngeally-produced sound" (Miller, 1977, p. 58).

This is complex language, but we have already studied the anatomy of the instrument, and thus understand that after the vocal sound is produced in the larynx, the breath pressure carries the tone through the *vocal tract* (the larynx, pharynx, mouth and, in some cases, the nose and sinuses). It is during this process that the vocal tone is actually resonated. During this process the fundamental tone is provided with overtones, and even some new pitches, whereas some aspects of the tone, as originally produced, are actually removed. The use of the term *timbre* then, "the quality of tone distinctive of a particular singing voice or musical instrument" (*Merriam Webster*, p. 1309), is very appropriate and relates very well to the resonation process. It is this filtering of the tone, as it passes through the vocal tract, which gives each singer his or her particular tone quality. The natural size and shape of the chest, neck, and head of the singer, along with the changes in the vocal tract as the singer produces various vowels will produce a very distinctive quality.

WHAT IS A RESONATOR?

Simply, a resonator is a secondary vibrator. Thus, it is not the originator of the pitch, but a column of air, or a solid surface, which will not only accept the original vibration, but will vibrate with it sympathetically, adding new properties to the original sound. As an example, think of the difference between singing in a very small carpeted room, filled with upholstered furniture and heavy window treatments (all of which muffle the sound you produce), and singing in an empty ceramic tiled room, where the sound is reflected off the tile and gives the singer, and listeners, the perception that the original

tone is not only louder, but more resonant. The room is actually adding new qualities to the originally produced sounds. If you sing in a large cathedral, where there are both hard surfaces and open spaces in which air and sound can spin freely, you will hear both types of resonators in action.

In the human body we have hard surfaces (bones, teeth), semihard surfaces (taut muscles, tendons, and ligaments), and soft surfaces (the lining of the mouth, organs, relaxed muscles). When a singer produces a vocal tone, the hard surfaces vibrate sympathetically through the process of *bone conduction* (the process whereby bones vibrate sympathetically with the original tone produced). The vibrations achieved through bone conduction, although helpful in the singing process, do not achieve sounds that can be heard beyond the singer's body. However, Johan Sundberg (1987) states:

> The sound from our voice organs propagates not only in air but also within the tissues of the speaker's body. The sound level in the vocal tract is extremely high during phonation, no less than 10 times, or 20 dB, higher than the threshold of pain. If we could shrink so that we could crawl into the mouth of a speaker, our ears would ache when the person phonated; our hearing might even be damaged by such loudness . . . sounds of such high amplitudes will travel through the walls of the vocal tract into the structures of the head just as the sound of noisy neighbors tends to travel through the walls of a house. The sound from the vocal tract will therefore reach the hearing organ with a quite considerable amplitude. This means that part of the sound one perceives of one's own voice has traveled directly from the vocal tract to the hearing organs by so-called bone (as opposed to air) conduction (pp. 159–160).

This, Dr. Sundberg states: "suggests a complication for voice training." If a student hears his or her own voice differently from that of the teacher, and attempts to create the sound which the teacher produces, it will still not be the exact same sound if heard by another listener. This is why many voice teachers choose not to demonstrate for their students, and why a student must understand, clearly, the difference between what she is hearing internally compared to that which is heard by others as she sings. "Auditory feedback," says Dr. Sundberg, "is not a very reliable source of information for the singer as to the voice use; it depends on the room acoustics, and it probably always differs from the sound perceived by the listeners" (Sundberg, 1987, p. 160).

The human body also has open cavities through which the sound is vibrated or resonated in columns of air, and it is these to which Richard Miller was referring, and which are the most important aspects of the singing process in achieving a resonant tone quality. It will be helpful here to return to Chapter 2—Anatomy of the Singer's Instrument, to review the human head and neck musculature, bone, and cavities, as seen in Figure 2-10. Note the positioning of the resonators described by Richard Miller in the excerpt above. A wide range of shapes and sizes is available to the vocal tract as each new vowel is produced in the human voice. The process of creating particular shapes with the vocal tract is both a learned and an unconscious process, which becomes a major part of the singing process.

HOW DO THE ARTICULATORS AFFECT THE RESONANCE PROCESS?

The resonating cavities, as outlined by Richard Miller, from the larynx up through the pharynx, and into the oro or mouth cavity, is generally referred to by voice teachers and voice scientists as the *vocal tract*. These individual and combined cavities form a long connected tubelike structure, the shape of which changes with the articulation of each vowel. In this way, the vocal tract helps to shape and resonate the vocal tone as produced in the larynx. Note the different shapes of the vocal tract in Figure 7-1, demonstrating the position of the tongue, jaw, and soft palate as various vowels are articulated.

As you study each of the illustrations for the production of a particular vowel, note that the vocal tract shape (from larynx to lips) changes primarily because of the movement of the tongue and lower jaw (*mandible*). Thus, learning to produce each vowel correctly is important not only to your diction, but to the production of a beautiful resonant

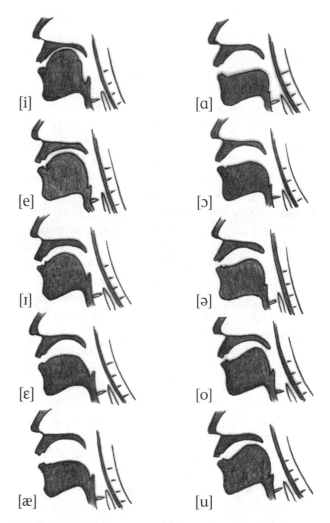

Figure 7-1. Tongue position and vocal tract shape on vowels. Each drawing represents a side view of the human head, showing the approximate position of the tongue and lower jaw as the singer produces the vowels (shown as IPA symbols next to the drawing). The left side demonstrates the tongue vowels from the highest arched position of the tongue to the lowest (*read top to bottom*). The right side demonstrates the lip vowels from the most open oro cavity to the least open oro cavity (*read top to bottom*). Note particularly the differing pharynx space beginning at the larynx up through the oropharynx, and oro cavity on each drawing.

tone quality as well. If the vowel is not correctly produced, for example if the singer has a "lazy" tongue, not only will the diction be unclear, but the tone will not have the most beautiful timbre, because the necessary space to resonate the particular tone is not correct. Thus, articulation and resonance cannot be separated in the process of singing.

Let us take a closer look at each of the illustrations in Figure 7-1, and note exactly how the vocal tract shape changes both the resonance area, and the vowel sound, as well as how the correct production of a pure vowel sound is an integral part of producing a beautiful vocal tone. First, look at the top left illustration under the "Tongue Vowels"—the shape for the vowel [i]. Note the high arch of the tongue so that most of the air column vibrating will be behind the tongue, and from the larynx to the oropharynx, rather than in the oro cavity. Note too the close proximity of the upper and lower jaws as well as the small amount of space between the arch of the tongue and the hard palate or roof of the mouth. Remember from the previous chapter on articulation, the tongue is arched high in the mouth— almost touching the hard palate—in the formation of the vowel [i]. Be sure to note the elevation of the soft palate for this vowel as well, as this also aids in the resonation of the vowel as it widens the pharynx cavity. This vowel resonates (vibrates freely) in the pharynx cavity, giving rise to sensations of facial resonance through both bone and air conduction.

Now, look at the second illustration for the vowel [e]. Notice that the tongue is lowered slightly, altering the vocal tract by opening the resonance area into the mouth or oro cavity somewhat more than for [i], and making a smoother and more elongated tube. Looking at the illustrations for the vowels [ɪ], [ɛ], and [æ] you will notice a further lowering of the tongue and elongation of the vocal tract for each of these tongue vowels. Thus, more and more of the oro cavity is utilized in the resonance process as the singer moves from the more closed to the more open vowels. Observing the illustrations from top to bottom, you can see the differences in each vowel in regard to the shape of the resonating tube. Remember, this tube is really a combination of resonators, responding to the tone produced in the larynx.

Now, look carefully at the right side of Figure 7-1—the Lip Vowels. Notice that as the singer moves from the most open vowel [ɑ] to the progressively more closed vowels [ə], (shwa), [o], and [u] and the tongue again rises, but further back in the oro cavity, allowing the sound to flow and resonate more

freely in the mouth than in the pharynx cavity. Even the most open of the lip vowels does not have the same pharynx resonating space as the tongue vowels. Because of the changes in the vocal tract as well as the innate pitch of each vowel, the vocal quality and overall characteristics of the vocal tone are affected each time we change vowels. Think of how many different vowels are contained on a single page of a song, and how many times and how rapidly the vocal tract changes shape to accommodate the demand of the singer's diction and pitch. This is why singers spend so much time vocalizing on vowels in the studio and practice room, and why many teachers will ask a voice student to read the text with a very resonant and dramatic voice. When speaking the text dramatically, the element of emotion is added to this process, further changing the quality of the tone, as discussed in Chapter 5 on the physiology of vocal tone production.

It is essential that every singer learn to establish the correct resonator shape for each vowel perfectly and easily as an unconscious action. The correct articulation must be practiced until it is second nature. Much studio lesson time and practice time should be spent on exercises which allow the singer to feel the changes in tone color as he or she moves through the different pure and mixed vowels. The more perfect the coordination between articulation and resonance, the more beautiful will be the tone quality produced. Of course, the quality of the fundamental tone produced in the larynx is of utmost importance as this is the tone which will be resonated in the vocal tract. This means that breathing for singing, including both inhalation and exhalation, must be perfectly controlled and coordinated as well. The interaction of the breath stream is extremely important in the production of a resonant vocal tone quality.

CAN THE INHALATION PROCESS AFFECT THE RESONATING ABILITY OF THE VOCAL TRACT?

The voice teachers of the Italian *bel canto* school would say yes. The *bel canto* inhalation process should be both through the nose and the mouth, inhaling gently as though smelling some wonderfully pleasing fragrance, and it is thought that this process opens the resonance areas (the vocal tract) and prepares them for the process of resonation. The *bel canto* exhalation process also has a strong affect on the resonance of the voice in that the airstream is consciously directed into the resonance areas and only then out toward the audience. Thus, the inhalation, exhalation, and phonation process are intimately intertwined with the resonating process. One hopes, it is evident at this point, that producing a beautiful vocal tone is a complex process which involves muscles, organs, bones, and air columns, as well as learning to control each of these body parts both physically and mentally.

SO, WHAT IS A "NATURAL VOICE"?

Of course we have all heard about people who are "born singers." They seem to require little or no training to produce a beautiful vocal sound. This means that the mental and physical coordination are innate, and these singers are gifted indeed. However, even the most gifted singer would do well to learn exactly how the sound is produced and resonated so that if a vocal problem occurs, or just as a matter of the aging process his or her voice changes, the singer will know exactly how to go about restoring the "natural" vocal sound. Even the most gifted athletes carefully develop the appropriate understanding and muscular coordination for their sport so there will be fewer injuries, and optimal performance levels can be maintained at all times. Singers should take heed, and emulate the practices of their athletic colleagues.

Why Do I Sound Different to Myself Than I Do to Others?

A large part of the learning and training process for singers includes learning how to "hear" your own voice. You know that when you hear your voice on a recording device, it does not sound the same to you as when you are actually speaking. This, according to Johan Sundberg (1987), is because:

. . . sounds traveling from the lip opening reach the ears with very different degrees of success, depending on the frequency of that sound; the higher the frequency, the more the radiation is concentrated along the longitudinal axis of the mouth . . . what reaches a speaker's own ears with negligible amplitude reduction are the low frequency components of the spectrum . . . speakers will not hear very much of their higher overtones unless they are close to a sound reflector (pp. 158–159).

This means the singer must learn to listen in a different way. Of course, we cannot stop listening; this would be disastrous for our pitch and ensemble control. But, we learn to listen to what comes back to us already resonated rather than to the sound sent through our *eustachian tubes* (connecting the middle ear with the nasopharynx), through bone conduction to our ears. We must also learn to "go by feel." Many teachers use the terminology *placement of the voice* in this regard. The teacher may ask you where you "feel" vibrations, and you will learn to recognize certain internal sensations or vibrations as being correct for the production of a strong and vibrant tone quality as identified by your teacher.

CAN A SINGER ACTUALLY "PLACE" THE VOICE?

No, this does not seem to be the case, but a singer can learn to feel vibrations in particular places, which will tell him or her that the tone is resonating correctly. The vocal tone fills all the cavities of the head, and through bone conduction, can even vibrate the skull, so the actual vocal sound is never in just one place. Of course, a singer must initially rely on someone listening to him or her to achieve any sort of accuracy in this process. This is the job of voice teachers and some vocal coaches. Only someone who knows your voice and your voice production technique can tell you when the tone is being produced well and is giving you the most optimal and beautiful sounds. A good voice teacher can tell you when the tone is too muffled, too bright or dark, too nasal, or lacking in "ring." When a teacher talks about "placing the voice," generally, he or she is referring to the placement and feel of body vibrations, which tell the singer that the tone is resonating correctly. As each vowel requires a different placement of the tongue, lips, and jaw, the resonance chamber is changed for each, thus sending vibrations through bone and air conduction into different parts of the head. These vibrations may be more or less intensely felt depending on the particular vowel. For example, the [i] vowel gives the feeling of vibrations very far forward in the facial structure. Some singers feel strong vibrations in the forehead area on the upper notes on the [i] vowel. At the opposite end of the spectrum, the [ɑ] vowel resonates in a totally different spectrum and does not present the singer with such easily identifiable vibrations in the facial structure or even within the mouth.

As you vocalize on each of the vowels, you will learn exactly where you should feel vibrations to produce the most beautiful tone quality for that vowel. Pay close attention to the "feelings" you achieve when your teacher tells you that you have just produced a particularly beautiful tone. Try to reproduce the same "feelings" or vibrations and you will achieve the same tone quality. On the other hand, if you attempt to produce the same tone quality, you may do this in many ways—some of which will surely be incorrect. It is always important to recreate the same sensations of tone quality so that you will teach the many parts of the vocal instrument to coordinate perfectly each and every time you produce a particular vowel. "Placing the voice" really means identifying the particular vibrations and sensations you feel when the tone is beautiful and free, so that you may reproduce those sensations and vibrations every time you produce a vocal tone.

WHAT IS "RING"?

According to William Vennard in his *Singing, the Mechanism and the Technic*, "'ring' in the voice comes directly from the larynx, and is the presence of a strong overtone averaging around 2800 to 2900 cycles for men, and higher, about 3200 cycles for women" (Vennard, 1967, p. 89). We think that "ring" in the voice comes from the width of the pharynx

cavity; the wider the opening at the larynx, the more resonant the vowel and tone produced. If you look again at Figure 7–1, you will note that the pharynx cavity is always open at the connection to the larynx. This is important because it is "ring" that allows a vocal sound to be projected over an orchestra, and what enables an opera singer to be heard in a very large auditorium without a microphone. It is the perfection of the vibratory and resonance processes.

Can the Resonator Be Consciously Affected?

Yes! We have already discussed the fact that changes in vowel as well as the correct production of vowels change the shape of the vocal tract from the larynx through the pharynx cavity. We can also change the resonance factors by changing the shape of the mouth and by lowering the larynx. Let us discuss the mouth changes first as they are more obvious and easier to control. Within the mouth, we have discussed the changes in tongue position, which change the vocal tract shape. Therefore, the tongue must be free to move into the appropriate shapes necessary for each vowel. Any tension in the tongue will affect the diction of the singer, and the ability to resonate the tone as well. The tongue must be relaxed and never "tight." A singer might think of the tongue as carpeting on the floor of the mouth— it is free, and resting there on the floor. There are many exercises that can help with the development of a relaxed and flexible tongue. Please see the exercises in Figure 7–2 for help in this area, as well as the exercises already listed in Chapter 6—Articulation for Singers.

The jaw can be moved up and down, side to side, as well as forward and back, and can be moved with or without tension. As tightening any muscle makes that muscle larger and less readily controlled, we will want to take care to keep the jaw muscles relaxed as well. The lower jaw (mandible) must be released from the *temporomandibular joint* (just forward of the ear), and opened enough to comfortably produce the tone with correct diction. Please see Figure 7–3 to locate the temporomandibular disk and joint. If the jaw and tongue muscles are tense,

Figure 7–2. Vocal exercises to aid in producing a resonant tone quality. Note that some text utilizes IPA, and some does not! Look for the brackets that tell you to read the International Alphabet symbols.

the vocal tract will not be in the proper shape for producing correct vowel sounds, resonating properly, or producing a balanced sound. Instead, the singer may produce a tone, which is overly dark. Generally, a relaxed jaw and tongue will help the singer to produce a "warm" beautiful tone which has both dark and light colors and which will project very well in a performance hall. The bel canto teachers and

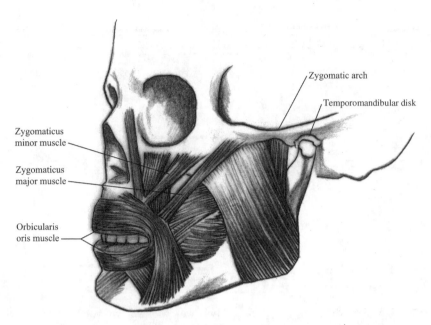

Figure 7–3. Important muscles in the creation of resonance. Note the position of the zygomaticus muscles, and the zygomatic arch in relation to the temporomandibular joint. Singers think about "lifting" the zygomatic arch on inhalation in order to create resonance space for the tone. Note the positioning of the orbicularis oris muscle, which is so important in focusing the singing tone.

singers will refer to this sound by the Italian term *chiaroscuro*—a term which literally translates *light/dark*. In other words, it is a perfectly balanced tone, possessing both light and dark qualities in order to achieve the desired vocal timbre. Professional singers generally attempt to develop and maintain this chiaroscuro color in their singing.

The lips and teeth are also an important part of the resonance process. The lips, as they are involved in the production of vowels and consonants, must never be tightly pulled forward or they will actually lower the pitch of the resonators, and remove "ring" from the tone. On the opposite side, if the lips are pulled back horizontally, they will actually raise the pitch of the resonator, and make the vocal sound too bright, possibly making the pitch sharp. This pulling back of the lips exposes the hard surface of the teeth and is the cause of the overly bright sound. Generally, the lips must be relaxed and slightly forward to project and resonate the tone correctly. Just the bottom edges of the upper front teeth should show as you sing. This position, in combination with the cor-

rect vowel production will help to give the singer the correct chiaroscuro effect.

At the base of the vocal tract is the larynx, and voice pedagogues continue to argue over its proper positioning. Most singing teachers agree that the larynx should lie naturally low. However, the key word here is naturally. Some singing techniques rely on forcing the larynx down, which can actually cause damage to the vocal instrument. On this subject William Vennard states: "Forcing the larynx down is futile, but at the same time I am convinced that the student must be conscious of its position, because it is a clear indication of how nearly the intrinsic musculature has achieved independence of the extrinsic . . . [the larynx] is bound to follow the motion of the tongue in forming vowels and consonants . . . also the larynx may rise for high notes . . . there are three ways of lowering "naturally" a larynx . . . with inhalation, with yawning, and after swallowing, the larynx descends by reflex action" (Vennard, 1967, p. 109). It is important for the student to learn to sing with a naturally lowered larynx, as this elongates the vocal tract and adds to the resonance of the voice. This takes time and patience and will require that the student learn to inhale in a relaxed manner, never attempting to find power in the inhalation process, but, rather, relaxation of the musculature and openness of the resonance cavities instead.

All of these ideas and processes may seem overwhelming at first. There are many activities to coordinate and all must function well at the same time for the voice to sound beautiful, warm, and rich. First and foremost, the student must establish excellent posture, breath control, and be comfortable with the actual phonation process. Then, the establishment of correct vowel production must be attended to. After gaining control over these elements of technique, it is appropriate to begin thinking about establishing "ring" in the voice and learning to resonate each and every tone produced in order to create the most beautiful vocal tone possible.

IMPORTANT TERMS TO DEFINE AND UNDERSTAND

Resonance

Vocal tract

Timbre

Resonator

Bone conduction

Auditory feedback

Fundamental tone

Natural voice

"Ring" in the voice

Placing the voice

Chiaroscuro

REFERENCES

Miller, R. (1977). *English, French, German and Italian techniques of singing—a study in national tonal preferences and how they relate to functional efficiency.* Metuchen, NJ: The Scarecrow Press.

Mish, F. C. (Ed.). (2005). *Merriam-Webster's collegiate dictionary.* Springfield, MA: Merriam-Webster.

Sundberg, J. (1987). *The science of the singing voice.* DeKalb, IL: Northern Illinois University Press.

Vennard, W. (1967). *Singing, the mechanism and the technic.* New York: Carl Fischer.

Chapter 8

HEALTH CONCERNS FOR SINGERS

Professional singers are much more vulnerable to infections or injuries of the vocal instrument, due to the nature of their work. They are in constant contact with large numbers of people, frequently have their mouths open, travel from one climate to another, are frequently tired, and often have problems finding a suitable diet in a new environment. Because of these facts, anyone intending on a professional or semiprofessional career as a singer must learn excellent nutritional and health care habits early on as a protective measure. Canceled singing engagements and/or auditions may otherwise lead to a very short career. The following information should be helpful in establishing a lifetime of good health and a long and productive career. It is highly recommended that anyone aspiring to a professional singing career or a career as a teacher of those who aspire to professional singing careers subscribe or gain access through a library to two important journals which offer sound advice on this area as well as others:

1. *The Journal of Voice*, the official journal of the Voice Foundation, previously published quarterly by Singular Publishing Group, Inc., San Diego, California. Now published by Elsevier. ISSN 0892-1997/ http://www.elsevierhealth.com
2. *The Journal of Singing*, the official journal of the National Association of Teachers of Singing (NATS), published five times per year by The National Association of Teachers of Singing. http://www.nats.org/journal_of_singing.php

In addition, the text *Keep Your Voice Healthy* by Friedrich S. Brodnitz, M.D. is an extremely important "guide to the Intelligent Use and Care of the Speaking and Singing Voice." A newer and more comprehensive book: *Vocal Health and Pedagogy* by Robert Thayer Sataloff, M.D., D.M.A., a well-known Professor of Otolaryngology at Jefferson Medical College and frequent speaker and publisher in the area of vocal health and pedagogy, has been published by Plural Publishing, Inc., in July 2005. Both books will be of interest to singers who are truly interested in maintaining excellent health and vocal well-being. There are countless other books and journals which will be of value to the singer and singing teacher. Some of these are listed at the end of this chapter. Students of singing should always be aware of the newest research and developments in vocal health care and nutrition, as they are extremely important.

Please Note: The information contained in this chapter is intended for educational purposes only. It is not provided to diagnose, prescribe, or treat any disease, illness, or injury. The author, publisher, printer, or distributor does not accept responsibility for such use. Individuals suffering from any illness, or injury should consult with a physician, perhaps specifically with an otolaryngologist, or an appropriate medical specialist.

THE ENVIRONMENT AND VOCAL HEALTH

Hydration

Given the ease with which we travel in the world today, one might wonder how a singer is affected by the varying environments (climate, temperature, air quality) in which we live and work. The human body responds quickly to changes in environmental temperature and humidity. Thus, climate conditions will affect greatly the body and vocal mechanism of the singer. It has frequently been said, "singing is a wet sport." In other words, the vocal mechanism must be well lubricated to work at its optimal capacity. The best climate for singers is one that is moderately warm and fairly high in humidity (approximately 40-50% humidity). The singer's throat much prefers a spring rainy day to a cold crisp day in December. In fact, a singer is more likely to contract a cold or viral infection in the cold and dry of winter than during the damp days of spring.

Dr. Friedrich Brodnitz suggests in his *Keep Your Voice Healthy* (Copyright 1988, Little, Brown and Company, Inc.), that it is best to keep heads cool, feet warm, and to stabilize humidity at a favorable level in your house. Don't overheat your home during the cold winter months, and be sure to add moisture to the indoor air to keep the humidity at a comfortable level (40-50%). It is better to wear a few layers of lightweight clothing than to be so bundled up that your skin is forced to perspire. The late Van L. Lawrence, M.D. otolaryngologist, former senior associate editor and author of the important column *Laryngoscope* for the NATS *Journal of Singing* until his untimely death, has written several articles on the importance of hydration, but one particular article is of significance here. Within this article Dr. Lawrence touches on several important issues for singers to remember. All voice students should read this entire article as well as others on the subject, which have been written by prominent otolaryngologists, speech pathologists, and teachers of singing. Following is factual information, upon which otolaryngologists and teachers of singing seem to agree at this time, as presented in Sermon on Hydration (the Evils of Dry), by Van L. Lawrence, M.D., 1986 (from *Journal of Singing.*March/April, 1986, pp. 22-23. Copyright 1986, National Association of Teachers of Singing, Inc. Reproduced with permission).

Excellent hydration is of utmost importance to all professional voice users as it is required for normal functioning of the respiratory and vocal tract. When you look into your mouth, you should see membranes that are pink, smooth, and covered with a thin, shiny and watery secretion. If you find yourself frequently clearing your throat to rid yourself of "postnasal drip," and feeling very dry when you sing or speak, you are probably dehydrated. The only lubrication required to keep this shiny "wet look" is water. Dr. Lawrence states that the normal nose alone will manufacture anywhere from a quart to a quart-and-a-half of watery thin mucus per 24-hour period. The majority of this is evaporated into the air one breathes in through the nose—this is how we moisten dry room air. There are three main points that come into play according to Dr. Lawrence:

1. Environmental water,
2. Induced salivation: artificially produced "spit," and
3. Maintaining body hydration.

Environmental Water

The important point here is to maintain your living and singing or working area humidity at 40 to 50%. This can be accomplished by using a humidifier during the heating season, or if unavailable, placing pans of water near heating ducts in order to raise the humidity level. If you are getting static electricity shocks from your carpeting, your humidity level is too low. In addition, taking long hot showers will help to provide necessary moisture to your mucous membranes. There are a number of steam inhalers on the market which can be used to increase the humidity level in your body during times of need—some are manufactured so they are very portable for travel needs, and others are larger and can also be used for adding room humidity. Choose one that seems right for your situation. Be sure to follow the cleaning directions provided by the manufacturer to keep bacteria levels down in your humidifier, vaporizer, or steam inhaler.

Air travel can be a problem for the singer, as the cabin humidity in air planes is approximately 10%; therefore, singers must remember to drink plenty of water while flying, and avoid alcohol, caffeine, and colas, which can act as diuretics (removing water from the body), and avoid milk products which produce thick mucus in most people.

Induced Salivation

Here, Dr. Lawrence suggests that anything that provokes salivation (biting your tongue for example) also promotes laryngeal mucous secretion as well. This indicates that the use of lozenges and hard candy will not only stimulate salivation, but more importantly, laryngeal secretions as well. However, singers must be careful not to choose a lozenge that may contain a medication, which would dry out the mucous membranes. Read the labels carefully, and know the drying agents. A list of medications and their effects are found later in this chapter. According to Dr. Lawrence, *mucolytic agents* can be extremely helpful in counteracting the effects of dryness. A mucolytic agent, or an *expectorant*, is a medication designed to thin the mucosal secretions. By their nature, mucolytics require an increased intake of water. Most of the popular mucolytic agents for singers seem to be forms of *guaifenesin* (some prescription brands include Fenesin, Humibid, Organidin, whereas over-the-counter forms—Robitussin, and Mucinex—all are available in liquid, gelcaps, and tablets). Even though these medications are thought to be relatively safe, and without side affects, singers would be wise to consult with their personal physicians before experimenting with any of the above mucolytics, to avoid possible interactions with other medications they may be taking.

In general, Dr. Lawrence states, antihistamines and aspirin-containing products should be avoided by singers whenever possible. Antihistamines have a drying effect on the upper respiratory passages, and can actually make the mucosal secretions thicker, making it extremely difficult to sing. Aspirin and aspirin-containing products not only impair the

singer's ability to feel pain, but predispose the singer to a vocal fold hemorrhage due to the thinning of the blood vessel walls caused by these analgesics.

Maintaining Body Hydration

You can monitor your own hydration level by checking the inside of your mouth for that shiny "wet look," and by checking your urine output. Dr. Lawrence also states that when one is well hydrated, the urine is very dilute, nonodorous, and almost invariably the color of tap water. Pay close attention to your liquid consumption, and try to drink 6 to 8 glasses (8 ounces in each glass) of water per day—more if you find yourself in a dry environment.

In summary, dry vocal cords are much more likely to be injured than wet ones, and common respiratory viruses will find it difficult to propagate in the presence of moisture. Keep yourself healthier by drinking more water.

POLLUTION

Environmental pollution occurs in the home, workplace, and of course, outdoors. The effect of atmospheric pollution on singers is just beginning to be studied. A preliminary article regarding the subject can be found in Pollution: Consequences for Singers, by Robert Thayer Sataloff, M.D., D.M.A., (from *Journal of Singing*. January/February, 1996, pp. 59-64. Copyright 1996, National Association of Teachers of Singing, Inc. Reproduced with permission). In his article, Dr. Sataloff states that vocal tract injury caused by inhaled pollution is the most obvious, causing pulmonary and/or laryngeal dysfunction. Some problems may even occur from the use of stage pyrotechnics or theatrical fogs. As singers, we must all be aware of potential vocal effects from potentially harmful substances and take necessary precautions. Dr. Sataloff states that if you think you are living and/or working in an area where the atmospheric pollutants may damage your singing instrument, do something about it immediately!

NUTRITION AND ITS IMPORTANT CONSEQUENCES FOR SINGERS

How Does Nutritional Intake Affect the Singer's Voice?

A diet containing lots of fresh fruits and vegetables, low in sugars and starches, and high in whole grains is, as we all know, good for us. But, it is difficult to stay away from foods that appeal to our taste buds; namely, those high in salt, sugar, and fat. Sweets and starches affect the voice in a negative way because they stimulate the mucous membranes. This may also be the case for some singers where dairy products are concerned. This is, of course, the source of the old saying "don't drink milk before you sing." In addition, a young singer should be aware that the age of the obese opera singer is over. Opera companies and musical directors want singers who look the part and are able to move well on stage. Many a young singer has lost the opportunity to sing a role that might have seemed perfect for his or her voice because he or she did not "look the part." In regard to human physiology and its relationship to vocal technique, singers must be careful not to eat heavily before singing which would inhibit breathing capacity. If necessary, return to Chapter 2, Figure 2–6 and note the anatomic position of the stomach in relation to the lungs and diaphragm, and then remember to plan on eating at least two to four hours prior to a performance or important rehearsal. This will ensure that food has left the stomach and will not interfere with the breath support process so important to excellent singing technique. Singers must also be concerned about eating after a performance, and must be careful not to overindulge late in the evening. These calories will quickly turn to fat and keep the singer from a good night's sleep. Obviously, these facts point to the need for a life of discipline and careful eating habits in order to establish and maintain a successful career as a professional singer.

There are a number of excellent books and articles on proper nutrition, vitamin, mineral, and antioxidant supplementation, as well as other areas of interest regarding health and nutrition. It would be wise for aspiring singers to look into some of these sources and learn the necessary discipline of healthful eating. Dr. Sataloff points out that vitamin or mineral deficiencies will quickly show up in the mucous membranes of the respiratory tract, and may cause problems with vocal technique. Do not hesitate to discuss your nutritional intake with your personal physician and your otolaryngologist.

Although there is increasing awareness and attention being given to the sustaining and healing powers of foods, many nutritionists and medical professionals seem to agree that we are no longer able to gain the required nutrients from foods as listed on the USDA Food Pyramid. There is an explanation for this phenomenon. First, modern farming techniques allow farmers to continue to grow and harvest the same produce year after year in soil that becomes depleted of essential minerals, rather than rotating crops from field to field. New farming technology also allows for genetic manipulation of seeds to ward off insects and disease in plants. There is much concern regarding this practice and the resulting mutations, which may occur in the future. In addition, much of our food is processed in some way to remove impurities. Unfortunately, this food processing also removes much of the nutritional value, which is then artificially replaced in some processed foods, particularly in breakfast cereals and breads. Thus, it is generally necessary to supplement even a good diet with vitamins, minerals, and antioxidants.

Most nutritionally conscientious Americans are at least aware of the existence of the USDA Food Pyramid, as it appears in Figure 8–1. This nutritional plan can be followed if one wishes to achieve an adequate nutritional intake. However, the newest research demonstrates an even better nutritional plan as might be found in the use of the *Mediterranean style of eating*. This food pyramid is also seen in Figure 8–1, and the differences between the two plans should be quite obvious to the reader. The use of organically grown foods will ensure the appropriate nutritional content in fruits and vegetables. In addition, every singer must know and understand his or her own body needs. Your nutritional intake should definitely be discussed with your health care professional as part of your overall health maintenance plan, as it will affect your vocal performance.

The United States Department of Agriculture Eating Right Pyramid

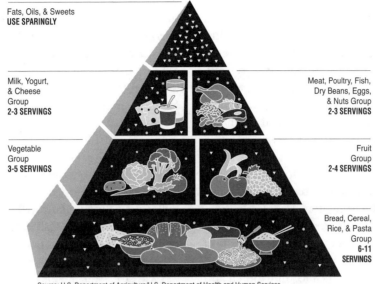

Fats, Oils, & Sweets
USE SPARINGLY

Milk, Yogurt, & Cheese Group
2-3 SERVINGS

Meat, Poultry, Fish, Dry Beans, Eggs, & Nuts Group
2-3 SERVINGS

Vegetable Group
3-5 SERVINGS

Fruit Group
2-4 SERVINGS

Bread, Cereal, Rice, & Pasta Group
6-11 SERVINGS

Source: U.S. Department of Agriculture/U.S. Department of Health and Human Services

Figure 8-1. USDA Food Pyramid and Mediterranean Diet Pyramid. Notice the differences between these two Food Pyramids, and decide which is more appropriate for your personal lifestyle. Note that the Traditional Healthy Mediterranean Diet Pyramid has as its base platform "Daily Physical Activity," and that meat, and products considered "sweets" are a very small part of this diet. Be sure to check your diet to make sure you are staying within the guidelines of the pyramid you choose above, as well as drinking 6 to 8 eight-ounce glasses of water daily. Excellent nutrition is necessary for sustaining the energy and good health required for a professional singer. The picture of the food pyramid is courtesy of the U.S. Department of Agriculture and can be found at http://www.mypyramid.gov/index.html. The Mediterranean Diet Pyramid is reprinted with permission from Oldways Preservation and Trust, available at http://www.oldwayspt.org/med_diet.html

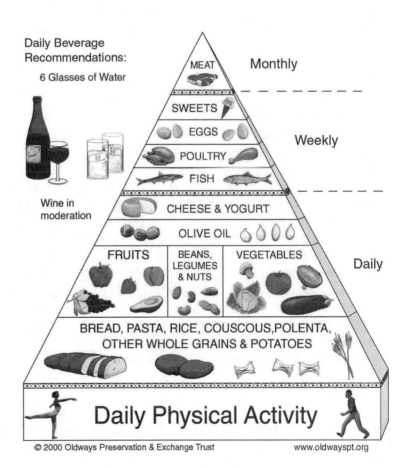

The Traditional Healthy Mediterranean Diet Pyramid

Daily Beverage Recommendations:

6 Glasses of Water

Wine in moderation

MEAT — Monthly

SWEETS
EGGS
POULTRY
FISH — Weekly

CHEESE & YOGURT
OLIVE OIL

FRUITS | BEANS, LEGUMES & NUTS | VEGETABLES — Daily

BREAD, PASTA, RICE, COUSCOUS, POLENTA, OTHER WHOLE GRAINS & POTATOES

Daily Physical Activity

© 2000 Oldways Preservation & Exchange Trust   www.oldwayspt.org

If your health care provider is uncomfortable with providing nutritional support, ask for a recommendation to a certified clinical nutritionist, or a registered dietitian with whom you may consult. Take responsibility for your own health and nutrition as well by reading current articles and books on the subject and discussing your findings with medical and nutritional professionals in the field. In this way, you will begin to identify the appropriate nutritional requirements of your body to maintain optimal physical and mental health. As a health care team, you, your personal physician, otolaryngologist, and nutritionist/dietitian can establish and maintain the physical well-being, high level of energy, and concentration necessary for a long and healthy singing career.

There are many fine sources for nutritional and supplement information. An excellent article specifically for vocal professionals can be found in Nutrition and the Professional Voice by Pamela L. Harvey and Susan H. Miller, 2006 (from *Vocal Health and Pedagogy Advanced Assessment and Treatment*, 2nd edition, Vol. II, Chap. 10, edited by Robert T. Sataloff, pp. 99–112. Copyright 2006, Plural Publishing, Inc. Reproduced with permission). In this book, the authors of the chapter state:

> There has been explosive growth in medical research regarding the relationships among nutrition, health, and disease. Scientific exploration has revealed a number of benefits related to micronutrition. Among these benefits are slowing of some of the physiological aspects of aging, enhanced athletic performance, increased protection against many forms of cancers, stronger defenses against cardiovascular disease, reduction in neural tube birth defects, protection from macular degeneration and cataracts, and bolstering of the immune system. As the science of nutrition matures and additional health benefits are revealed, the nutritional advice given to singers will expand and solidify. One can predict that research will explore the nutritional status of healthy and injured singers and the inclusion of an informed nutritionist into the professional voice care team (p. 103).

Portions of this chapter also appeared in an earlier article in the *Journal of Singing* (September/October [Part I], Vol. 54, No.1, pp. 41–48, and November/December [Part II] Vol. 54, No. 2, pp. 43–49, 1997 issues, listing guest authors: Pamela L. Harvey, MA, CCC-SLP, Dave E. David, M.D., and Susan H. Miller, R.D). It is stated within the article that performers should obtain medical clearance from their personal physician, discuss thoroughly the basic elements of nutrition and gain some understanding of some of the current findings in nutritional science, and then begin to establish nutritional goals for themselves. Within Parts I and II of this article, you will find "Nutritional Goals." Following are eight examples of nutritional goals found here, and some highlights of the information found in the article.

1. Eat at least four servings of fruits and vegetables per day.
2. Take a quality comprehensive antioxidant, vitamin, and mineral supplement.
3. When eating meat, eat a portion smaller than your portion of vegetables.
4. Check the nutritional panel on packaged foods
5. Choose foods that derive 20% or less of their calories from fat.
6. Limit fat intake to 30 to 40 grams per day.
7. Drink eight 8-ounce glasses of water daily.
8. Eat 25 to 30 grams of fiber daily.

This is an excellent article, and I recommend it highly to anyone interested in improving vocal technique, and the life style and energy needed for achieving a singing career. Figure 10–1 in Chapter 10 of Dr. Sataloff's *Vocal Health and Pedagogy*, is an excellent chart of nutrients and their functions, requirements, signs of deficiency, and food sources. This is a perfect place for any singer to begin his or her study of nutritional guidelines, in addition to the many books devoted to nutrition and nutritional healing. Begin to explore this and other books to gain knowledge and understanding of this most important subject.

Please pay careful attention to the list of essential nutrients and their functions as provided in Table 8–1. This list will make you aware of the functions of each essential nutrient, and will help you to know if you are eating well enough to gain the necessary bodybuilding and maintenance tools necessary for good health. Table 8–2 offers information on sources of these essential nutrients.

Table 8-1. Essential Nutrients and Their Function

The more than 45 essential nutrients are grouped into categories: Macronutrients, and micronutrients. Each nutrient has a specific role to play in good health. Energy is derived from protein, fat, and carbohydrate. Vitamins and minerals do not provide energy, but aid in the chemical reactions that allow the conversion of protein, fat, and carbohydrate to energy. All nutrients are dependent on the others; none function totally independently. Study the following list so that you will understand some of the functions of the essential nutrients.

MACRONUTRIENTS

Protein	Builds and repairs all body tissues—builds antibodies (blood components that fight infection) Builds enzymes and some hormones
Fat	A concentrated energy source Supplies essential fatty acids Aids in the absorption of fat-soluble vitamins
Carbohydrate	The body's main source of energy Spares protein
Water	Necessary for adequate fluid balance Involved in body temperature regulation

MICRONUTRIENTS

VITAMINS

Vitamin A	Aids in normal bone and tooth formation Aids in normal vision Maintains the health of skin and mucous membranes for normal resistance to infections
B Vitamins: (B Complex)	
Thiamine (B1)	Assists energy release from carbohydrate Aids in normal growth and appetite
Riboflavin (B2)	Maintains healthy skin and normal vision Maintains normal function of the nervous system Releases energy to body cells during metabolism
Niacin (B3)	Involved in the release of energy from carbohydrate, protein, and fat Aids normal growth and development Maintains a normal nervous system and digestive tract
Pyridoxine (B6)	Aids in the utilization of protein, production of antibodies and red blood cells, the normal function of the nervous system
Folacin (Folic Acid)	Aids in blood cell formation (both red and white)
Vitamin (B12)	Aids in red blood cell formation Maintains healthy functioning of the nervous system and gastrointestinal tract
Biotin	Functions in the metabolism of fats and carbohydrates
Pantothenic acid	Involved in the utilization of macronutrients in energy production
Para-aminobenzoic acid (PABA)	Occurs in combination with folic acid, and stimulates the intestinal bacteria, enabling them to produce folic acid, which, in turn, aids in the production of pantothenic acid. Functions in the breakdown and utilization of proteins and formation of blood cells.

continues

119

Table 8-1. *continued*

Vitamin C	Maintains healthy gums and teeth
	Maintains strong blood vessel walls, promotes healing of wounds
	Required for the production of collagen, a protein substance found in all fibrous tissue including connective tissue, cartilage, and skin
Vitamin D	Aids in the absorption and utilization of calcium in the formation and maintenance of strong bones and teeth
Vitamin E	Maintains health of membranes (An antioxidant—binds with oxygen to prevent unwanted changes). Protects Vitamin A
Vitamin K	Required for normal blood clotting
MINERALS	
Sodium	Involved in body fluid distribution and nerve and muscle function
Potassium	Involved in body fluid distribution—Required for proper nerve transmission and muscle contraction—Plays a role in protein and carbohydrate metabolism
Chloride	Helps maintain the body's acid-base balance
Calcium	Aids in the formation and maintenance of strong bones and teeth, muscle tone and normal heart beat, proper blood clotting, and healthy nerve function
Iron	An important component of hemoglobin (the red blood cell component that transports oxygen and carbon dioxide)
	Plays a role in maintaining the immune function and resistance to infection
Phosphorus	Aids in the formation and maintenance of strong bones and teeth
	Regulates the release of energy
Magnesium	Aids in the formation and maintenance of strong bones and teeth
	Aids in normal muscle and nerve function
Zinc	Required for normal growth and development, wound healing, and normal sense of taste
Iodine	Aids in the function of the thyroid gland
Copper	Involved in hemoglobin and connective tissue formation
Fluoride	Important for strong teeth
Chromium	Aids the action of insulin (the hormone that helps cells take up sugar from the blood and use it for energy)
Selenium	Helps protect vitamin E
Manganese	Plays a role in brain function
Molybdenum, lithium, cobalt, boron, nickel, vanadium, silicon	Possibly necessary in very small quantities; the role of some of these elements remains unclear

Always check with your physician and nutritionist to learn appropriate nutritional supplement guidelines for your particular body type. Attempt to gain nutritional value from foods first—when this cannot be achieved, use supplements as necessary to complete your nutritional intake.

Table 8-2. Sources of Essential Nutrients

MACRONUTRIENTS	
Protein (12–15% of daily calories)	Requirement: 0.5–1 g. per kg of body weight Complete proteins are found in foods of animal origin, such as eggs, milk, cheese, fish, chicken, pork, and beef. Incomplete protein is low or deficient in one or more of the essential amino acids and is found in foods of vegetable origin such as fruit, vegetables, grains, seeds, and legumes
Fat (less than 25% of daily calories)	Sources are divided into visible and invisible fats. Visible fats include butter, margarine, lard, vegetable oil, visible fat on meats. Invisible fats include cream, whole milk and its products, cheese, egg yolk, avocado, nuts, and seeds. In general try to avoid saturated fats. *Saturated fat* is the main dietary cause of high blood cholesterol. The American Heart Association recommends that you limit your saturated fat intake to 7–10% of total calories (or less) each day. *Polyunsaturated and Monounsaturated fats* are the two unsaturated fats. These fats may actually help lower your blood cholesterol if you use them in place of saturated fats. They are found primarily in oils from plants. Polyunsaturated fats include safflower, sesame and sunflower seeds, corn and soybeans, many nuts and seeds, and their oils. Monounsaturated fats include canola, olive and peanut oils, and avocados.
Carbohydrate (60-65% of daily calories)	Recommended intake is 60–65% of the total daily energy intake. The major sources are the sugars and starches obtained from plant sources, including fruits, vegetables, nuts, grains as well as refined sugars and concentrated sweets. Some animal source foods contain carbohydrates—primarily those found in the milk group. Plant sources are the best for you!
Water	Drink 6 to 8 eight-ounce glasses of water a day. Some of this can come from fruit juices, herbal teas, and some soft foods such as Jello.

MICRONUTRIENTS	
VITAMINS	
Vitamin A	Fat-soluble vitamins can be obtained from plant and animal sources One of the richest sources of vitamin A is fish-liver oil (a supplement). Some animal products, such as cream and butter, may contain both preformed vitamin A and carotene. Carotene is abundant in carrots, and certain green leafy vegetables such as broccoli and spinach
B Vitamins: (B Complex)	Water-soluble substances found in brewer's yeast, liver, and whole-grain cereals. When in good health, the body produces B vitamins within the intestinal bacteria
Thiamine (B1)	A component of the germ and bran of wheat unless milled away
Riboflavin (B2)	Difficult to obtain a sufficient supply without supplementing the diet. Sources include liver and other organ meats, or brewer's yeast
Niacin (B3)	Generally obtained in the diet through lean meats, poultry, fish, and peanuts as well as wheat germ and brewer's yeast.
Pyridoxine (B6)	The best sources are meats and whole grains
Folacin (Folic Acid)	Folic acid is easily destroyed by high temperature, exposure to light, and being left at room temperature for long periods of time. The best sources are green leafy vegetables, liver, and brewer's yeast
Vitamin B12	Animal protein is almost the only source in which B12 occurs naturally in foods in substantial amounts. Muscle meats, fish, and dairy products are other good sources
Biotin	Appears in trace amounts in all animal and plant tissue. Some rich sources of Biotin are egg yolk, beef liver, unpolished rice

continues

Table 8-2. *continued*

Pantothenic acid	Found in organ meats, brewer's yeast, egg yolks, and whole-grain cereals (33% of pantothenic acid content is lost during cooking, and 50% is lost in the milling of flour
Para-aminobenzoic acid (PABA)	Found in liver, yeast, wheat germ, and molasses—supplement only under physician or certified clinical nutritionist's direction due to toxicity to liver, heart, and kidneys
Vitamin C	The least stable of vitamins and is very sensitive to oxygen. Potency can be lost to light, heat, and air. Most commonly found in fresh fruits and vegetables
Vitamin D	A fat-soluble vitamin, can be acquired either by ingestion or exposure to sunlight. Found in both plant and animal tissue. Fish liver oils are the best natural source of vitamins A and D
Vitamin E	This fat-soluble vitamin is composed of a group of 7 forms of tocopherols which occur in highest concentrations in cold-pressed vegetable oils, all whole raw seeds and nuts, and soybeans.
Vitamin K	Fat soluble and manufactured in the intestinal tract in the presence of certain intestinal flora (bacteria). Natural sources include green plants, leafy green vegetables, cow's milk, yogurt, egg yolks, safflower oil, fish liver oils, and other polyunsaturated oils.

MINERALS

Sodium	Found in virtually all foods, especially table salt. High concentrations can be found in seafoods, carrots, beets, poultry, and meat.
Potassium	Sources include all vegetables, especially green leafy vegetables, oranges, whole grains, sunflower seeds, and mint leaves. Large amounts can be found in potatoes and bananas.
Chloride	Provided almost exclusively in the diet by table salt. It can also be found in rye flour, ripe olives, and sea greens.
Calcium	The most abundant mineral in the body, and present in significant amounts in a limited number of foods, including milk and dairy products. Can also be obtained from certain breads and cereals, as well as some fruits and vegetables.
Iron	The best source of dietary iron is liver, with oysters, heart, and other lean meats as good choices. Leafy green vegetables are the best plant sources.
Phosphorus	The second most abundant mineral in the body, and found in every cell. Foods rich in protein are also rich in phosphorus, and include meat, fish, poultry, eggs, whole grains, seeds, and nuts.
Magnesium	Widely distributed in foods, especially fresh green vegetables. Other sources include soybeans, figs, corn, apples, and oil-rich seeds and nuts.
Zinc	The best source appears to be in unprocessed foods, preferably those grown in organically enriched soil.
Iodine	Obtained from salt water sea life, both plant and animal
Copper	Whole grain products, almonds, green leafy vegetables, dried legumes, and most seafoods
Fluoride	Rich sources include seafoods, gelatin, and fluoridated drinking water.
Chromium	Good sources include corn oil, clams, whole grain cereals, and meats.
Selenium	Found in the bran and germ of cereals, some vegetables, such as broccoli, onions and tomatoes, and tuna fish
Manganese	Found in whole-grain cereals, egg yolks, and green vegetables
Molybdenum, lithium, cobalt, boron, nickel, vanadium, silicon	The best sources of all trace elements in proper balance are natural unprocessed foods.

Be sure to note the importance of leafy green vegetables for nearly all essential nutrients. You will find more comprehensive tables in Dr. Sataloff's *Vocal Health and Pedagogy* (second edition, volume II, pp. 113–120).

SLEEP AND REST REQUIREMENTS FOR SINGERS

How Much Rest Is Enough Rest?

This is a very individual need, and will differ for each person. However, some general guidelines can be provided:

1. The average person needs between 7 and 8 hours of sleep per night, more if under stress or fighting an infection.
2. Undisturbed sleep is essential.
3. Performing artists must rest before a performance.
4. Follow your own body's signals—be aware of your average sleep need in order to function at your best and don't let yourself get "run-down."

Pamela L. Harvey and Keith G. Saxon state:

sleep is now understood to be an essential element of human existence that affects mood, cognition, problem solving, memory, performance, productivity, accident rates, and general health, including endocrine, cardiovascular, and immune function . . . it appears that for optimal learning to occur, we not only must be well rested before training, but that post-training sleep, particularly the first sleep that occurs after training, is essential to consolidate newly learned skills or demonstrate improvement"(from Sleep and the Vocal Performer by Pamela L. Harvey and Keith G. Saxon, 2006, *Vocal Health and Pedagogy Advanced Assessment and Treatment*, 2nd Edition, Vol. II, Chap. 11, edited by Robert T. Sataloff, p. 122, copyright 2006, Plural Publishing, Inc. Reproduced with permission).

It is quite common for performers to have difficulty sleeping on the night prior to an important performance. It is also common to have difficulty sleeping on the night following such a performance.

What Can the Singer Do to Promote Healthy Sleep Patterns?

First, avoid caffeine—even a cup or two of a caffeine containing drink during the day can cause insomnia at night. Avoid alcohol consumption. Although a drink or two of an alcoholic beverage seems to help some people relax enough to fall asleep, even moderate amounts of alcohol can distort normal sleeping patterns (from Insomnia, edited by David E. Larson, M.D., 1990, *Mayo Clinic Family Health Book*, Chap. 33, Mental Health, p. 1028. Copyright 1990, by HarperCollins Publishers).

The primary cause of sleep disturbance for most singers is the stress, and perhaps anxiety over an upcoming performance. Harvey and Saxon refer to important research regarding vocal performers and their sleep habits in Sleep and the Vocal Performer by Pamela L. Harvey and Keith G. Saxon, 2006 (from *Vocal Health and Pedagogy Advanced Assessment and Treatment*, 2nd edition, Vol. II, Chap. 11, edited by Robert T. Sataloff, p. 127, copyright 2006, Plural Publishing, Inc. Reproduced with permission). Here they state:

Most vocal performers reported sleeping approximately 7.25 hours per night when not rehearsing or performing and indicated that they believed this was adequate sleep . . . During rehearsals and performances, the performers reported sleep time was substantially less. The mean duration of reported sleep time was 6 hours with a large majority, 96%, indicating that this was not adequate sleep and that they frequently experienced difficulty in falling asleep. They attributed these difficulties most frequently to an inability to relax (being too "revved up") and also to feelings of stress/anxiousness. Vocal consequences of poor sleep were reported as difficulty with breath support (82%), reduced vocal endurance/voice tiring easily (36%), huskiness/roughness to the voice (18%), and greater time needed for warm-up (8%). The most frequently described impact of sleep loss on total performance was reduced focus and ability to concentrate (86%), and increased frustration and irritability (37%) (Sataloff, p. 127).

Of course it is imperative that you are well prepared for rehearsals and performances. Excellent preparation will generally relieve the anxiety associated with the performance itself (see Chapter 1—process for learning a song). If you are feeling well prepared, but are still unable to sleep, consider the following aids:

1. Avoid strenuous exercise in the hours prior to bedtime. However, regular exercise during the day should contribute to sound, restful sleep.
2. Take a warm bath to help you relax.
3. Take a long, leisurely walk to relax you.
4. Try drinking warm milk, or chamomile tea to relax you.

In general, over-the-counter or prescription sleep aids are not particularly good for performers as they actually disturb the natural sleep pattern, and should be avoided as much as possible. If you are having a long-term problem (more than two weeks) with your sleeping pattern, you should consult your personal physician about the problem as soon as possible.

PHYSICAL CONDITIONING AND HEALTH MAINTENANCE FOR THE SINGER

Is Exercise Good for a Singer?

Yes! Regular, moderate exercise is good for general health and helps reduce the effects of stress on your physical and psychological wellbeing. Brisk walking and swimming are two excellent forms of exercise for singers, stimulating the flow of blood and deep breathing. Also, any exercise that helps a singer to relax and reduce tension is good. Sports that increase tension and stress or cause heavy muscular fatigue, such as playing football, soccer, or wrestling, are best

left to nonsingers. Recent research shows, however, that some weight bearing and aerobic exercise is good for singers and even promotes healthier and higher quality singing.

In Exercise Physiology: Perspective for Vocal Training by Carole M. Schneider, Keith G. Saxon, and Carolyn A. Dennehy, 2006 (from *Vocal Health and Pedagogy Advanced Assessment and Treatment,* 2nd Edition, Vol. II, Chap. 25, edited by Robert T. Sataloff, pp. 301-303. Copyright 2006, Plural Publishing, Inc. Reproduced with permission), the authors make several important suggestions regarding exercise for singers:

The enhancement of any physical performance is directly related to the level of fitness and conditioning of the performer . . .Vocal performers can expect to benefit from general and specific physical conditioning in this regard . . . Improvement in physical fitness or condition leads to increased performance capacity, particularly as it pertains to the cardio-respiratory and skeletal muscle systems (Sataloff, pp. 301–303).

In this chapter on exercise physiology, the authors discuss four basic principles for appropriate physical conditioning:

Overload Principle: " . . . physiologic adaptations will occur in the working muscles with the appropriate stimuli. Appropriate stimuli include workloads that are greater than workloads encountered in daily life"(Sataloff, p. 302). In other words, a person must go beyond the norm in daily life in order to feel the benefits of exercise. Then, after the body adapts to this new level of stimulation, the stimuli must again be increased to continue to experience continued development and renewal.

Specificity: "The training program must be appropriate for the activity or performance" (Sataloff, p. 302). Here, the authors discuss the training of particular muscle groups and movement patterns as appropriate for the activity to be developed.

Individuality Principle: "The physiologic responses to training vary between individuals.

Similar training routines will not produce exactly the same physiologic benefits to all athletes" (Sataloff, p. 303). This, of course, is true for singers as well. It is necessary to adapt the exercise program to the specific body type and development. A personal trainer can be of great assistance here, or when possible, utilize the athletic trainer in the sports department of your college or university.

Reversibility Principle: 'The majority of physiologic benefits from training are lost within a short period of time when training is discontinued" (Sataloff, p. 303). In other words, if you stop exercising, the benefits achieved will be lost rather quickly over the time period of inactivity, making it more difficult to achieve the same physical results.

A book by Keith G. Saxon, M.D., and Carole M. Schneider, Ph.D. entitled *Vocal Exercise Physiology*, and published by Singular Publishing Group, Inc. in 1995, is one of the first to discuss the parallel natures of sport-related activities and the principles involved in the training of professional singers. This book would be very valuable for the voice teacher and student in understanding the scientific basis of fitness and training. Two additional articles would be well-worth reading: Peggy Brunner's "Fit or Fat: The Singer's Challenge" found in the *Journal of Singing* (Vol. 44, May/June 1988, p. 29), and Nora Sirbaugh's article entitled "The Effects of Exercise on Singing" found in the *Journal of Singing* (May/June 1995, pp. 27–29). issue. Both articles will be helpful in convincing singers that physical exercise performed three times a week will be highly beneficial.

In general, the newest research is proving that regular exercise can be very beneficial to singers for both physical and psychological reasons. It not only develops the body physically so that the vocal support system is positively affected, but allows and enables stress reduction as well. If singers are carefully guided by exercise physiology professionals, and remember to pay close attention to breathing during exercise so as not to place too much subglottic pressure on the vocal cords, they can benefit enormously from regular physical exercise.

DOES IT MATTER IF I SMOKE?

Yes! Nicotine has a toxic effect on the heart and blood vessels, which are vital to every human being. It causes direct irritation and drying out of mucous membranes, making it difficult for the vocal mechanism to function. In addition, nicotine leaves deposits of coal tar on the mucous membranes of the respiratory system making it difficult for the lungs to work at full capacity and frequently causing a "smoker's cough." If you wish to be a singer, don't smoke! Those planning on careers in singing should also avoid areas where others are smoking so as not to be affected by second-hand smoke.

WHAT ABOUT DRINKING ALCOHOLIC BEVERAGES?

There is probably nothing wrong with an occasional alcoholic drink (assuming you are of the legal age), but in combination with singing, alcohol has several negative effects:

1. Alcohol interferes with judgment and muscular coordination.
2. Alcohol dilates blood capillaries causing an increased production of mucus.
3. Alcohol causes hoarseness because of the drying effect.
4. Alcohol may cause an allergic reaction, (especially beer and wine) which will congest the nasal cavities.

On a day when a singer must perform, it is best to avoid alcohol completely!

HOW DO ALLERGIES AFFECT THE VOICE?

The majority of allergic reactions are caused by inhaling something to which the body responds negatively, such as pollen, dust, animal dander, or mold. The body's reaction is to produce such symptoms as a runny nose, nasal congestion, itchy throat, sneezing, coughing, or wheezing. The combination of these symptoms will make singing at least less comfortable and at worst impossible. Untreated allergies can lead to asthmatic symptoms that are even more serious.

Allergies can be dealt with in three common ways:

1. Avoid those things to which you are allergic
2. Build up a resistance by taking desensitizing shots
3. Use prescriptive medicines to inhibit the allergic reaction.

As completely avoiding those things to which one is allergic is nearly impossible and prescriptive aids, such as antihistamines or steroids, have so many negative side effects, the best solution is probably to seek out a good Allergist, determine through testing, what triggers allergic reactions in your system, and begin the process of desensitization.

Note: Steroids (methylprednisolone, dexamethasone) can very effectively restore your voice after a bad case of allergy-caused laryngitis, but this treatment should not be used frequently or without a doctor's supervision. This is a treatment used only when a singer is absolutely desperate. For more information about medical diagnoses, and treatments, please see *Vocal Health and Pedagogy,* second edition, Robert T. Sataloff, editor.

FIGHTING THE COMMON COLD

The average person gets two "colds" a year, no matter where they live or in what climate. We get a cold because we have been exposed to a virus and our resistance has dropped too low from poor nutrition, lack of sleep, or living under too much stress to suppress it with the immune system. Getting "chilled" does not, in and of itself, cause a cold, but it does diminish the body's resistance and thus the mucous membranes are left open to infection. Colds should always be taken seriously, especially by singers. Colds weaken the body's resistance and open the door to other bacterial infections such as tonsillitis, laryngitis, bronchitis, and pneumonia.

What Should I Do to Avoid Colds?

1. Get enough rest. (7–8 hours each night).
2. Eat a balanced diet, rich in protein and unprocessed carbohydrates, and include lots of fruits and vegetables.
3. Don't let yourself get "run down."
4. Keep your hands clean by thorough washing several times a day, using an antibacterial soap.
5. Drink lots of fluids (avoid caffeine); especially water (6–8 eight-ounce glasses per day).

What Should I Do When I Get a Cold?

1. Don't ignore it. Take it seriously.
2. Stay home, preferably in bed for a day or two if at all possible.
3. Apply localized, moistened heat to create *hyperemia*—this will increase the flow of blood to the infected area and may speed recovery.
4. Inhaling steam is helpful in soothing dry membranes.
5. Drink plenty of fluids; especially water. Avoid products containing alcohol or caffeine, including colas, coffee, and tea. Herbal teas have no caffeine and may be of help in achieving appropriate hydration levels.
6. Eat lightly.

Gargling with warm water mixed with a small amount of baking soda will stimulate the flow of mucus and soothe dry membranes. It will not kill germs. Do not use salt for gargling. It is too drying for the delicate throat tissues. Lozenges have little effect on the throat and frequently the contents have a tendency to dry out mucous membranes. Lozenges do stimulate the flow of saliva, which feels soothing to the throat. Hard sugarless candy and chewing gum will also stimulate the flow of saliva and will cause less trauma to the throat tissues. Eucalyptus creates a sensation of coolness in the mucous membranes of the throat; however, this is irritating to the nasal passages and should be avoided. *Antihistamines* suppress allergy symptoms and do not cure or prevent colds. Although they may make it easier to breathe for a short time, they are generally too drying for the delicate membranes of the singer's throat. It is not recommended that singers experiment with antihistamines. See your medical professional for a proper diagnosis and recommendation in this regard.

Aspirin, NSAIDS (ibuprofen), and acetaminophen are good pain relievers if you have a headache or severe pain. However, the slight fever associated with the common cold is part of the body's method of fighting the infection. Raising the body temperature kills germs and fights infection. Thus, lowering the body temperature interferes with this natural method of fighting infection. Take aspirin only if absolutely necessary or recommended by your doctor. Dr. Robert Sataloff states: "The platelet dysfunction caused by aspirin predisposes an individual to bleeding and even hemorrhage, especially in vocal folds traumatized by excessive voice use in the face of vocal dysfunction. A vocal fold hemorrhage can be devastating to a professional voice user; and for this reason, the laryngologist (RTS) prohibits aspirin use and recommends minimal use of NSAIDs in his singers and all voice patients" (from Medications and the Voice by Robert Thayer Sataloff, Mary J. Hawkshaw, and Joseph Anticaglia, 2006, *Vocal Health and Pedagogy Advanced Assessment and Treatment*, 2nd Edition, Vol. II, Chap. 16, edited by Robert T. Sataloff, p. 200. Copyright 2006, Plural Publishing, Inc. Reproduced with permission).

In the category of alternative medicine or nutritional medicine is supplementation with *zinc gluconate* to aid in shortening the period of the active cold virus. During double-blind studies, adults and youngsters weighing at least 60 lbs. were told to suck on 2 tablets (23 mg elemental zinc or placebo) for at least 10 minutes at the onset of a cold, followed by 1 tablet every 2 waking hours up to a maximum of 12 tablets daily for adults and 9 tablets daily for younger children. Smaller children were limited to a maximum of 6 tablets daily. Treatment was to stop 6 hours after symptoms ceased, and no other treatments were permitted. Whereas cold sufferers receiving zinc completely recovered in an average of 3.9 days, those receiving placebo took 10.8 days to become symptom free. The treatment was equally effective for both mild and severe infections, and was beneficial even if supplementation was delayed. Many subjects became asymptomatic

within hours and one-fifth of the zinc-treated group fully recuperated within one day as reported in "Reduction in Duration of Common Colds by Zinc Gluconate Lozenges in a Double-Blind Study," by G. A. Eby, D. R. Davis, and W. W. Halcomb, 1984, (from *Antimicrobial Agents and Chemotherapy*, Volume 25, pp. 20–24. Copyright 1984, Society of Microbiology). Singers should be aware that zinc must not be taken on an empty stomach as it causes extreme nausea. Zinc gluconate lozenges are available over the counter and in several flavors. The best way to prevent colds is to build a healthy body, which will resist infections.

HEALTH CONCERNS FOR WOMEN

The respiratory tract is quite sensitive to hormonal changes in the body; thus, the menstrual cycle as well as pregnancy and menopause will have an effect on the vocal mechanism. Many women suffer from nasal and upper respiratory congestion immediately before and at the beginning of their menstrual periods. In addition, abdominal cramps may interfere with free breathing and support. Building a superior vocal technique is the best compensation for any temporary vocal impairment, but don't expect to be at your best during your menstrual period. If possible, avoid important auditions and performances at this time.

Premenstrual Syndrome

Melvyn R. Werbach, M.D., Assistant Clinical Professor at the UCLA School of Medicine has compiled a number of abstracts regarding recent publications and papers regarding the use of certain nutritional aids in treating illnesses and conditions. This "Sourcebook of Clinical Research" is entitled *Nutritional Influences on Illness* and was first published by Keats Publishing, Inc. New Canaan, Connecticut in paperback form in 1988. Third Line Press published the second edition in 1996.

In the section entitled "Premenstrual Syndrome" by Melvin R. Werbach, M.D., 1988 (from *Nutritional Influences on Illness*, pp. 364–369. Copyright 1988,

Melvin R. Werbach, M.D.), the female singer will find some very interesting facts tested through research, as well as resulting suggestions that the basic diet can be changed in several ways to avoid premenstrual syndrome as divided into four subgroups: PMT-A (anxiety), PMT-D (depression), PMT-C (cravings), and PMT-H (hyperhydration). Among these suggestions are the following:

1. Reduce caffeine at least 3 days prior to symptom onset. (Women who consume large amounts of caffeine are more likely to suffer from PMS).
2. Reduce sugar at least 3 days prior to symptom onset. Sugar intake is significantly greater in women with PMT than in normals. (PMT-A, PMT-C)
3. Reduce salt to 3 gm/day at least 3 days prior to symptom-onset. (PMT-C, PMT-H)
4. Reduce intake of dairy products and calcium. (PMT-A)

In regard to supplementation with certain nutrients, the clinical findings as presented here demonstrate:

1. Mixed results when Vitamin B6 is given.
2. Positive results when supplements of Vitamin A were given.
3. Positive results when supplements of Vitamin E were given.
4. Positive results when Magnesium supplements were given.
5. Positive results when supplements of Omega-6 Fatty Acids were given.

Menopause and Singing

In an additional section of *Nutritional Influences on Illness*, the reader will find abstracts concerning nutritional and other supplementation during menopause. In an article presented in the March/April 1996, pages 39 to 42, *Journal of Singing*, Dr. Robert Sataloff discusses "The Effects of Menopause on the Singing Voice." Within the article, Dr. Sataloff cites several studies and articles, including his own previous writings on this subject. He also gives excellent general information regarding the men-

strual years and the effects of the menstrual cycle on the singing voice. This is a very informative article for those interested in the topic.

Pregnancy and Singing

It is generally thought that for most women, pregnancy rarely interferes with vocal performance during the first five to six months. However, it is best to avoid professional singing engagements in the last trimester of pregnancy. At this time, hormonal influences on the mucous membranes become pronounced and the growth of the baby interferes with the abdominal motion necessary for the use of the diaphragmatic-costal breathing process. After delivery, abdominal muscles must be exercised so that they return to full strength and breathing exercises should be begun as soon as possible.

Female singers should feel free to discuss appropriate treatments and nutritional supplementation for PMS and other symptoms of the menstrual cycle, as well as asking for specific directions during pregnancy, and when approaching menopause. There is still controversy over hormone replacement therapy (HRT) due to the possible link to breast and ovarian cancer associated with the supplementation. Be sure to discuss supplements and HRT with your personal physician, gynecologist, and otolaryngologist to be sure that you have made the wisest choice for your body and family genetic history. Also an excellent choice today is the use of *phytoestrogen*, the plant alternative to estrogen replacement therapy. This has proven effective for many women, and research continues to prove the results.

VOCAL MISUSE AND ABUSE

Contained in two articles written for the Laryngoscope column in the September/October 1985, (pp. 23–26), and September/October 1986, (pp. 22–26) *Journal of Voice*, Dr. Robert Sataloff lists and counsels singers about 20 ways "to abuse their voices, damage their health and shorten their careers." All singers should read both articles in full, and remember all 20 points. Here, in summary fashion, are the 20 points for quick reference.

From "Ten Good Ways to Abuse Your Voice: A Singer's Guide to a Short Career" (Part I) by Robert T. Sataloff, M.D., 1985 (from *Journal of Singing,* September/October 1985, pp. 23–26. Copyright 1985, National Association of Teachers of Singing, Inc. Reproduced with permission).

1. Do not warm up before you use your voice (this includes singing and speaking). Dr. Sataloff suggests vocal warm-ups first thing in the morning for singers, teachers of singing, and professional voice users.
2. Do not study singing. This point includes both popular and classical singers. He admonishes the "sick" or "injured" singer especially to see the voice teacher on a regular basis.
3. Do not exercise. Dr. Sataloff states that singing is an athletic activity and requires excellent respiratory conditioning, endurance, and good general health. "Overweight, poor general conditioning, avoidance of some form of aerobic exercise regularly, and failure to maintain good abdominal and thoracic muscle strength undermine the power source of the voice and predispose the singer to vocal difficulties."
4. Speak as you would never dare to sing. Singers should carry over the formal training learned as singers into the use of the speaking voice. Vocal injury from incorrect use of the speaking voice will be carried over into the singing voice.
5. Wear yourself out. "When we wear ourselves out, we interfere with the body's ability to repair, replenish and balance the components of our vocal mechanisms."
6. Sing the wrong music. "Attempts to make the voice something that it is not, or that it is not yet, often stress the voice and may produce significant harm."
7. Sing in noise. "Classical singers are trained to compensate for such problems (over an orchestra, outdoors, etc.) by learning to monitor their performance with proprioceptive feedback (by feel) rather than auditory feedback (by ear). Popular singers are required to sing in the presence of extreme noise produced by electronic instruments and exuberant audiences." Sataloff admonishes the singer to remember that "choirs are among our noisiest environments,"

and to "sing as if you are giving a voice lesson to the person standing on either side of you." when you are singing with a choir.
8. Speak in noise. Here, he refers to the noise at parties following vocal performances, the noise of cars, airplanes, or other background noise.
9. Conduct. Here, conductors of amateur ensembles should be careful not to sing all the individual parts in order to teach, nor should the conductor attempt to speak over the singing choir. Be aware of hoarseness following a rehearsal and take it as a warning!
10. Teach voice. "Teachers also have a tendency to demonstrate vocal materials in their students' ranges, rather than their own. If a singing teacher is hoarse or has neck discomfort, or if soft singing control deteriorates at the end of the day (assuming the teacher warms up before beginning voice lessons), voice abuse should be suspected."

There are many other important informational facts in this article and every student of singing should read the entire article. These are only the highlights.

From "Ten More Good Ways to Abuse Your Voice: A Singer's Guide to a Short Career" (Part II) by Robert T. Sataloff, MD, 1986 (from *Journal of Singing,* September/October 1986, pp. 22–26. Copyright 1986, National Association of Teachers of Singing, Inc. Reproduced with permission).

1. Smoke. The adverse effects of tobacco smoke are well documented and incontestable. The immediate effects include inflammation, which alters the vocal cords themselves, and later may produce cancer, emphysema, blood vessel disease, and other major illnesses.
2. Drink alcohol. Alcohol opens up blood vessels (including those in the voice box) and alters mucosal secretions, which are so important to singing; it alters awareness and fine motor control in small amounts. Some mild allergic reactions may take place as well.
3. Take drugs. Most street drugs alter sensorium; the decreased awareness and impairment of accurate analytic abilities undermine good vocal technique.

4. Eat, drink, and be merry. Singers must remember that they are athletes constantly in training. Excessive eating and "partying" may be hazardous, especially late in the evening. It predisposes to reflux laryngitis and weight gain.

5. Prescribe your own medicines. For the most part, medicines are chemicals. In the right doses at the right time, they may work miracles. However, in the wrong doses, for the wrong duration, at the wrong time, or in the wrong person, they may be harmful or even poisonous.

6. Only see your doctor when you're desperate. The longer a singer waits before visiting a doctor, the worse his condition will be. Moreover, the more time between the doctor visit and a performance commitment, the better the chances of effective medical care and safe singing.

7. Choose the wrong doctor. Not all doctors are voice specialists. The subject of care for the professional voice user is fairly new in physician training. It is important for singers to be as well educated as possible about all aspects of the voice and its maladies, not only so they may help a good laryngologist reach an expeditious and correct diagnosis, but also so they know when their doctor's advice doesn't make sense.

8. Choose the wrong voice teacher. Vocal training consists of muscle development and coordination. Once muscles are shaped and contoured, they maintain their shape for many years. The importance of expert training for the beginner cannot be overemphasized.

Dr. Sataloff suggests the following reasonable expectations regarding what should and should not happen during the course of vocal training with a "good teacher:"

a. Abdominal and back muscle strength and breathing ability should improve.

b. The voice should improve, but not necessarily immediately. Often, as a singer abandons "bad habits," the voice actually sounds worse for a time while strength is being developed in appropriate muscles.

c. Singing should not hurt the throat. If the singer has pain in the neck, throat, or larynx, that may be a danger signal.

d. Hoarseness following voice lessons is also a danger signal. It does not ordinarily occur after proper singing. It is not reasonable for a singer to expect that even a singing teacher who is known to be superb will necessarily be right for him or her. If the teacher and student are not communicating effectively and making progress, discussions of referral to another voice teacher at least for evaluation and possibly for training are reasonable.

e. Beware the voice teacher who is too secretive. Most good teachers have no compunction about having their lessons observed occasionally, about having their students listened to under proper circumstances, and about having them evaluated by a qualified laryngologist.

9. Choose the wrong schedule. When we try to rush nature, she frequently rebels. Each singer needs to be honest with himself and to seek the advice of experienced teachers and coaches. Conservative, slow progression and development with appropriate repertoire predispose to strong, healthy voices. Impatience, bad advice, and self-deception predispose to an early career change.

10. Choose the wrong career. Dr. Sataloff affirms that virtually everyone can sing. A singer who chooses a career for which his [her] voice is not suited may damage his [her] voice box and ruin him [her] self for an equally gratifying and attainable career (singing different repertoire).

THE SINGER'S MEDICINE CHEST

After having reviewed the summary section of Dr. Sataloff's articles on abuse of the voice, and many others, it is also important for the singer, during training and education, to gain as much knowledge about certain over-the-counter and prescription medications as possible, so that when a drug is prescribed, the singer will have some idea of what the effects will be on the body, and specifically on voice production and technique. In a 2005 book entitled *Treatment of Voice Disorders*, Sataloff devotes an entire chapter to "Medications and the Voice." In addition, his *Vocal Health and Pedagogy*, 2nd edition also contains two chapters, which are important sources here: Chapter 16 *Medications and the Voice*, and Chapter 17 *Medications for Traveling Performers*. Both these chapters and *Treatment of Voice Disorders* are coauthored with Mary J. Hawkshaw, and Joseph Anticaglia among others. Additional information on important medications and herbal remedies can be found in these books.

More recently, in the January/February 1999 *Journal of Singing* (Vol. 55, No. 3, pp. 53–63), and in conjunction with Garyth Nair, founding Music Director of the Chamber Symphony of New Jersey, and former professional singer and conductor, Sataloff provides research information in an article entitled: Vocal Pharmacology: Introducing the Subject at Drew University. This information was taken from a 1997 presentation given by Mr. Nair in regard to the "specific treatment protocols needed for our University student singers and actors." Included in the article is a "Table of Possible Prescription and OTC Agents That Can Adversely Affect the Performing Voice." This table will be extremely helpful for singers and teachers of singing, and should be obtained and utilized with care. The table, Mr. Nair explains, "is a compilation drawn from Robert Sataloff's excellent book, *Professional Voice: The Science and Art of Clinical Care*, second edition. He states that he has made additions to include more drugs, both prescriptive and OTC. Some of the most common medications from this chart (Table 8–3) are included here for informational purposes, and not to prescribe or attempt to diagnose or treat any medical conditions. As of July 2005, *Professional Voice: The Science and Art of Clinical Care* has been published in a three-volume set (third edition) by Plural Publishing, Inc. This important reference work should be in the library of every university where students are studying to be professional singers.

Of course a singer could and should read as much about health care research and developments as possible, but remember to consult your personal physician, nutritionist and/or otolaryngologist before taking over-the-counter medications, and do not prescribe your own medicines. Where appropriate, attempt to solve chronic health problems with good nutrition and natural products.

For singers, excellent mental health and emotional control is as important as strong physical wellbeing. The professional performance lifestyle and the process of preparing for a career in performance can be very stressful. Students aspiring to be professional singing musicians are generally very aware of the obstacles associated with establishing themselves as professional performers. First, there is mastering the language of music, then developing the physiologic and technical aspects of vocal production, followed by gaining in-depth knowledge of historical performance practice, learning several languages, gaining acting, interpretive, and audition skills, and a multitude of other skills. The process of acquiring all this knowledge as well as learning to use it wisely can be very stressful. How does the singer deal with this stress?

Of course each singer is different, and handles the stresses of everyday life differently. In general, a singer will be able to cope with the stresses of training for and maintaining a performance career through the discipline of good nutrition, proper rest, and exercise, as previously stated. When the stresses seem to require more than normal maintenance, singers might think about the following:

Psychosomatic factors definitely enter into the physical performance arena for singers. Anxiety, anger, sadness, tension, and depression can affect the singer and the vocal instrument in a negative way. When a singer is feeling depressed, angry, or anxious about something completely unrelated to singing or a particular performance, these feelings may appear physically as muscular tension and reduced control of vocal technique. It is best, when a singer finds himself or herself in such a "mood," not to continue to practice or perform through it, but to "take a step back," to evaluate the situation and to determine what it is that is causing the negative emotional impact. It may be necessary to get professional help in extreme cases, but generally, singers just need to talk through the problem with a friend or colleague, to discuss it rationally and attempt to solve or reduce the problem that is causing the emotional reaction. There are many psychologists who act as stress management counselors and who can be of significant help in solving such problems.

Table 8–3. Health Concerns: Prescriptions and Over-the-Counter Agents That Can Adversely Affect the Voice A Summary Chart

Class	Common Medication Name	Effects and Notes
Antihistamines	Benadryl, Chlor-Trimeton, Allegra, Claritin, Vicks Formula 44, Robitussin DM	drying effect on upper respiratory tract secretions, OTC's may have a sedative effect; those containing codeine are especially drying unless balanced with a wetting agent like guaifenesin
Mucolytic Agents	phenylephrine Guaifenesin (Fenesin, Humibid, Guaifid)	expectorant and vasoconstrictor—some drying may occur, thins and increases secretions
Corticosteroids		useful in managing acute inflammatory laryngitis
Diuretics	hydrochlorthiazide (Didronal, Dyazide)	should not be used for vocal fold symptoms related to menses. Dehydrates singers.
	caffeine (coffee, tea, certain soft drinks)	can be a powerful diuretic and produces the same effects as diuretic medications
Other Anti-Edema Agents (sprays)	epinephrine (Bronkaid, Primatene) pseudoephedrine (Sudafed)	often used for respiratory edema action involves reduction in diameter and volume of vascular structures in the submucosal area. May produce rebound effect that is counterproductive
Topical Laryngeal Sprays	diphenhydramine (Benadryl) oxymetazoline (Afrin)	not recommended due to analgesic effect, very effective for severe edema immediately prior to performance—better at restoring speech than singing!
	propylene glycol (Saline)	provides lubrication for dry climates, or following travel—should be used in conjunction with oral hydration
Topical Nasal Sprays	Beconase, Vancenase, Rhinocort, Nasacort, Flonase	no apparent harm to voice, reduces nasal and nasopharyngeal edema, may reduce airborne allergy sensitivity
Moist Oral Inhalers		may develop contact inflammation from sensitivity to the medications or the propellants—may cause mucosal drying
Steroid Inhalers	(Flovent, Vanceril, Beclovent)	dysphonia occurs in up to 50% of patients due to aerosolized steroid may be capable of causing wasting of the vocalis muscle!
Antiviral Agents	Acyclovir	used for herpes, can be useful in patients with herpetic recurrent superior laryngeal nerve paresis or paralysis
	Amantadine	may cause agitation, tachycardia, and extreme dryness.
Antitussives		often have agents which have a secondary drying effect, especially if they contain codeine or dextromethorphan/ may also contain antihistamines (drying agent)
Antihypertensives		Almost all dry mucous membranes of the upper respiratory tract, especially if they contain a diuretic agent
Gastroenterologic Medications	antacids histamine H2-receptor antagonists	occasionally have a drying effect useful in the treatment of gastric acid reflux laryngitis, occasionally cause drying effects

Table 8–3. *continued*

Class	Common Medication Name	Effects and Notes
		avoid any with diphenhydramine (Benadryl) due to drying effect
Sleeping Medications		
Analgesics		Pain at the vocal folds is an important protective physiologic function. Should not be used just prior to performance!
	Aspirin	*causes platelet dysfunction and predisposes one to hemorrhage. Should be avoided by singers whenever possible.*
	Ibuprofen	may inhibit clotting mechanism
	Acetaminophen	**Recommended for Singers!**
	Narcotic analgesics	Do not use shortly before performance
Beta-Blockers	propranolol	have been used to lower anxiety levels in performers—*are not indicated for singers!*—potentially dangerous as they can affect heart rate, blood pressure, and may induce asthma attacks in those susceptible

Source: From "Vocal Pharmacology: Introducing the Subject at Drew University," by G. Nair and R. T. Sataloff, 1999, January/February, *Journal of Singing, 55*(3), pp. 53–63. Copyright 1999, National Association of Teachers of Singing. Reproduced with permission.

WHAT ARE THE MAIN SOURCES OF STRESS OR ANXIETY FOR SINGERS?

They are the same worries which trouble everyone —fear of failure, perfectionism, lack of self-esteem, or repressed emotions which have little or nothing to do with an upcoming performance. Fear of failure is probably the most common negative emotion for a performer. This is the fear that causes so much anxiety prior to a performance. If the singer is well prepared for the performance, much of the anxiety can be removed with ease. This is sometimes called "stage fright." In experiencing stage fright, the singer has already decided that something will go wrong during the performance. For example, forgetting the words, the notes, or not being able to make pleasing sounds. We actually cause our own anxiety and sometimes failure when we allow ourselves to continually dwell on these negative aspects without providing a cure for the mostly irrational thoughts we have regarding the performance. A possible solution for this is the visualization technique already discussed in Chapter 1 of this book. I have personally found it quite helpful, through an exercise, to place myself in a state of "stage fright" two to three weeks prior to a big performance. At this early date, there will still be plenty of time to repair any possible threats to a successful performance as identified during the stage fright exercise.

In doing this exercise, the performer should find a quiet spot where concentration will not be disturbed, and one by one go through all (even the most absurd) possibilities worrying you about the performance (your "fears"). Then, one by one, rid yourself of the possibility of this happening through rational and logical self-talk. For example, if you are worried about forgetting words, be sure you have prepared yourself well, that all of the words are memorized carefully, and that the literal translation for each foreign word as well as the context of each phrase is well in hand. If you cannot remember all of the words when not under the stress of performance, the chance of forgetting on the stage is very real. If, however, you have no difficulty in remembering the words, and are able to interpret and phrase the text easily, you will not need to worry about forgetting words. You must prove to yourself that you are prepared appropriately for the performance in order to feel absolutely at ease on the stage. Choosing a more frivolous anxiety, if you are worried about falling on stage, check that you are wearing shoes that fit you well, are comfortable, and appropriately "scuffed" on the bottom. Then, practice in the hall where you will sing the performance (while wearing the shoes) several times in order to achieve an appropriate comfort level. This method takes a little time, but is well worth the effort in maintaining a comfort and concentration level on stage, which allows you the freedom of expression necessary for an outstanding performance.

WHAT SHOULD I DO TO PREVENT STAGE FRIGHT BEFORE A PERFORMANCE?

The late Madame Sonja Sharnova, noted Chicago voice teacher and contralto with the Chicago Opera Company, outlined several steps for preventing stage fright, which she distributed to her students regularly. Following are Madame Sharnova's ten tips to prevent stage fright before a performance.

First of all, she states: "Fear is the basic condition to be dealt with. What produces fear? Four basic causes are: uncertainty, ignorance, self-consciousness, and lack of concentration. To eliminate these, have the pupil explore and confront every aspect of a singing performance so that familiarity may take the place of uncertainty, knowledge may replace ignorance, poise may replace self-consciousness, and sustained single-mindedness correct faulty concentration." Here are her ten suggestions:

1. Rehearsals should simulate the conditions of actual performances. Visit the auditorium or recital hall beforehand, if possible, to familiarize yourself with the dimensions and acoustics thereof. Frequent preliminary short exposures to an audience, small or large, will also be helpful.
2. Detailed knowledge of the song and text is indispensable. Memorization and performance standards must be trained beyond minimum requirements so that margin of security and ease may be built into the final performance. It is better to relax down into the desired standard than to stretch and strain up to it. Hence, the policy of overbuilding a technique promotes self-confidence.
3. Proper diet, rest, recreation, and relaxation exercises should not be overlooked during the days and period preceding the performance date.
4. Vigorous spoken declamations of the text will be helpful. An intelligent English translation of a foreign text may be recited and sung aloud, as a practice device, to help capture the essential message of the song or aria. Try paraphrasing the text in ordinary conversational English until the meaning and communicative intent is fully realized. Cultivate conversational ease of expression, not bombast, so that the communicative aspects of singing may be realized. Sing it as if you were saying it. Singing will seem sterile unless there is communicative contact with the listener.
5. Avoid stiffness of posture. Freedom of movement during rehearsal will help to relax the body and prevent awkwardness and stiffness while singing.
6. Try out several different transposed keys so that a sense of tonal fitness and ease may be realized suited to the tessitura of the voice. Avoid foolhardy extremes of pitch, or dynamics of phrasing which might invite a sense of insecurity or incompetence.
7. Be certain that a phrase-wise and not a note-wise reading of the song is developed. Learn to sing through the song without stopping a number of times. Ignore the errors. Don't always chop it up into repeated fragments. Note the errors, if any, separately, and then isolate them for separate treatment without violating the continuity of the song. The final performance should not seem like a series of problems to be overcome. Try to capture the wholeness of the song, its meaning, and its mood. There must be a resolute continuity of forwardness to a song, not hesitancy or uncertainty about what is coming next. The sustained effect must be built into the performance pattern.
8. Know the accompaniment thoroughly and be able to stop or continue at any point of the song, without confusion. Above all, be able to sing

through it mentally or silently, then audibly, without any accompaniment at all.

9. Don't overwork the song but use similar arias and texts that embody similar vocal problems. Flexibility and versatility of expression in the particular idiom will thus be cultivated.
10. Visualize success, not failure. Practice seeing yourself before an audience.

These ten suggestions will help a singer to achieve control over not only the emotions, but the entire situation. They, along with excellent technical preparation, will help the singer in alleviating the need to be a perfectionist, as well as improving low self-esteem. The key to success on the performance stage is appropriate preparation and understanding of the task at hand. When training has been appropriate, the singer will be able to control the emotional as well as the physical aspect of performing.

SINGING WHEN SICK

What Should a Singer Do When Awaking the Day of a Performance with a Sore Throat?

To sing or not to sing, that is the question! The answer to this question, of course, can vary greatly from one singer to another. But, some general suggestions might include the following:

Evaluate the problem. Can you determine a cause for the sore throat? Does it relate to overuse or abuse of the voice previously, or is it a viral or bacterial infection? You may need the help of a physician to make this determination. Do not hesitate to call your personal physician or otolaryngologist in such an instance. If the problem is bacterial, you may need an antibiotic, and you would be doing yourself and everyone else you come in contact with a favor by not exposing them to your ailment. Although viral infections do not respond to antibiotics, you may still want to consult your physician if you think you have a virus. A viral infection can lead to a bacterial infection, which will prolong your recovery time. Always ask your voice teacher and physician for advice on whether you should sing a

performance or an audition on a "sick throat." Frequently, singers cause themselves extensive damage by singing on swollen vocal folds, which should not have been forced to sing. You must trust the advice of your voice teacher and your doctor, so be sure you have both to rely upon in times such as these. In general, the advice for "singing sick" has always been and continues to be—if you could cause damage to your voice by singing, don't sing! If you will sing a bad audition or performance, don't sing! It is far better to cancel a performance than to leave a bad impression as a professional singer.

If the vocal problem seems to be related to too much singing or speaking (overuse or abuse of the voice) rather than to a viral or bacterial infection, there are several things which may help to reduce the effects as follows:

1. Take a hot shower and allow the steam to penetrate your nasal and respiratory passages as much as possible.
2. Try placing a washcloth soaked in tolerably hot water over the nose and mouth and inhale through this to penetrate the nasal passages with moisture and create hyperemia.
3. Drink lots of fluids; warm water, or herbal tea will help to rehydrate the injured membranes.
4. Reduce use of your speaking voice to a minimum; allowing the vocal folds to rest as much as possible.
5. Rest as much as possible, and eat a moderate amount of foods rich in protein and carbohydrates to aid the body in healing the injured area.
6. Avoid any caffeine containing products, as well as salty and highly seasoned foods.
7. Vocalize carefully and gently later in the day to prepare the vocal folds for singing. You should be able to recognize whether you will be able to sing or not after a few hours of rest and hydration.
8. Some singers find yoga and meditation helpful in relieving the muscle tension found in neck and shoulder muscles following a day of "bad singing" technique.

This chapter could go on without pause, as new information on physical and mental health care is discovered and presented every day. The aspiring singer needs to remember that he or she is responsible for his or her own health and well-being. Read and educate yourself as well as possible in the areas of nutrition, appropriate physical and mental health care, alternative medicine, and exercise physiology, and become part of your own health care team. Be alert to new discoveries, and be patient with a sick body. Never hesitate to consult a professional in regard to a health question, especially in the case of illness with an upcoming performance. Early intervention is always best!

BASIC INFORMATIONAL SOURCES ON HEALTH CARE/ NUTRITION FOR SINGERS

Balch, Phyllis A., & Balch, James F. *Prescription for Nutritional Healing A-to-Z Guide to Supplements*, Avery Publishing Group, Garden City Park, NY, 1998. ISBN 0-89529-816-3

Brodnitz, Friedrich S. *Keep Your Voice Healthy*, Little, Brown and Company Inc., Boston, 1988 (First edition published by Harper & Row in 1953; a reprint edition was published by Charles C. Thomas in 1973. ISBN 0-316-10902-9

Deglin, Judith Hopfer, Vallerand, April, & Russin, Mildred. *Davis's Drug Guide for Nurses*, F. A. Davis Company, Philadelphia (a new edition is issued each year).

Gershoff, Stanley. *The Tufts University Guide to Total Nutrition*, Harper Collins Publishers, Inc., New York, 1996. ISBN 0-06-271588-7

Kirschmann, Gayla J., & Kirschmann, John D. *Nutrition Almanac* (4th edition), McGraw-Hill, New York, 1996. ISBN 0-07-034922-3

Larson, David E. *Mayo Clinic Family Healthbook*, William Morrow and Company, Inc., New York, 1990. ISBN 0-688-07819-2

Murray, Michael T., N.D. *Encyclopedia of Nutritional Supplements*, Prima Publishing, Rocklin, CA, 1996. ISBN 0-7615-0410-9

Sataloff, Robert Thayer. *Professional Voice, The Science and Art of Clinical Care*, Plural Publishing, Inc., San Diego, CA, 2005. ISBN 1-59756-001-4

Sataloff, Robert Thayer, M.D., D.M.A. *Vocal Health and Pedagogy*, 2nd Edition, Plural Publishing, Inc. San Diego, CA, 2006. ISBN 13: 978-1-59756-087-0 (softcover: v. 1) ISBN 10: 1-59756-087-1 (softcover: v. 1)

Saxon, Keith G., & Schneider, Carole M. *Vocal Exercise Physiology*, Singular Publishing Group, Inc., San Diego, CA, 1995. ISBN 1-56593-159-9

Werbach, Melvyn R., M.D. *Nutritional Influences on Illness—A Sourcebook of Clinical Research*, Keats Publishing, Inc. New Canaan, CT, 1988. ISBN 0-87983-531-1

IMPORTANT TERMS TO DEFINE AND UNDERSTAND

Hydration

Proper environmental humidity

Mucolytic agent (Guaifenesin)

Antihistamine/decongestant

Proper nutrition

Otolaryngologist

USDA Food Pyramid versus Mediterranean Food Pyramid

Nutritionist/dietitian

Weight bearing and aerobic exercise

Exercise physiology

    Overload principle

    Specificity principle

    Individuality principle

    Reversibility principle

Steroids

Aspirin, NSAIDs, and acetaminophen

Zinc gluconate

Phytoestrogen

REFERENCES

Journal Articles

Brunner, P. (1988, May/June). Fit or fat: The singer's challenge. *Journal of Singing*, p. 29.

Eby, G. A., Davis, D. R., & Halcomb, W. W. (1984). Reduction in duration of common colds by zinc gluconate lozenges in a double-blind study. Antimicrobial agents and chemotherapy. *American Society of Microbiology*, 25, pp. 20-24.

Lawrence, Van L. (1986, March/April). Sermon on hydration (The evils of dry). *Journal of Singing*, pp. 22-23.

Nair, G., & Sataloff, R., (1999, January/February). Vocal pharmacology: Introducing the subject at Drew University. *Journal of Singing*, pp. 53-63.

Sataloff, R. T. (1996, January/February). Pollution: Consequences for singers. *Journal of Singing*, pp. 59-64.

Sataloff, R. T. (1996, March/April). The effects of menopause on the singing voice. *Journal of Singing*, pp. 39-42.

Sataloff, R. T. (1985, September/October). Ten good ways to abuse your voice: A singer's guide to a short career (Part I). *Journal of Singing*, pp. 23-26.

Sataloff, R. T. (1986, September/October). Ten more good ways to abuse your voice: A singer's guide to a short career (Part II). *Journal of Singing*, pp. 22-26.

Sataloff, R. T., David, D., Harvey, P., & Miller, S. (1997, September/October). Nutrition and the professional voice user (Part I). *Journal of Singing*, 54 (1), pp. 41-48.

Sataloff, R. T., David, D., Harvey, P., & Miller, S. (1997, November/December). Nutrition and the professional voice user (Part II). *Journal of Singing*, 54(2), pp. 43-49.

Sirbaugh, N. (1995, May/June). The effects of exercise on singing. *Journal of Singing*, pp. 27-29.

Books

Brodnitz, F. S. (1988). *Keep your voice healthy*. Boston: Little, Brown.

Deglin, J. H., Vallerand, A., & Russin, M. (2006). *Davis's drug guide for nurses*. Philadelphia: F. A. Davis.

Gershoff, S. (1996). *The Tufts University guide to total nutrition*. New York: Harper Collins.

Kirschmann, G. J., & Kirschmann, J. D. (1996). *Nutrition almanac* (4th ed.). New York: McGraw-Hill.

Larson, D. E. (1990). *Mayo Clinic family healthbook*. New York: William Morrow.

Murray, M. T., (1996). *Encyclopedia of nutritional supplements*. Rocklin, CA: Prima.

Sataloff, R. T. (2005). *Professional voice, The science and art of clinical care*. San Diego, CA: Plural.

Sataloff, R. T., (2006). *Vocal health and pedagogy* (2nd ed.). San Diego, CA: Plural.

Saxon, K. G., & Schneider, C. M. (1995). *Vocal exercise Physiology*. San Diego, CA: Singular.

Werbach, M. R., (1998). *Nutritional influences on illness—A sourcebook of clinical research*, New Cannan, CT: Keats.

Web sites

The Traditional Healthy Mediterranean Diet Pyramid, Oldways Preservation and Exchange Trust, Boston, 2007, available at: http://www.oldwayspt.org

The United States Department of Agriculture Eating Right Pyramid, U.S. Dept. of Agriculture Web site is available at: http://www.mypyramid.gov/index.html

Chapter 9

BEYOND VOCAL TECHNIQUE—
BECOMING AN
ARTISTIC PERFORMER

DO I NEED TO STUDY MORE THAN VOCAL TECHNIQUE?

Yes! Once a singer feels that vocal technical matters are under control, basic breathing and support mechanics are in place, and physical skills are developing well, it is time to think about interpretation, and performance skills. This is true whether the singer intends to sing on the opera or Broadway stage, in the concert hall, or as a popular singer on the stages of the entertainment industry.

WHAT IS INVOLVED IN THIS PROCESS?

Many things are included. To be an artistic vocal performer, a singer must have a very well-rounded education. Studying the *liberal arts*, in addition to music, will be helpful to the aspiring singer in achieving the necessary social, psychological, political, scientific, and economic understanding needed to interpret music from different historical eras and parts of the world. The liberal arts include the *Fine and Performing Arts* (music, art, dance, photography, etc.), the *Humanities* (languages, literature, philosophy, history, and religion), the *Social Sciences* (sociology, psychology, economics, and political sci-

ence), *Quantitative Studies* (mathematics, computer sciences), and the *Natural Sciences* (biology, chemistry, physics, geology, astronomy). Studies in science and mathematics will enable a singer to develop the "other side of the brain." A well-rounded education is essential to the preparation for a professional performance career.

A singer must be well trained in the areas of musicianship as well, including excellent sight-reading skills, strong listening skills, and skills in music analysis. The singer will need competent piano skills to learn chosen song or operatic literature, as well as to be able to play basic accompaniments. This will enable the singer to develop an appreciation for and an understanding of the accompaniment (whether orchestral, chamber, keyboard, or other). It is essential that the singer be able to study and understand the song or opera role as an integrated whole rather than as one line of music around which others are adding support. The singer must be able to confidently study and interpret the melodic and harmonic structures of the vocal line as well as the accompaniment in order to achieve a cohesiveness of presentation. A singer should never be forced to rely on an accompanist or musical coach to teach him or her the music. If a singer must utilize someone else's skills to learn music, he must be very wealthy, and willing to be fully dependent on someone else for an entire career. Neither should a singer need to rely on recordings for learning music. If a singer learns all of his music through listening to someone else's interpretation, how will he develop his own ideas in regard to the presentation of a song? What if there is no recording of the song the singer must perform?

Perhaps even more important than the required theoretical and piano skills for the aspiring classical singer is the acquisition of historical knowledge regarding composers, compositional style, and performance practice, in order to achieve a correct stylistic presentation of an art song or operatic role. In this regard, singers should spend as much time as possible in the study of the history of music, its style, and performance practice. Singers must seek out courses in general music history, particularly the history of the Baroque, Classical, Romantic, and Contemporary periods, so they will be fully prepared for the necessary study and research required of them as professional performers. The musical theater and more popular music oriented singers also need this background to understand where the popular music of today has come from. Knowing and understanding the past is extremely important to a strong understanding of the present and future, and will be a great aid in developing the interpretive skills necessary to becoming a professional singer. In addition, courses in art song and operatic literature should also be a major component of a degree program in vocal performance, and should introduce undergraduate students to a wide variety of styles and practices in the composition of vocal music.

An entire chapter of this book has been devoted to the International Phonetic Alphabet and the correct pronunciation and translation of the Italian and English languages, but aspiring singers will need to have a basic foundation and understanding of at least two more western European languages—French and German. In the past, colleges and universities routinely required students to enroll in six credits of a foreign language to complete the requirements for an undergraduate degree. This is no longer the case in many colleges and universities, where students now study foreign culture. Although this may be appropriate for some, it is not enough for the aspiring classical singer, who will find it extremely important to acquire excellent skills in at least four languages. It is strongly recommended that aspiring singers acquire at least a basic knowledge of two languages while studying at the college level, and that they become fairly fluent in at least one secondary language. Generally, vocal music programs require that singers take courses in a foreign language, but singers should use their undergraduate elective credits to continue their language study if they intend to perform professionally. All classical singers will find themselves performing in the Italian, German, French, and English languages on a day-to-day basis. If the singer intends to sing professionally in choral ensembles, whether as a secular or sacred chorister, Latin will also be an appropriate language with which to be comfortable. Most college and university vocal performance degree programs also require a student to acquire some skills in what used to be considered an "exotic" language. These might include Spanish, Russian, Polish, Swedish, Chinese, Japanese, or other languages beyond those western European languages already discussed. In studying language, an aspiring singer must attain much more than good pronunciation skills in the languages as she will need to be able to correctly translate, phrase, and interpret poetic literature from the Baroque though the Contemporary period in several languages. Thus, the lyric diction classes offered at the undergraduate level are merely a stepping stone to the more intense study required for a professional career in the singing world.

The best education for an aspiring singer is a complete one. Even if it takes a little longer to complete undergraduate studies, you will find your liberal arts studies very valuable as you go on to graduate school and a professional performance career.

THE INTERPRETATION OF VOCAL MUSIC

As singers, we are in the unique position of being required to interpret two creators rather than one, the composer, and the poet. Instrumentalists, of course, are not generally placed in this position. Only rarely, as in the vocalise intended for concert performance, are singers given the luxury of interpreting only one person's ideas. So, how does a singer go about the process of deciding on an appropriate interpretation? There are some general guidelines, which will be helpful to the singer in this endeavor.

Interpreting the Poetry

1. Using the guidelines from Chapter 1 on "How to Learn a Song" will be of great help here. This includes, creating a literal translation of the poem if it is in a foreign language, and detailed work on pronunciation and phrasing of the language.
2. Even in our native language, we frequently have questions about the poet's meaning of a text. A singer must read the poem many times, using different inflections, and finding hidden meanings which might be expressed if the poem is presented in a way which may have been intended by the poet. It is the responsibility of the singer to express and convey the meaning of the poem in the way in which the poet intended. Frequently in poetry and theatrical works, there is a *subtext,* which will be understood only by doing research on the poet, the full work from which an aria or art song comes, and "reading between the lines."
3. The singer must research the poet and study other poetry of the same and differing genres to gain a full understanding of the particular poem being studied.
4. The singer must carefully study the way in which the composer has set the poem to enhance its meaning, and then utilize those aspects which point to the true meaning of the words when performing the song.

Interpreting the Music

1. Of course the singer's study of theory, music history, and vocal literature will come into play here, as she explores the historical placement of the music and its composer. Using her knowledge of historical style and performance practice will enable the singer to achieve a stylistically correct interpretation of the song or aria.

2. The singer must research the composer in the same way as the poet, looking not only at the particular song, aria, or opera, but also at the relationship of this composition to others in the composer's output.
3. Achieving the best interpretation of the music is fully entangled with the interpretation of the poetry and visa versa. Most often, the composer is setting a poem, which he has borrowed from a literary artist. Only rarely has the music been composed first, and then words placed around the notes. Thus, the singer must study the poem in depth, and carefully note how the composer has interpreted the words; demonstrated in the way the melodic line, rhythms, phrasing, dynamics, and so on have been written to enhance the text.

German Soprano, Lilli Lehmann (1848-1929) was known as "one of the first great international superstars of opera." She was much admired for her dramatic presence and for her great repertoire, said to have included at least 600 Lieder and 170 operatic roles. "In *How to Sing* (1902, Public domain. Reprint by Dover Publications, Inc., 1993), Madame Lehmann draws upon her vast experience and a profound understanding of her vocal art to offer inspiration and sound advice in every phase of singing, from how to breathe correctly, produce a ringing head tone, and execute a proper trill to important nuances of vocal expression and role interpretation." (Publisher's note on the Dover edition) In the new paperback edition of Mme. Lehmann's book, the singer will find a brief statement "Concerning Expression." The entire book is quite interesting, and offers insight into vocal technique and the interpretation of music, and should be read by aspiring vocal performers. Some of her words are worth repeating here as they relate to this topic:

When we wish to study a role or a song, we have first to master the intellectual content of the work. Not till we have made ourselves a clear picture of the whole should we proceed to elaborate the details, through which, however, the impression of the whole should never be allowed to suffer. The complete picture should always shine out through all. If it is too much broken into details, it becomes a thing of shreds and patches . . . A word is an idea; and not only the idea, but how that idea in color and connection is related to the whole, must be expressed . . . Every elaboration of a work of art demands the sacrifice of some part of the artist's ego, for he must mingle the feelings set before him for portrayal with his own in his interpretation, and thus, so to speak, lay bare his very self (p. 132).

In a subsequent chapter, entitled "Before the Public," Mme. Lehmann writes about performing in general, and makes these important comments which still apply today:

If I have put my individuality, my powers, my love for the work, into a role or a song that is applauded by the public, I decline all thanks for it to myself personally, and consider the applause as belonging to the master whose work I am interpreting . . . In any matter relating to art, only the best is good enough for any public. If the public is uncultivated, one must make it know the best, must educate it, must teach it to understand the best . . . It is the artist's task, through offering his best and most carefully prepared achievements, to educate the public, to ennoble it; and he should carry out his mission without being influenced by bad standards of taste (pp. 133–134).

These words speak for themselves, and offer the young singer important thoughts on the responsibility of interpreting the works of great composers and poets. In the 21st century, we have become somewhat more concerned with our own egos, and having a "personal style." If we accept Mme. Lehmann's writings, in interpreting the works of the great composers, we must put our own egos away, and devote ourselves to the discovery of the composer's, and poet's ideals. It is those ideals that must be presented to and understood by the audience when the performance comes to an end.

Those singers who aspire to the popular music stages and recording studios are much more concerned with the attainment of a personal style and a carefully defined interpretation which acknowledges the performer rather than the composer in its presentation. Thus, the composer's and lyric writer's names are generally unknown in popular music of the 20th and 21st centuries. This is an important distinction for those wishing to become known through the performance of popular rather than classical music. A singer wishing to perform in clubs and through the popular media will need to develop a very well-defined personality which appears in the singing of every song. The classical singer does not usually need to be so concerned with this aspect of the performance art.

In their excellent book, *The Art of the Song Recital*, Shirlee Emmons and Stanley Sonntag offer the singer "extensive, thoroughgoing, and definitive insights into the attributes that can render it at once a great art and a magnificent entertainment" (Emmons, Sonntag, 1979, p. xv). In a chapter on research, they offer the following which has been reprinted by permission of Waveland Press, Inc. from (Shirlee Emmons and Stanley Sonntag, *The Art of the Song Recital*, first edition, Long Grove, IL; Waveland Press, Inc., 1979 [reissued 2001]. All rights reserved).

A singer cannot consider scholarship an end in itself, although knowledge does result from such work. Rather, the reason for this activity is a totally pragmatic one: a singer's primary goal is to "get inside the song" and "make it his own." Margaret Rae, in a speech before the New York Singing Teachers' Association, pointed out that "empathy is a word borrowed from modern psychology. It means a "feeling into" and is defined as "the imaginal and mental projection of oneself into the elements of a work of art." When a person projects himself into a piece of music or literature, he responds emotionally to its contents *in addition to comprehending it logically* [italics ours]. We suggest that the artist can never truly make the song "his own" until he understands every aspect of the music and the poem (p. 172).

Another quote in the Emmons/Sonntag book comes from the important American opera conductor and pianist, James Levine:

The goal of producing a performance as faithful to the composer's intentions as possible requires more than literal fidelity to notation; it means somehow fathoming the depth, breadth, and complexity of the most imaginative impulses of men, many of whom lived hundreds of years ago.

To approach this goal . . . [one] must steep him-self in a number of other things—as much of that composer's output as possible, as well as language, culture, human experience, psychology, perform-ance practices of the period (pp. 172-173).

An artist-singer will have carefully studied the full text from which only a portion may have been used for a song setting, will study the composer, the times, and the environment in which that composer worked. This same singer will bring to his or her interpretation, a lifetime of personal experiences, a wealth of musical and literary knowledge, and a real desire to allow the poet and composer to speak through his or her voice in performance. It takes tremendous discipline to become such an artist, but one only need have the desire to make it happen.

THE ACCOMPANIST, YOUR PARTNER IN INTERPRETATION AND PERFORMANCE

Singers do not generally have the opportunity to perform in a truly "solo" manner. The interpretation of concert vocal literature requires partnership with a pianist, an organist, or harpsichordist, an instru-mental ensemble, an orchestra, or some other varia-tion of accompanying instruments. For the most part, young singers find themselves rehearsing and performing with pianists more often than any other accompanying instrument. It is important, then, for the singer to establish a strong working relationship with the accompanist, and indeed a musical and interpretive partnership. The singer must feel free to share verbally the knowledge she has gained through research and study of the poetry and music so that the two performers may achieve a unified form of expression on the stage.

Are There Guidelines for Rehearsals with an Accompanist?

If both the singer and pianist come to the rehearsal prepared (having completed the appropriate research, knowing the music and poetry quite well, and having a fairly well-established idea about the interpretation), respect one another as equal partners in the music, and are willing, through cooperative effort, to achieve the best possible performance, the rehearsal will be a success. The singer and accompa-nist should discuss interpretive ideas verbally first, and then come to some agreement following some attempts at different interpretive readings of the song. Each must be open-minded and willing to try the ideas of the other. Although both may be open regarding likes and dislikes of interpretive ideas in the studio, once they take the stage for a perform-ance, they must be absolutely supportive of one another. There will be no acknowledgment of musi-cal or technical errors on the part of either musician during a performance. On the performance stage, each must demonstrate to the audience an obvious admiration and respect for the other.

As a singer generally sings from memory, and the accompanist has the music to refer to, when the singer experiences the occasional memory slip, the accompanist can be a big help, in repeating a phrase, or coming to a recognizable cadence. This is one of the most difficult aspects of the accompa-nist's job, and requires intimate knowledge of the music, text, and the interpretive direction the singer has chosen to follow. Generally, singers wish to rehearse more for a performance than other musi-cians. Throughout the extensive rehearsal period, the accompanist should gain a very firm knowledge of interpretation, musical phrasing, breath require-ments, and perhaps vocal technical inefficiencies. Together, the singer and accompanist learn to listen and interact in a manner suggesting the intimate shared musical knowledge they possess. When the team of singer and accompanist have reached this level, they will be quite comfortable on the stage together. It is worth the extra time and effort to try to achieve this state.

Below is a list of musical and interpretive com-ponents, which should be discussed within rehearsals for a recital or performance. This is just a suggestive list, and is not exclusive. There are many other things that might be beneficial to discuss, and both the singer and accompanist should remain open to communication of ideas. Both must remain patient and understanding as each works out technical and interpretive aspects of the music.

1. Tempo and variations of tempo (rubato)
2. Composer's interpretive markings

3. The use of vocal effects such as portamento, straight tone, breathy tone, and so on
4. Breath markings and phrasing
5. Stylistically correct performance practice
6. Length of pauses to be taken between songs (particularly within a song cycle)
7. The interpretation of dynamic markings
8. The use of any overtly dramatic gestures involving the accompanist
9. The approach to and departure from the stage
10. Accepting audience applause (bows and acknowledgment).

THE "NUTS AND BOLTS" OF A PERFORMANCE

Performance Attire

Your choice of attire depends on the type of program or recital you will be singing of course, but there are some general rules which you can use as a guideline. *The Art of the Song Recital* (Emmons, Sonntag) has a full chapter on *Recital Tactics and Strategies* which the young singer will find extremely helpful in making decisions regarding attire, makeup, hair styles, and so forth. Following is a summary of some of those guidelines, reprinted by permission of Waveland Press, Inc. from Shirlee Emmons and Stanley Sonntag's *The Art of the Song Recital* (first edition, Long Grove, IL; Waveland Press, Inc., 1979 [reissued 2001]. All rights reserved). Every aspiring professional singer should own a copy of this book, and refer to it frequently in the preparation of a recital or professional performance.

A Formal Appearance (Recital or Orchestral Soloist): MEN

Men should generally wear, either a formal black tuxedo, tails, or a dark suit and tie for an evening recital performance or when appearing as a soloist with an orchestra. Ties should always be somewhat conservative, and must be comfortable around the neck so as not to inhibit vocal technique. Emmons suggests that males err on the side of conservatism in choosing a look for the stage. The male singer

wants a look that projects elegance rather than the avant garde, so as not to offend the more conservative members of the audience. Your attire should not detract from your performance, but should add to it.

All parts of the outfit should fit comfortably and be clean and neatly pressed. Coat and pants should be properly tailored, with pants being a bit on the long side. The fit of the suit coat should allow for comfortable arm motion so that interpretive gestures can be achieved with ease. The most conservative look would include a white long sleeve wing tip collar shirt with black button studs. If the recital or performance is a lengthy one, men might consider having a second shirt to change into following the intermission so that they feel fresh and approachable at the end of the recital. Tux shirts in colors and with ruffles are available, but give a much more casual look to the outfit. *You don't want to look like you're going to the prom, but rather like you are a singer who is ready for the professional stage.* Be sure that socks (which should always be dark) and shoes (dress shoes, not rubber-soled shoes meant for day wear) match the color of the suit. If you are wearing tails or a tuxedo, shoes must be black. Shoes should always be well-shined and heeled.

Men have the choice of wearing a cummerbund or a vest on the stage. Either is acceptable; however, the male singer must be sure to choose a vest length that does not leave a gap between the waistline and the bottom of the vest. Vests have a tendency to slim the singer and are perhaps more comfortable for singing than the cummerbund for the heavier singer. Vests should be constructed of the same color and fabric as the tuxedo.

A Formal Appearance (Recital or Orchestral Soloist): WOMEN

Women should generally wear a full-length gown for an evening performance. There are many fabric types and styles to choose from, and each individual must make the correct choice for her body type. In general, Emmons/Sonntag suggest in *The Art of the Song Recital* that women:

1. Coordinate dress color with the accompanist if the accompanist is a female. Choose a color that is becoming to your complexion, and test it

under the stage lights. *Darker colors project better under stage lights than pastels.*

2. Check both front and back to be sure you will present a professional image when entering and leaving the stage area.

3. Check the fit carefully so that you will have freedom of expression for interpretive gestures, and breath support.

4. Don't choose a dress with such a low décolleté (plunging necklines) that it distracts from your performance demeanor.

5. Consider the size of the auditorium; you want a dress that will make you look and feel elegant and professional.

6. Be sure that clothes do not fit too tightly; this will cause wrinkles, and will attract attention to the technical aspects of your performance, especially if you are not a fully trained singer.

7. Remember that dull fabrics subtract body weight and shiny fabrics add body weight. Dark colors subtract body weight and light colors add body weight. Large patterns in fabric add size to the figure, whereas solid colors subtract weight and slim the body.

Female singers should attempt to match shoe color to dress color and be sure that shoes are well broken in; appropriate scuffing on the bottom of newer shoes will keep you from slipping on a freshly polished stage floor. Do not wear heels that are higher than you are accustomed to, as they will be uncomfortable and will impact your overall performance. For the same reason, "open toe" shoes are generally uncomfortable on the stage because the singer must stand for a long period of time in one position, and the feet will swell due to the heat on the stage. Jewelry should be conservative and should complement the chosen gown, not detract from it. Do not choose earrings, which dangle and shine so much that they will sway with your every move and distract the audience from your interpretive presentation.

Semiformal Attire (Afternoon Performance, Master Class, or Audition Attire): MEN

Either a dark suit or a dark blazer and pants are appropriate. Sport jackets are generally felt to be too casual. A turtleneck seems to be an acceptable alternative to a shirt and tie these days if the singer can wear it well. Turtlenecks are becoming on tall men with long necks, but not on short men with short necks and stocky bodies. Be fairly conservative with colors. If you choose to wear the blazer and slacks, note that this will make you appear shorter—if you are a tall man, this may be perfectly acceptable, but for the shorter male attempting to look taller, the look will be wrong. If the coat and pants are of the same color, the effect is to make the singer look taller.

As with the formal performance, a darker, solid color, vested look that fits well and is clean and neatly pressed will make the most elegant presentation. Be sure that the shirt and tie are conservative, using the guidelines above, and that dark socks and dark well-polished shoes complement the ensemble. Be sure that your socks are long enough that if you must be seated on the stage, no leg skin should be visible.

Semiformal Attire (Afternoon Performance, Master Class, or Audition Attire): WOMEN

For female singers, a street-length (below the knee to midcalf) dress or stylish skirt and blouse are appropriate. Wearing a skirt and blouse will generally look somewhat more casual and may have a tendency to make you look shorter if they are belted. Wear colors that look nice on you, but are not difficult to look at for long periods of time. In general, women can use the same guidelines regarding colors, fabric types, and patterns as given previously for the formal attire. Shoes should be carefully coordinated with the outfit, and nylons should be flesh colored, or darker to coordinate with the ensemble. As with the formal attire, all attire should be well tailored, clean, and neatly pressed.

College or University Performance Class Attire (Recital Class or In-School Performance): MEN

A suit is always acceptable, but a sport coat and pants with shirt and tie or turtleneck are appropriate. Use the same rules that you would use for a semiformal performance or audition as listed above and you will be comfortable on the stage.

College or University Performance Class Attire (Recital Class or In-School Performance): WOMEN

A street-length (below the knee to midcalf) conservative dress or skirt and blouse are appropriate. Be careful that the length of the dress or skirt is long enough to compensate for the fact that the stage is above the audience. Be a bit on the conservative side, and utilize the information as presented under the semiformal performance or audition as listed above.

Remember, the better you feel about your appearance, the easier it will be to walk out on stage feeling good about yourself and confident in your ability to perform.

Look well = Feel well = Sing well!

SOME DRESS "DO'S AND DON'TS"

1. Never wear a tuxedo without a tie.
2. Never wear colors that will make you look "washed out" (for example, the color yellow under bright lights makes nearly everyone look somewhat ill).
3. Check the color of the stage curtains to be sure your outfit doesn't "clash."
4. Never wear uncomfortably tight shoes or clothing—it gets hot on stage and clothes and shoes will get tighter!
5. Plan a rehearsal in your recital attire—especially shoes.

THE FINISHING TOUCHES: HAIR AND MAKE-UP

Both men and women need to remember that a becoming hairstyle is much more appropriate than attempting to wear whatever style is the current fad. Your hair should be clean, neatly combed, and should never cover your face, particularly your eyes. Styles that allow portions of your hair to fall onto your face will be extremely distracting for the audience, and will detract from your overall performance

and concentration. Your eyes are the most expressive part of your face, and can really help you with conveying the text and music—do not let your hair get in the way of this.

All females should wear make-up under stage lights, especially if all the lighting is "white." In some performance halls, the lighting technicians will insert gels into the lighting fixtures, giving you extra color. You can check to see if this is the case, by looking up at the lights, it will be evident if gels are in place or not. Pure white light will "wash you out" and make it very difficult for the audience to distinguish your features. The amount of make-up depends on the size of the performance hall; a small space obviously requires less make-up than a hall that seats 2,000 people. Your make-up, like your attire and hair, should always enhance your appearance and make you appear elegant and professional. In general, you wish to accentuate your good features, especially your eyes. I suggest that, a few weeks prior to a big recital, you go to a professional make-up artist for suggestions and ideas. Sometimes professional photographers can refer you to such people for suggestions in how and what make-up to use. Think somewhat conservatively regarding make-up as you did with your attire.

CHECKING OUT THE PERFORMANCE SPACE

Rehearsals in the Performance Hall Prior to the Performance

In this regard, again please refer to the Emmons/Sonntag *The Art of the Song Recital* for much more detail. Some of the following information has been reprinted by permission of Waveland Press, Inc. from Shirlee Emmons and Stanley Sonntag's *The Art of the Song Recital* (first edition, Long Grove, IL; Waveland Press, Inc., 1979 [reissued 2001]. All rights reserved).

In general, every singer should plan at least one rehearsal in the recital hall or room where he or she will perform and to check the stage floor for obstructions, slippery spots, or loose boards. Your accompanist will need to check the tuning and action of the piano to make sure it is in perfect working order. Be sure to check the piano bench as well to determine if there are squeaks or adjustment problems, and be sure there is a chair for your page-turner if you have one.

You will want to check the acoustics of the hall, in order to decide what the best position for the piano and yourself will be for the performance, so that you may take full advantage of the performing area and hall acoustics. You will want to check the lighting to be sure the stage is well lit, and check that the lighting gels are appropriate for a recital. Also, it will be important to find the singer's and accompanist's dressing rooms, determine if you can vocalize in the dressing room, or if you should move to a "green room" for this purpose. Locate the quickest and most comfortable route to the stage from the dressing room. Be sure you have access to a bathroom and water. Of course you will want to sing in the hall so that you have an idea of how it feels and sounds to you and your accompanist, and to determine if you can hear and communicate well with each other. Making these determinations may seem inconsequential in light of all the research and preparation that goes into the musical preparation, but it will make you feel more comfortable and in control of the situation so that your concentration can be placed fully on the performance at hand.

STAGE DEPORTMENT

Getting On and Off the Stage Gracefully

On the subject of stage deportment, singers should remember that practice makes perfect. Singers are willing to spend hours vocalizing in a practice room, but when it comes time for the performance, they seem to feel that knowledge of appropriate movement on the stage should be automatic. This is definitely not the case. Singers must practice their entrances to and exits from the stage just as they practice every other aspect of the performance in order to feel perfectly comfortable. It is also wise to plan and practice these moves to and from the stage with the accompanist and a page-turner if there will

be one, so that there are no collisions on stage during the performance.

Always plan rehearsal sessions in the shoes you will wear for the performance to be sure they are comfortable. It is difficult enough to concentrate on singing and interpreting without the added burden of pinching shoes. When walking onto the stage, the singer always precedes the accompanist regardless of gender. Both performers walk in front of the piano, generally entering from the stage right side, so that they enter at the keyboard end of the piano. Then, the accompanist moves closer to the keyboard, and the singer moves to the center of the stage. When both have arrived in the designated space, they bow together.

When entering the stage, smile and act as though you would not want to be anywhere else at this moment. Remember, you like to sing and you have something of importance to present to your audience, or you wouldn't be here. The audience wouldn't be there either if they didn't want to hear you sing. Walk quickly and confidently to your position; turn to the audience, acknowledging their welcoming applause with a bow. If you learn to lift your sternum and assume an attitude of confidence, you will have set yourself up for a successful performance before even one note is played or sung.

At the close of any program section, or at the conclusion of the program, as the performers are leaving the stage, the accompanist will wait for the singer to move past him or her and then follow close behind. If the singer is a male and the accompanist a female, it is common for the singer to allow the accompanist to exit ahead of him.

Where Should I Stand?

Formal and Informal Recitals with Piano

When singing a formal recital with piano, it is customary for the singer to stand in the "crook" or bow of the piano (Figure 9–1). This position allows for communication between singer and accompanist, is a good place from which to hear the piano clearly, allows the accompanist to hear and see your breaths, and gestures, and allows you various options for hand positioning, such as resting one hand on the

Figure 9-1. Recital singer with piano. It is customary for the classical singer to take a position in the bow or "crook" of the grand piano; this allows for excellent communication with both the accompanist and the audience, and provides a good place from which the singer may hear the piano clearly.

piano, and so on. Do not, however, use the piano as a crutch. It should not be leaned on nor should the singer drape him or herself on it. This latter type of positioning may be used sparingly for specific interpretive reasons. Singing an art song recital requires musical and literary interpretation of the highest caliber. This interpretation should be evident to the audience in the vocal sound, on your face, and from your physical gestures. However, this is not an operatic or "staged" performance and thus does not require a great deal of movement or gesturing. A few well-chosen hand gestures will serve the recitalist better than many dramatic movements that might actually detract from the overall performance. All gestures should be in keeping with the appropriate historical style and performance practice, and should aid the singer in conveying the text and music.

Singing with an Orchestra or Band

It is common for a singer to stand to the conductor's left when singing with an orchestra (near the con-

cert master) or band (near the first clarinetist generally). This gives both singer and conductor good communication possibilities throughout the performance, and allows the singer to hear the full orchestration. It is best if the conductor is not behind the singer but just to the singer's left. On some smaller stages, it is occasionally necessary, but not suggested, that the singer be farther forward than the conductor. This makes it very difficult for the conductor and singer to communicate, and should be avoided if at all possible.

USING YOUR SPEAKING VOICE FROM THE STAGE

Singers sometimes have an aversion to speaking from the stage; they are more comfortable singing, because they have rehearsed the singing more. If you are uncomfortable because the singing has been practiced more than the speaking, then there is a simple solution—practice the spoken portions too. In any case, when you speak from the stage, remember the following rules:

1. Support your speaking voice as you would your singing voice.
2. Enunciate clearly and carefully as you do when you sing.
3. Say what you have to say as precisely as possible in the least amount of time. The audience is here to listen to you sing.
4. Project your voice with breath energy to the back of the performance hall.
5. Have the same confidence about your speaking voice that you have about your singing voice!

HOW LONG SHOULD I WAIT BEFORE I BEGIN SINGING?

First of all, remember that time on stage seems to move at a different pace. This is because of the amount of adrenalin present for a performance. If things are going very well, it may seem that a one-hour recital has gone by in a "flash." On the other hand, if you have a memory lapse, this lapse may seem to go on for several minutes, when it may in reality have been a few brief seconds. The key words here are relax, concentrate, and breathe!

After entering the stage, acknowledge your audience, and take your position in the bow of the piano or at the conductor's left. Lower your eyes and take time for two or three good deep breaths. Think about the first song you will sing, its opening phrase, the poem, the emotion to be conveyed, any specific dynamic markings or musical phrases you have discussed in rehearsal. Think carefully about the character singing the song and attempt to become that character. All of this will take under 15 seconds, during which time the audience has had a chance to settle into their seats, look at the first section of your program, and glance at a program note or two. They should now be ready for you to begin. When the room seems quiet and you have had time to set all of these things in motion, lift your head, letting your accompanist know that you are ready to begin. Letting your accompanist know you are ready to begin may be as simple as this lift of your head, a slight nod, a smile, or some other small gesture, which should be prearranged during the rehearsal preparation for the performance.

An accompanist/singer team will have carefully rehearsed the beginning of each song and will be sure to communicate verbally with one another a good starting gesture. These gestures should be very simple and should never detract from the mood that is set up as the singer lifts his or her head. A nod, for example, should not be curt or quickly executed if the song is to be slow and introspective. The audience sees everything the singer does as part of the performance, so gestures must be memorized and practiced right along with the recital program and should also convey meaning to the audience. A simple smile, slight nod of the head, lifting the head, or focusing on one area of the audience section is enough to tell the accompanist or conductor and audience that you are ready to begin.

Years ago, a young baritone who was studying with me gave his first art song recital. The program was well prepared, and everything went as planned, but his parents had never been to a formal vocal recital before. Following the recital, after the congratulations had been given, I overheard this student's father ask him what he was doing when his head was down like that before he began to sing. The student replied: "I was calling 911!" Even though now we look back and laugh about this, it is not atypical for a young student on the stage for the first time to feel this sort of anxiousness. A certain amount of anxiety is going to be present when a student presents a full length recital for the first time—the moments just prior to beginning a new song cycle or song group are extremely important to the establishment of the control necessary for fine artistic singing.

RELATING TO THE AUDIENCE

Singing a recital is quite different in this aspect than singing to a nightclub audience or performing with a wedding band. In the last two instances, the popular singer is expected to "sell" the song and thus sometimes sings directly to a particular audience member, making direct eye contact with that person. This is not generally the case when singing a formal classical voice recital. A recital is almost always presented on a stage or in an area set up in a manner that divides the audience from the performer, and defines the roles of each. A popular singer seems to attempt to put him or herself on the same level as the audience, making members of the audience feel they are right next to the singer, that the singer is there just for them. The popular performer tries very hard to draw the audience in and to make them feel they are a part of the performance. A classical singer's responsibility is to interpret the words and the music of the poet and composer, and to convey these to the audience to the best of his or her ability. To do this, the singer spends years studying vocal technique, music history, theory, foreign languages, performance practice, and style, as well as doing in-depth research on the compositions to be presented. All of this study and research allows the singer to feel that he or she is singing the song to the exact specifications of the poet and composer. It is the singer's responsibility to convey the message of the song and the poem as best he can without really adding his own "style."

Thus, the classical singer never really "sells" a song. As a matter of fact, most classical singers feel that because the song is well composed and the singer is interpreting what the composer and poet wrote, the song needs no "selling." The audience, then, is there to experience and hear this particular singer's interpretation of these songs. Members of the audience do not expect the same type of "delivery" they expect in a more popular type music program; they may even be offended if a singer attempts to "sell" a song by Schumann or Brahms or one of the many classical art song composers.

This difference has a lot to do with the performer's delivery of classical recital music. It allows the singer to, on occasion, look off to the side, seemingly ignoring the audience, in order to capture a particular ethereal moment. It does occasionally allow for direct eye contact with members of the audience, but generally the singer focuses his eyes directly above the heads of the audience. This gives the audience members the impression that there is eye contact when there really is not, and it is not as distracting for the younger singer particularly.

A singer must decide what facial expressions or glances will best convey the meaning of the text and music throughout the song and then actually choreograph these into the presentation. Facial and hand gestures are rarely automatic for a singer and must be studied and practiced along with the song. Remember that the singer and accompanist are partners in this interpretation. Both must work closely together in rehearsals and during the recital to be sure the interpretation is presented well as a team.

Figure 9–2. Formal bow from the stage. Singers must be sure to thank their audience members by giving a full bow as demonstrated in this drawing. Notice that the singer's eyes and head are down, rather than looking up at the audience.

ACKNOWLEDGING APPLAUSE AND BOWING FROM THE STAGE

Your exit from the stage is as important as your entrance and the performance is not over until you have returned to your dressing room. Thus, your acknowledgment of audience appreciation is extremely important and will greatly influence your audience when they are deciding if they would like to attend another of your performances. When acknowledging applause, always bow from the waist (Figure 9–2), allowing your head to lower and your eyes to see the floor. Allow your hands to fall gracefully together in front of you or you may, if you are tall, leave one hand on the piano. It is not necessary or advisable to keep your eyes and head up as you bow. The bow is a thank you for the applause

and a "humbling" of one's self in the eyes of the audience. For ladies, curtsies are generally used only on the theater or opera stage and not on the recital stage with the exception of the great divas.

It is certainly easy to acknowledge applause when you feel you have given a good performance. A smile naturally comes to your lips, you feel happy, and you bow gracefully. What about those times when you don't feel you did your best? At these times also you must smile and give a graceful bow. Remember that no matter what goes on in your mind, the average audience member is there to see you succeed. They want to see you do your best, so mistakes are quickly erased from their minds as they move on to more positive thoughts. They are not there to criticize you, but to cheer you on. No matter what kind of a performance you feel you have given, give your audience a smile, a gracious bow, and thank them for their support. In some instances, a smile and slight nod of the head is enough, such as when the audience applauds in the middle of a song cycle or an extended work. This lets them know you appreciate the applause, but do not wish to interrupt the continuing emotional flow of the work. When you have completed the song group, cycle, or complete work, give a full bow in acknowledgment of applause. Do not forget to acknowledge your accompanist graciously as well! It is customary to turn directly to the pianist, and "give the stage" to him or her for a full bow, as in Figure 9-3.

It is always recommended that you give the audience as much help as possible within the written program regarding appropriate places for applause. You might write something like: Please hold your applause until the end of a group of songs or the end of a song cycle. This will help audience members, who are unfamiliar with the traditions of the art song recital, know exactly when to applaud, so that they too will be more comfortable in attending your performances in the future.

Overall, good stage deportment requires the use of common sense along with knowledge of what

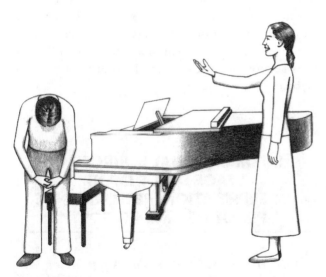

Figure 9-3. Acknowledging the accompanist. Singers should always acknowledge their accompanist at the end of a group of songs, a song cycle, and certainly at the end of a program. Turn your body completely toward the accompanist and gesture toward him or her so audience members know they are applauding for the accompanist.

the common practices of performance are in your area. Be gracious and respectful to the composer, the poet, your accompanist, the audience, and yourself and you can't fail.

BACKSTAGE AT THE PERFORMANCE

Here, I just wish to give singers a few pointers on backstage etiquette, and some suggestions for maintaining your composure and concentration throughout the performance. First of all, remember that the backstage personnel have a very important job to do; they are in charge of moving props or equipment on the stage, setting and operating the lights, setting and operating any video or audio equipment, and so forth. They have been taught to respect you as the artist performer. You must also respect these important people; attempt to stay out of the way of moving sets, lighting instruments, and sound equipment; be polite; and do not expect them to be your servants. Do not ever move anything on a stage that has been set for a performance without consulting with the stage manager. Generally, you will find the stage manager and stagehands very helpful and polite. Backstage personnel appreciate and respect your art and you as the artist, and you must respect and appreciate their art as well.

Shirlee Emmons and Stanley Sonntag have given some wonderful advice in regard to the do's and don'ts backstage (p. 162) during and immediately prior to a performance. These are repeated here for your convenience, but I highly recommend that you read their entire book, particularly Chapter 8, entitled Recital Tactics and Strategies (pp. 149–170). Reprinted by permission of Waveland Press, Inc. from Shirlee Emmons and Stanley Sonntag's *The Art of the Song Recital* (first edition, Long Grove, IL; Waveland Press, Inc., 1979 [reissued 2001]. All rights reserved).

The Do Not List!

1. Do not allow visitors backstage before the concert or during the intermission.
2. Do not waste your energies by talking.

3. Do not fret about letting down your voice teacher.
4. Do not try to be "great." Just try to use well the skills you have spent so much time acquiring—vocal, musical, dramatic.
5. Do not chastise yourself about your responsibility toward family or friends.
6. Do not arrive at the hall so early that you become psychologically drained before performing nor so late that, through anxiety, you will lose composure.

The Do List!

1. Quiet concentrated reviewing of musical and technical points from the recital is helpful.
2. Sing full voice before going out, if it has (during the rehearsals and rehearsal concerts) been judged to be useful or necessary.
3. In short, keep your mind on what you are going to do and not on what might happen.

PUBLIC RELATIONS

Janice Papolos has written a very insightful book regarding the business side of establishing yourself as a professional performer, entitled *The Performing Artist's Handbook*. This book will be helpful for singers and instrumentalists as well, and deals with the careful development and printing of a resumé, publicity photos, professional correspondence, music and theatrical unions, demo tapes, management, publicity, audition attire, and more. This is a must have book for anyone planning on becoming a professional performer, and is available at most major libraries and bookstores. You will find full bibliographic information regarding this book at the end of this chapter.

In general, student singers need to remember that what they put in print prior to a recital will give the public and the audience a particular impression regarding their talents and personality. If you are publicizing a recital, make the materials as professional as possible. If you are writing program notes for a concert, do the necessary research, and make the notes an educational experience for your audience. Do not wait until the last moment and "throw something together" because you have run out of time. If you present a professional image prior to the performance, your audience will anticipate a professional performance!

When you are ready to begin auditioning and doing competitions, you must also remember that the paperwork is your reader's first impression of you—the singer! Be sure that all the information on applications is typed or printed as neatly as possible. If you have only one copy of an audition or competition application, make a photocopy and save the original so that you will not have to erase or whiteout mistakes. Always be sure that applications are presented on time and have been carefully prepared. If you have questions regarding the application, ask your voice teacher, or use the contact phone number listed on the application. Many students have been disqualified from competitions or auditions due to late or improperly completed applications. Don't let this happen to you. There are many things to remember when attempting to present a polished and professional image as a performer that have little to do with your talent, but each one is essential to your success. Be sure that you learn to perform the business duties of your profession as well as you learn to sing. Following this section is a list of some helpful books on the subject of performance.

INFORMATIONAL SOURCES ON STAGE DEPORTMENT, INTERPRETATION, PERFORMANCE PRACTICE, AND SO FORTH

Balk, H. Wesley. *The Complete Singer-Actor: Training for Music Theater*, Second edition, University of Minnesota Press, Minneapolis, 1988. ISBN 0-8166-1418-0 (pbk)

Balk, H. Wesley. *Performing Power A New Approach for the Singer-Actor*, University of Minnesota Press, Minneapolis, 1985. ISBN 0-8166-1367-1 (pbk)

Bernac, Pierre. *The Interpretation of French Song*, W. W. Norton & Company, Inc., New York, 1978. ISBN 0-393-00878-9

Brown, Howard Mayer, & Sadie, Stanley, Editors. *The Norton/Grove Handbooks in Music Performance Practice-Music After 1600*, W. W. Norton & Company, Inc. New York, 1990. ISBN 0-393-02808-9

Craig, David. *On Singing Onstage*, Schirmer Books, New York, 1978. ISBN 0-02-870580-7 (pbk)

Crocker, Richard L. *A History of Musical Style*, Dover Publications, Inc. New York, 1986. ISBN 0-486-25029-6

Cyr, Mary. *Performing Baroque Music*, Amadeus Press, Portland, OR, 1992. ISBN 0-931340-49-7

Dornemann, Joan (with Maria Ciaccia). *Complete Preparation—A Guide to Auditioning for Opera*, Excalibur Publishing, New York, 1992. ISBN 0-9627226-3-4 (pbk)

Emmons, Shirlee, & Sonntag, Stanley. *The Art of the Song Recital*, Waveland Press, Long Grove, IL, 2001. ISBN 1-57766-220-2

Harrison, Donna Esselstyn. *Poetry in Song Literature: A Handbook for Students of Singing*, Wm. Caxton Ltd., Sister Bay, WI, 1989. ISBN 0-940473-07-0

Kimball, Carol. *Song: A Guide to Style and Literature*, Pst. . . Inc., Redmond, WA, 1996. ISBN 1-8777761-68-0

Kirkpatrick, Carol. *"Aria Ready" The Business of Singing*, Bancroft Publications, 2003. ISBN 0-9770524-3-5

Lehmann, Lilli, *How to Sing*, Dover Publications, Inc., New York, 1993. ISBN 0-486-27501-9 (pbk)

Lehmann, Lotte. *More Than Singing, The Interpretation of Songs*, Translated by Frances Holden) Dover Publications, Inc., New York, 1985. ISBN 0-486-24831-3

Lehmann, Lotte. *Eighteen Song Cycles, Studies in Their Interpretation*, Praeger Publishers, New York, 1972. LC 73-171026

Miller, Philip (translator). *The Ring of Words— An Anthology of Song Texts*, W. W. Norton & Company, Inc. 1973. ISBN 0-393-00677-8

Miller, Richard. *On the Art of Singing*, Oxford University Press, New York, 1996. ISBN 0-19-509825-0

Moore, Douglas. *A Guide to Musical Styles From Madrigal to Modern Music*, W. W. Norton & Company, New York, 1962. ISBN 0-393-00200-4

Papolos, Janice. *The Performing Artist's Handbook*, Writers Digest Books, Cincinnati, OH, 1984. ISBN 0-89879-143-X

Prawer, S. S. (editor/translator). *The Penguin Book of Lieder*, Penguin Books, Baltimore, 1965.

Vinquist, Mary & Zaslaw, Neal, Editors, *Performance Practice: A Bibliography*, W. W. Norton & Company, Inc. New York, 1970. ISBN 0-393-00550-X

IMPORTANT TERMS AND CONCEPTS TO UNDERSTAND

Liberal arts

Performance practice

Historical style

Exotic language

Interpreting poetry and music

Portamento

Song cycle

Stage deportment

Backstage etiquette

Program notes

Publicity materials

REFERENCES

Emmons, S., & Sonntag, S. (2001). *The art of the song recital*. Long Grove, IL: Waveland Press.

Lehmann, L. (1993). *How to Sing.* New York: Dover.

Papolos, J. (1984). *The performing artist's handbook.* Cincinnati, OH: Writers Digest Books.

Appendix I

MUSICAL TERMINOLOGY FOR THE VOICE STUDENT

The following terms appear in music frequently and should become part of your vocabulary as a singing musician. Try to memorize as many of them as possible. Always consult a music dictionary for terms appearing in your music, which you do not understand!

TEMPO (THE RATE OF SPEED OF THE MUSIC)

Term	Meaning of the Term
Lento	Very slow
Grave	Slow
Largo	Slow and broad
Adagio	At ease, leisurely
Andante	Moderately slow (a walking tempo)
Andantino	A little faster than Andante
Moderato	The mid point, moderately
Allegretto	A little faster than Moderato (a little slower than Allegro)
Allegro	Merry, lively (a relatively fast tempo)
Vivace	With life and energy (faster than Allegro)
Presto	Quick (a very fast tempo)
Prestissimo	As fast as possible

When a metronome marking is indicated, it is advisable to check the metronome for an accurate tempo—especially if the marking is that of the composer, and not the editor of the music. Every musician should own a metronome and use it regularly in practice.

CHANGES IN TEMPO (TERMS WHICH ALTER THE SPEED OF THE MUSIC)

Term	Abbreviation	Meaning of the Term
Accelerando	Accel.	Getting faster
Stringendo	String.	Pressing forward
Piu mosso		More motion (Faster)
Allargando	Allar.	Gradual broadening of the tempo
Rallentando	Rall.	Gradually becoming slower
Ritardando	Rit.	Gradually becoming slower
Meno mosso		Less motion (slower)
A Tempo		At the original tempo (found after a Rit., Rall., etc.)
Ad libitum	Ad. lib.	At the performers pleasure (take time if you wish)
A piacere		As you wish (tempo at the discretion of performer

DYNAMICS (HOW LOUD OR SOFT)

Term	Abbreviation		Meaning of the Term
Pianissimo	PP	(pp)	Very soft
Piano	P	(p)	Soft
Mezzo piano	MP	(mp)	Moderately soft
Mezzo forte	MF	(mf)	Moderately loud
Forte	F	(f)	Loud
Fortissimo	FF	(ff)	Very loud
Fortississimo	FFF	(fff)	Extremely loud

These terms are quite subjective and will change according to the century in which the music is written, the style of the music, and the interpretation of the piece.

CHANGES IN DYNAMICS

Term	Abbreviation	Meaning of Term
Crescendo	Cresc.	Gradually louder
Sforzando	Sfz.	Louder, accented
Rinforzando	Rfz.	Re-enforcing the tone (forceful)
Forzando	Ffz.	Forcing the tone
Descrescendo	Decresc.	Gradually softer
Morendo		Dying away
Perdendosi	Perd.	Dying away

TERMS REFERRING TO STYLE

Term	Meaning of Term
A cappella	In church style—unaccompanied
Affetuoso	Affectionately
Agitato	In an agitated manner
Animato	Animated, lively
Ben marcato	Well accented
Cantabile	In a singing style - legato
Con amore	With love
Con brio	With vigor or spirit
Con expressione	With expression
Con fuoco	With fire
Con forza	With force
Con grazia	With grace
Con moto	With motion
Dolce	Sweetly
Grandioso	Grandly, majestically
Marcato	Accented
Rubato	An elastic, flexible tempo involving slight accelerandos and ritardandos that alternate according to the requirements of musical expression.
Semplice	Simply
Serioso	Seriously
Sostenuto	Sustained

TERMS USED TO ALTER THE MEANING OF OTHER TERMS

Term	Meaning of Term
Poco a poco	Little by little
Assai	Always, very
Attacca	Go on at once without pause
Con	With
Ma	But
Mezzo	Moderate, Half
Non	Not
Troppo	Too much

For example, a composer may write:
Allegro ma non troppo—the translation would be: Merry, Lively (Fast), but not too fast

Can you translate the following examples?

Morendo poco a poco   Molto espressivo con rubato

Appendix II

MUSIC READING SKILLS FOR BEGINNING SINGERS/MUSICIANS

This appendix will help you begin to understand the language of music. In order to be a competent and skillful singer, you will need to go well beyond the information presented here. Most colleges and universities and many high schools offer courses in the fundamentals of music reading as well as advanced coursework in music theory and composition. A student wishing to become a singer should definitely enroll in such courses as well as courses in keyboard studies. Gaining knowledge in both areas will be vital to your development as a musician. If such courses are not available to you, there are also many self-help books and computer software packages which are designed to allow you to teach yourself the basics.

For now, study the following information and use as much of it as is comfortable for you. Singers should never be dependent on someone else to teach them their notes for songs and arias, nor should they be dependent on recordings of the songs they wish to sing. It would be expensive indeed to hire a musician to teach you every note of every song you wish to sing, and it would not give you the musical freedom you need for interpretation to learn each of your songs from a recording. So, begin now to learn how to read music and to develop your skills as a singer/musician.

THE LANGUAGE OF MUSIC: THE STAFF

Music is written on a five line and four space staff as shown here:

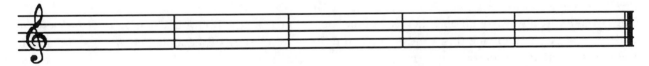

Composers utilize the lines and spaces of the staff to indicate the relative high and low pitches of music. The higher the placement of the note on the staff, the higher the pitch; the lower the placement, the lower the pitch. For example:

Low   High

THE LANGUAGE OF MUSIC: THE CLEFS

At the beginning of each staff you will find a symbol, which is referred to as a *Clef*. There are several different clefs, which have been used throughout the history of music. The most common clef is the *Treble Clef* (or *G Clef*). The Treble Clef looks like this on a staff:

The staff is known as the *Treble Staff* when a treble clef is placed on it. The treble clef has a loop, which establishes the pitch G on the second line of the treble staff, and this is why it is also known as the G clef. As notes are named after the first seven letters of the alphabet (A through G), we can now see where each note is placed on the treble staff as follows:

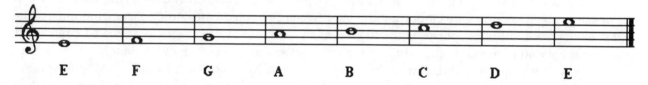

For singers, the treble clef and the treble staff are generally used for the vocal line, placed above the piano accompaniment. To help you remember the names of the notes on the treble staff, many different mnemonics have been created. For example, the first letter of the notes placed on the lines (from bottom to top or, lowest to highest) **E**very **G**ood **B**oy **D**oes **F**ine. The first letter of the notes placed in the spaces (from bottom to top or, lowest to highest) spell the word **FACE**. Of course, eventually, you will want to memorize the names of each of the notes on the staff so you can recognize them quickly and without thinking.

Sometimes, when writing for lower men's voices, the composer will utilize the *Bass Clef* and *Bass Staff*. The Bass Clef looks like this:

The two dots are always found on either side of the fourth line from the bottom, which on the bass clef staff is the note F. Again, knowing this, we can utilize the first seven letters of the alphabet (A–G) and name all the notes on the Bass Clef staff as follows:

Of course there are mnemonics for the lines and spaces of the bass clef staff as well. The most common mnemonic for the first letters of the notes on the lines of the Bass Clef staff is: **G**ood **B**oys **D**o **F**ine **A**lways. The mnemonic for the notes found in the spaces is: **A**ll **C**ows **E**at **G**rass. Again, memorize the note names as quickly as you are able.

THE LANGUAGE OF MUSIC: THE GRAND STAFF

The treble staff and the bass staff can be joined together by a *brace* consisting of a straight line and a curved line—this is combination of the staves is then called a *Grand Staff*. This is the staff you are accustomed to seeing for piano music as well as for the accompaniment to your songs. Generally, the composer of songs places an additional treble staff over the top of this grand staff, and this is where the singer's line is found. Here's an example:

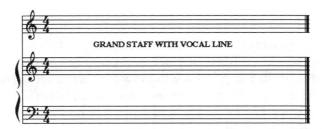

GRAND STAFF WITH VOCAL LINE

There is a note on the grand staff, which happens to be between the treble and bass staves (the plural of staff). This note is known as *Middle C*. This note can also be located on the piano keyboard—approximately in the middle of the 88 key piano keyboard. Below is a Grand Staff showing the Middle C.

Middle C

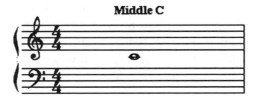

THE LANGUAGE OF MUSIC: LEGER LINES

There are many more notes available to the composer than those that can be placed directly on the grand staff. Pitches played by the flute and piccolo, for example, can be found far above the treble staff, and pitches played by the tuba and bass violin can be found below the bass staff. When a composer wishes to indicate these notes, she or he uses what is known as a *leger line*. This is a line, which helps us to extend the staff in either an upward or downward direction. Note the use of leger lines both below and above the staff in the following example:

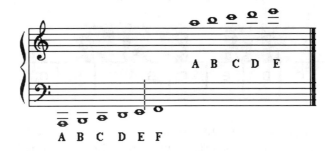

For the most part, singers utilize the treble or bass staves for the notes they sing. However, a coloratura soprano sings quite high above the treble staff, and a basso profundo sings below the staff. Some singers may occasionally find themselves singing notes written with leger lines, and some singers will use them frequently—this depends on your voice category.

THE LANGUAGE OF MUSIC: MORE ABOUT PITCH

So far, we have only spoken of pitch names contained on the white keys of the piano. What about the black keys? As you look at the keys of a piano, you will notice that there is a repeating pattern of white and black keys. As you move from one adjacent pitch to another (one piano key to the next), the distance between these pitches is termed a whole or half step. Moving from a white key to the adjacent black key on the right is moving a half step. Moving from the black key to the adjacent white key on the right is also a half step. Therefore, moving from one white key to the adjacent white key on the right (when there is a black key between them) is a whole step. Two black keys with a white key between is also a whole step, and two white keys without a black key between is a half step.

Flats

The black keys are named in relationship to the white keys. In musical notation, a flat sign lowers the pitch of a note by a half step. If we use the piano keyboard to visualize this concept, you will see that a black key to the left of a white key is a half step lower. Also, two adjacent white keys (E and F; B and C) are separated by a half step rather than a whole step. Thus, if we move from white key "D," to the black key on its left, we will find D flat (see diagram below).

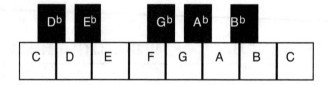

Sharps

A sharp raises the pitch of a note by a half step. Looking again at the simulated piano keyboard, we can see that the black key to the right of a white key is a half step higher. Thus, moving from white key "D" to the adjacent black key will give us "D" sharp (see diagram below).

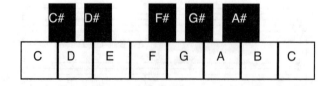

When comparing the examples for flats and sharps, you will notice that C# and Db are the same note as are D# and Eb, and so forth. When a composer uses flats or sharps in the music, however, they will appear before the note to which they are applied in a measure. If, within the same measure, the composer wishes to change the note back, he or she must use what is called a *natural sign*. A natural sign will be placed in front of the note to which it is applied. A natural sign cancels the effect of a flat or sharp which has preceded it in the same measure.

A natural sign looks like this:

KEY SIGNATURES

To make music reading easier, all the flats or sharps used throughout a composition are placed at the beginning of each line of a composition. This is called a *Key Signature*. If the key signature upon which the composition is based changes during the piece, the composer must either show a new key signature, or if it changes for only a short period, *accidentals* (sharp, flat, or natural signs) will appear before each note to be changed. A key signature with one flat (B flat) (see below) means that every B is sounded as B flat, a key signature with two flats (B flat and E flat) means all the B's and E's are flatted. The same concept applies to each of the flat and sharp signatures. Typical flat and sharp key signatures are shown below.

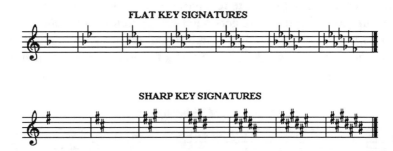

THE LANGUAGE OF MUSIC: DURATION OF SOUND AND SILENCE

Notes and Rests

The duration of musical sounds and silences (long or short) is indicated by different types of notes. The types of notes and rests are seen below. All the note and rest values are very carefully calculated mathematically. A course in fundamentals of music or music theory will help you to gain an understanding of how the notation system works.

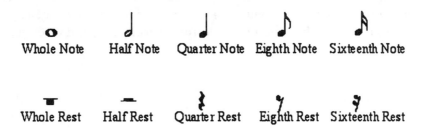

Measures and Bar Lines

Music is divided into equal parts called measures. Bar lines indicate the beginning and the end of a measure. The distance between the two bar lines is called a measure. There are many types of bar lines and each has a particular meaning. For example, a double bar line with a thin and a thick line tell the musicians that this is the end of a piece. A double bar line with two dots placed before it tells the musician to repeat a section either from a previous repeat sign, or all the way from the beginning as in the following examples:

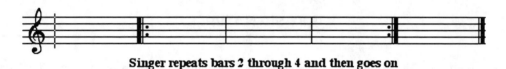

Singer repeats bars 2 through 4 and then goes on

Time Signatures

In order for the notes to have very specific duration values, the composer utilizes a *Time Signature*. Time signatures are placed at the beginning of a composition. Each contains two numbers placed in the form of a fraction (one number over the top of the other). The top number tells us the number of beats in each measure and the bottom number tells us which note receives one beat. For example, 4/4 tells us that there are four beats in each measure, and a quarter note gets one beat. Therefore, a whole note receives four beats, a half note two beats, and so on. The most common time signatures are seen below, but there are many possibilities; particularly in modern times when the duration of a note can be calculated very precisely with computers and digitalized equipment.

Some Examples of Time Signatures

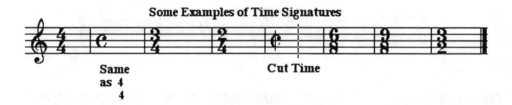

Another way of writing/reading time signatures can be seen below. Note that the bottom number or note head symbol always represents one beat in a measure.

$$\frac{2}{2} = \overset{2}{\underset{}{\jmath}} \qquad \frac{2}{4} = \overset{2}{\underset{}{\jmath}} \qquad \frac{4}{8} = \overset{4}{\underset{}{\jmath}}$$

Learning to count rhythms (the combination of sounds and silences) in a composition is very important and requires study on the part of the developing musician. It is frequently the rhythm of a song that makes it so exciting and interesting, and the rhythms must be interpreted exactly so that the composer's intentions are followed.

THE LANGUAGE OF MUSIC: MUSICAL SYMBOLS

Composers use certain musical symbols to guide the performer in the performance and correct interpretation of the music as written. Some of these symbols are shown, named, and defined for you below.

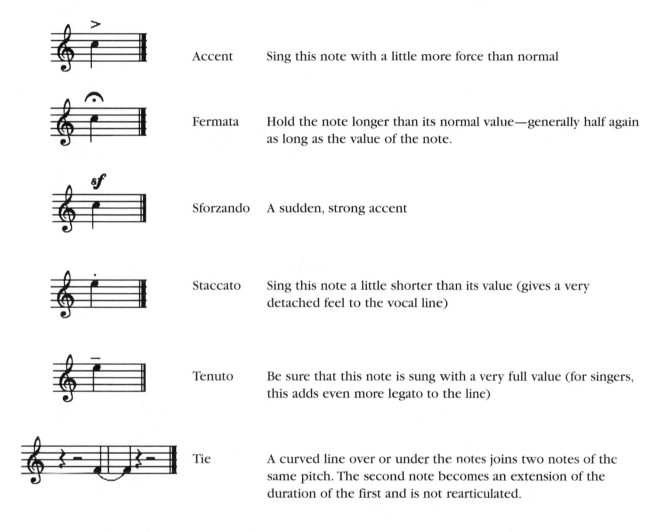

	Accent	Sing this note with a little more force than normal
	Fermata	Hold the note longer than its normal value—generally half again as long as the value of the note.
	Sforzando	A sudden, strong accent
	Staccato	Sing this note a little shorter than its value (gives a very detached feel to the vocal line)
	Tenuto	Be sure that this note is sung with a very full value (for singers, this adds even more legato to the line)
	Tie	A curved line over or under the notes joins two notes of the same pitch. The second note becomes an extension of the duration of the first and is not rearticulated.

Remember that the information presented here is only a beginning. In order to become an excellent musician and singer, you will want to take a course in the *Fundamentals of Music* and then go beyond to study music theory, develop your own keyboard skills, and study the history and style of music as well.

Appendix III
VOCAL PERFORMANCE EVALUATION

The form on the following page will be used to evaluate your vocal performances in this class. More important than the letter grade will be the comments made regarding certain aspects of your presentation. Of course, the most important initial priority in a class such as this will be on correct posture, diaphragmatic-costal breathing, and the correct production of vocal sound. Only after the vocal technique is somewhat comfortable will you be able to work intensely on interpretation and presentation. Do not be frustrated by the fact that you must think about the technique so much initially. Within a short period of time, with regular concentrated practice, you will be able to think about the interpretation of the song more than the technical aspects.

Use this evaluation in preparing a song for presentation. Watch in a mirror, or videotape yourself in a practice session, and then evaluate your own performance. In this way you will find you make faster progress. You can be your own best teacher if you will be a careful observer of the aspects on the evaluation sheet and correct the problems you see and hear in your own singing.

VOCAL PERFORMANCE EVALUATION

Name: _____   Song Title: _____

Date: _____   Overall grade: _____

A = Excellent—No major problems   B = Good—Problems under control and being corrected

C = Average—Specific technical or musical problems need more work but are fixable

D = Poor—Problems need much work—Lack of practice or effort is evident!

Area Considered	Grade	Comments
Concentration:	_____	
Taking the Stage:	_____	
Positive Thinking:	_____	

Preparation: _____
1. Poem translation comes through
2. Poem diction is clear
3. Rhythm is learned correctly
4. Pitches are learned correctly
5. Vocalization of song is correct

Posture: _____
1. Head, neck, and shoulders
2. Mouth position
3. Rib cage and sternum
4. Abdominal muscles
5. Overall stance
6. Hands

Breathing: _____
1. Diaphragmatic-costal process used
2. Opens and relaxes on inhalation
3. Rib cage stays expanded
4. Breathes at correct points
5. Overall process

Vocal sound: _____
1. Tone is clear and ringing
2. Tone is easily produced
3. Tone is focused well

Overall Performance _____

Comments:

Bibliography of Selected Reference Books

Arbitol, M.D. (2006). *Odyssey of the Voice*. San Diego, CA: Plural Publishing, Inc.

Balch, James F., M.D., & Balch, Phyllis A., C.N.C. (1998). *Prescription for Nutritional Healing A-to-Z Guide to Supplements*. Garden City Park, NY: Avery Publishing Group.

Bennett, Bev, & Van Vynckt, Virginia. (1997). *Dictionary of Healthful Food Terms*. Hauppauge, NY: Barron's Educational Series, Inc.

Benninger, Michael S., M.D. (2006). *The Performer's Voice*. San Diego, CA: Plural Publishing, Inc.

Boone, Daniel R. (1997). *Is Your Voice Telling on You?* (2nd edition). San Diego, CA: Singular Publishing Group, Inc.

Bricklin, Mark. (1990). *The Practical Encyclopedia of Natural Healing* (Rev. edition). New York: Penguin Group.

Brodnitz, Friedrich S., M.D. (1988). *Keep Your Voice Healthy* (2nd edition). Boston: College-Hill Press.

Brown, Oren. (1996). *Discover Your Voice How to Develop Healthy Voice Habits*. San Diego, CA: Singular Publishing Group, Inc.

Caesari, E. Herbert. (1951). *The Voice of the Mind* (2nd edition; 1971). Boston: Crescendo Publishing Company.

Caruso, Enrico, & Tetrazzini, Luisa. (1909). *Caruso and Tetrazzini on The Art of Singing*. Dover Edition (1975). New York: Dover Publications, Inc.

Chapman, Janice L., AUA, OAM. (2005). *Singing and Teaching Singing A Holistic Approach to Classical Voice*. San Diego, CA: Plural Publishing, Inc.

Coffin, Berton. (1989). *Historical Vocal Pedagogy Classics*. Lanham, MD: The Scarecrow Press, Inc.

Dayme, Maribeth Bunch. (2006). *The Performer's Voice*. New York: W. W. Norton and Company.

Dornemann, Joan, with Ciaccia, Maria. (1992). *Complete Preparation A Guide to Auditioning for Opera*. New York: Excalibur Publishing, Inc.

Deglin, Judith Hopfer, Pharm.D., & Vallerand, April Hazard, Ph.D., RN. (2004). *Drug Guide for Nurses* (9th edition). Philadelphia: F. A. Davis Company.

Elliott, Martha. (2006). *Singing in Style A Guide to Vocal Performance Practices*. New Haven, CT: Yale University Press

Emmons, Shirlee, & Sonntag, Stanley. (2001). *The Art of the Song Recital*. Long Grove, IL: Waveland Press, Inc.

Gershoff, Stanley, Ph.D. (1996). *The Tufts University Guide to Total Nutrition* (2nd edition). New York: Harper Collins Publishers, Inc.

Gray, Henry, F. R. S. (1974). *Anatomy, Descriptive and Surgical*, 1901 edition. Philadelphia: Running Press Book Publishers.

Hines, Jerome. (1982). *Great Singers on Great Singing*. Garden City, NY: Doubleday & Company.

Hixon, Thomas J., Ph.D. (2006). *Respiratory Function in Singing A Primer for Singers and Singing Teachers*. San Diego, CA: Plural Publishing, Inc.

Kimball, Carol. (1996). *Song, A Guide to Style and Literature*. Redmond, WA: Pst. . . Inc.

Kirkpatrick, Carol. (2003). *"Aria Ready" The Business of Singing* (2nd printing). Bancroft Publications.

Kirschmann, Gayla J., & Kirschmann, John D. (1996). *Nutrition Almanac* (4th edition). New York: McGraw-Hill.

Larson, David E., M.D., Editor in Chief. (1990). *Mayo Clinic Family Health Book*. New York: William Morrow and Company, Inc.

Lehmann, Lilli. (1902). *How to Sing,* 3rd revised and supplemented edition, (1993), translated from the German by Clara Willenbücher. Mineola, NY: Dover Publications, Inc.

Lehmann, Lotte. (1945). *More Than Singing: The Interpretation of Songs*, translated by Frances Holden. Mineola, NY: Dover Publications, Inc.

Mader, Sylvia S. (1991). *Understanding Human Anatomy and Physiology*. Dubuque, IA: Wm. C. Brown Publishers.

Manén, Lucie. (1974). *The Art of Singing*. Bryn Mawr, PA: Faber Music LTD.

Marshall, Madeleine. (1953). *The Singer's Manual of English Diction*. New York: Schirmer Books.

McKinney, James C. (1994). *The Diagnosis and Correction of Vocal Faults*. Nashville, TN: Genevox Music Group.

Miller, Philip L. (1963). *The Ring of Words An Anthology of Song Texts*. New York: W. W. Norton & Company, Inc.

Miller, Richard. (1977). *English, French, German and Italian Techniques of Singing: A Study in National Tonal Preferences and How They Relate to Functional Efficiency*. Metuchen, NJ: The Scarecrow Press, Inc.

_____ (1996). *On the Art of Singing*. New York: Oxford University Press, Inc.

_____ (1986). *The Structure of Singing System and Art in Vocal Technique*. New York: Schirmer Books.

Monahan, Brent Jeffrey. (1978). *The Art of Singing A Compendium of Thoughts on Singing Published Between 1777 and 1927*. Metuchen, NJ: The Scarecrow Press, Inc.

Moriarty, John. (1975). *Diction Italian Latin French German . . . The Sounds and 81 Exercises for Singing Them*. Boston: E. C. Schirmer Music Company.

Murray, Michael T., N.D. (1996). *Encyclopedia of Nutritional Supplements*. Rocklin, CA: Prima Publishing.

Nair, Garyth. (2006). *The Craft of Singing*. San Diego, CA: Plural Publishing, Inc.

_____ (1999). *Voice Tradition and Technology A State-of-the-Art Studio*, San Diego, CA: Singular Publishing Group, Inc.

Papolos, Janice. (1984). *The Performing Artist's Handbook*. Cincinnati, OH: Writer's Digest Books

Reid, Cornelius L. (1974). *Bel Canto Principles and Practice*, (2nd printing). New York: Joseph Patelson Music House.

Sataloff, Robert Thayer, M.D., D.M.A. (2005). *Professional Voice The Science and Art of Clinical Care* (3rd edition). San Diego, CA: Plural Publishing, Inc.

_____ (2006). *Vocal Health and Pedagogy, Vol. I Science and Assessment* (2nd edition). San Diego, CA: Plural Publishing, Inc.

_____ (2006). *Vocal Health and Pedagogy, Vol. II Advanced Assessment and Practice* (2nd edition). San Diego, CA: Plural Publishing, Inc.

_____ (2005). *Voice Science*. San Diego, CA: Plural Publishing, Inc.

Saxon, Keith G., M. D., & Schneider, Carole M., Ph.D. (1995). *Vocal Exercise Physiology*. San Diego, CA: Singular Publishing Group, Inc.

Sundberg, Johan. (1987). *The Science of the Singing Voice*. DeKalb, IL: Northern Illinois University Press.

Titze, Ingo R. (1994). *Principles of Voice Production*. Englewood Cliffs, NJ: Prentice-Hall, Inc.

Tortora, Gerard J. (1995). *Principles of Human Anatomy* (7th edition). New York: Harper Collins College Publishers.

Vennard, William. (1967). *Singing the Mechanism and the Technic* (4th edition). New York: Carl Fischer, Inc.

Ware, Clifton. (1998). *Basics of Vocal Pedagogy The Foundations and Process of Singing*. Boston: McGraw-Hill.

Werbach, Melvyn R., M.D. (1987). *Nutritional Influences on Illness A Sourcebook of Clinical Research*. New Canaan, CT: Keats Publishing, Inc.

_____ (2000). *The Pharmacist's Guide to Vitamins, Minerals, Herbs and Other Nutrients*. Pharmavite LLC, Northridge, CA.

Index